THE INTERPELLATIONS

THE CATHOLIC UNIVERSITY OF AMERICA
CANON LAW STUDIES
No. 172

THE INTERPELLATIONS

BY

EDWARD MARTIN WOEBER, M.A., J.C.L.
Priest of the Archdiocese of Denver

A DISSERTATION

Submitted to the Faculty of the School of Canon Law of the Catholic University of America in Partial Fulfillment of the Requirements for the Degree of

DOCTOR OF CANON LAW

THE CATHOLIC UNIVERSITY OF AMERICA
WASHINGTON, D. C.
1942

NIHIL OBSTAT:

CLEMENS V. BASTNAGEL, J.U.D., S.T.L.

Censor Deputatus

Washingtonii, die 8a maii 1942

IMPRIMATUR:

✠ Urbanus Ioannes Vehr, D.D.

Archiepiscopus Denveriensis

Denveri, die 15a augusti, 1942

PRINTED IN THE UNITED STATES OF AMERICA
BY THE REGISTER COLLEGE OF JOURNALISM
DENVER, COLO.

DEO DICATUM
IN HONOREM
BEATAE MARIAE VIRGINIS

TABLE OF CONTENTS

PART TWO—THE LEGISLATION OF THE CODE ON THE INTERPELLATIONS

CHAPTER III

CHAPTER IV

CHAPTER V

CHAPTER VI

CHAPTER VI *(Continued)*

APPENDIX

FOREWORD

The title of this monograph suggests its contents. The subject, however, cannot be broached without some preliminary consideration of the doctrine of marriage and of the Pauline Privilege, for the licit and valid use of which the interpellations are an important factor. The question of the Pauline Privilege and of the concessions accorded by reason of canon 1125 has been specifically treated in two previous Catholic University of America Canon Law Studies, both of which embrace summarily the matter of the interpellations. It is the hope of the writer in the present work to particularize the discussion of this phase of the doctrine as touched upon so capably by the Very Reverend Monsignor Donald J. Gregory, J.U.D..[1] and the Reverend Francis J. Burton, C.S.C., J.C.D.[2]

The method followed in this treatise is partly historical, partly doctrinal. The purpose is to show certain stages of the development of the doctrine of the interpellations through history and to give the practice of the Church in their regard under the present legislation.

Of necessity the historical section is brief, because the allusions to the Pauline Privilege prior to Gratian are sketchy. Roman law is silent on the question. There is only St. Paul's statement for the privilege.[3] until the fourth century, when the Fathers began their commentaries on the Epistles of the Apostle. Even then the patristic information lacks definite conclusions on the privilege, for either the Fathers were loath to allow its use or they failed to appreciate its implications. From then until the eighth century, with one alleged exception, there is almost a total absence of testimony in the Western Church. One may hazard the opinion that in a Christian society there was little need to invoke it, or possibly that the struggle to maintain the indissolubility of marriage, regarding which there were many abuses, may have led ecclesiastics in the Church to adopt a

[1] *The Pauline Privilege,* The Catholic University of America Canon Law Studies, n. 68 (Washington, D. C.: The Catholic University of America, 1931). Burton, C.S.C.[2]

[2] *A Commentary on Canon 1125,* The Catholic University of America Canon Law Studies, n. 121 (Washington, D. C.: The Catholic University of America Press, 1940).

[3] I Cor., VII:12-16.

rigoristic view, refusing to recognize even the exception permitted by St. Paul. In the ninth century the import of the doctrine began to be realized and interest in it blossomed anew. Three centuries later the doctrine was incorporated into the canonical legislation of the Church by Pope Innocent III, but it was not until the early seventeenth century that the necessity of the interpellations was officially recognized and legally prescribed as the proper juridical procedure to prove the departure of the unbelieving spouse. From then until the Code the teaching was uniform in the main, with particular problems reaching a solution through decrees of the Pontiffs, decisions of the Roman Congregations and the opinions of the canonists.

The present study does not pretend to give an exhaustive treatment of the doctrine of the interpellations, but simply a conspectus of the historical antecedents of the present Code law and of the legislation on the interpellations as incorporated in the Code.

The writer wishes to take this occasion to express his gratitude to His Excellency, the Most Reverend Urban J. Vehr, D.D., Archbishop of Denver, for the opportunity of advanced study which his promotion of clerical scholarship has afforded and for his many kindnesses in the preparation of this work. He is likewise deeply appreciative of the graciousness and helpful direction of the members of the Faculty of the School of Canon Law of the Catholic University. To these and other cherished friends, sincere thanks are expressed.

HISTORICAL CONSPECTUS

INTRODUCTION

PRELIMINARY DISCUSSION

Article I. Fundamental Notions of Marriage

Marriage is a stable contractual union entered by one man and one woman by which each mutually gives and receives conjugal rights which are perpetual and exclusive, having in view primarily the generation and rearing of children and secondarily the reciprocal services of domestic life.[1] Both the natural law [2] and the positive divine law as given in Sacred Scripture [3] postulate the essential character and the fixed terms of the marital contract as mentioned in the definition. But even the casual student of ancient history knows that the pristine idea of exclusiveness and indissolubility suffered through the ages and that divorce with remarriage, as well as polygamy, was permitted and practiced by Hebrew and pagan alike. The Mosaic law, by divine dispensation, tolerated simultaneous polygamy,[4] and for a cause allowed a man to repudiate his wife by giving her a bill of divorce.[5] Likewise Roman law, under the widespread use of which Christianity was born, regarded marriage as capable of dissolution.[6] It must be stated, however, that both the Mosaic and Roman laws intended indissoluble unions, divorce and remarriage being permitted only by way of exception. But with the advent of Christ the exception had almost become the rule, and since He came "to save, not to destroy," His was the burden of making men once more conscious of the dignity and sacredness of marriage,[7] and of bringing them to

[1] De Smet, *Tractatus Theologico-Canonicus de Sponsalibus et Matrimonio* (4. ed., Brugis: Car. Beyaert, 1927), n. 75, (hereafter cited as *De Spons. et Matrim.*).

[2] Cf. St. Thomas Aquinas, *Contra Gentiles,* lib. III, cap. 122, coll. *Summa Theologica,* IIa, IIae, q. 154, art. 2; Joyce, *Christian Marriage, an Historical and Doctrinal Study* (New York: Sheed and Ward, 1933), pp. 1-25, (hereafter cited as *Christian Marriage*).

[3] Genesis, I:27-28, II:23, Matt. XIX:4-5.

[4] Genesis, XVI:3.

[5] Deuteronomy, XXIV:1-4.

[6] D. (24.1) 60.1; 61; 62; D. (24.4) 4; D (24.3) 22.7; Leage-Ziegler, *Roman Private Law* (2 ed., London; Macmillan and Co., Ltd., 1937), p. 107.

[7] Matt., V:32; Mark, X:11-12; Luke, XVI: 18.

the realization that the prevailing custom was not intended from the beginning. "Have you not read that the Creator, from the beginning, made them male and female, and said, 'For this cause a man shall leave his father and mother, and cleave to his wife, and the two shall become one flesh'? What therefore God has joined together, let no man put asunder."[8] Since the natural law allowed of no dissolution at any time for pagans, and since the Mosaic dispensation given in favor of the Chosen People was herewith revoked,[9] the doctrine of the permanence and of the unity of marriage was once more established for all people regardless of religious or non-religious conviction. The promulgation of this evangelical law made all marriages which were entered into in the absence of any impediment of the natural and positive divine law and by the free and deliberate consent of the contracting parties, and then consummated by them, exclusive and indissoluble, with the important exception divinely committed to the Church over non-consummated Christian marriages[10] and on the valid baptism of one party over non-sacramental unions under specified conditions.

This dissertation is indirectly concerned with the latter unions. The power of the Church to permit the convert to contract a second marriage, thereby dissolving the union entered in infidelity, is known as the Pauline privilege, of which the interpellations are usually a necessary factor.

[8] Matt., XIX:4-6; Mark, X:6-7—*The New Testament* (Confraternity of Christian Doctrine edition, Paterson, N. J.: St. Anthony Guild Press, 1941).

[9] Matt., XIX: 7-8; Mark, X:3-6; cf. also Sanchez, *Disputationum de Sto. Matrimonii Sacramento Libri Decem* (2 vols., Venetiis: Guerilium, 1614), lib. II, disp. XIII, n. 3; lib. X, disp. I, n. 9, (hereafter this work will be cited as *De Matrim*).

[10] Conc. Trident. sess. XXIV, *de matrimonio,* can. 6—"If anyone says that matrimony contracted but not consummated is not dissolved by the solemn profession of religion by one of the married parties, let him be anathema."

§1. *The Pauline Privilege Defined*[11]

The Pauline privilege, or the *Casus Apostoli* as it is sometimes called, is concerned with the dissolution of valid marriages,[12] entered into between the unbaptized, on the subsequent conversion of one party. Such unions contracted and consummated in infidelity are true marriages, possessing the attributes of unity and indissolubility, but they lack that supreme degree of stability[13] that belongs to consummated Christian marriages.[14] No civil authority can dissolve them,[15] for if civil powers other than that of the Jews ever did possess a divine privilege, it was abrogated by Christ. But to His Church God has granted a certain control over them. Properly understood, the Church has no jurisdiction over the unbaptized nor do her laws affect them,[16] but if a married infidel receives baptism, the convert becomes a subject of the Church and under certain conditions may be free to enter new nuptials with a Christian, thus being released from

[11] For an appreciation of the historical development of the doctrine of the Pauline privilege consult: Esmein-Généstal-Dauvillier, *Le Mariage en Droit Canonique* (2. ed., 2 vols., Paris: Sirey, 1929-1935), II, 270; Freisen, *Geschichte des Canonischen Eherechts bis zum Verfall der Glossenliteratur* (Paderborn: Druck und Verlag von Ferdinand Schöningh, 1893), p. 769.

[12] S.C.S. Off. (Siouxormen.), 18 maii 1892, ad 1, 2—*Codicis Iuris Canonici Fontes, cura Emi. Petri Card. Gasparri editi* (9 vols., Romae: Typis Polyglottis Vaticanis, 1925-1939. (Vols., VII-IX, *ed. cura et studio Emi. Iustiniani Card. Serédi*), n. 1155, (hereafter this work will be cited as *Fontes*). Cf. also S.C.S. Off., instr. (ad Ep. S. Alberti), 9 dec. 1874, ad 2, II—*Fontes*, n. 1036.

[13] St. Thomas Aquinas asserts: "Matrimonium infidelium est imperfectum, ut dictum est. Sed matrimonium fidelium est perfectum, et ita est firmius."—IV Sent., d. XXXIX, q. 1, art. 5, ad 1; IV Sent., d. XXXIII, q. 2, art. 2; cf. also Sanchez, *De Matrim.*, lib. II, disp. XIII, n. 4; Gregorius XIII, const. "*Populis*," 25 ian. 1585, *Appendix ad Bullarium Pontificium Sacrae Congregationis de Propaganda Fide*, I, 103; *Codex Iuris Canonici* (Romae: Typis Polyglottis Vaticanis, 1934), Documentum VIII. (In the future when the Code is cited simply the canon will be listed, and if other sections of the Code are quoted or cited the abbreviation *C.I.C.* will be used).

[14] Romans, VII:2-3; I Cor., VII:10.

[15] Schmalzgrueber, *Ius Ecclesiasticum Universum* (5 vols. in 12, Romae, 1843-1845), lib. IV, tit. XIX, n. 18, (hereafter this work will be cited as *Ius Eccles. Universum*). Pius IX, *Syllabus*, prop. 67—H. Denzinger-C. Bannwart, *Enchiridion Symbolorum Definitionum et Declarationum de Rebus Fidei et Morum* (18-20. ed., Friburgi Brisgoviae: Herder, 1932), n. 1767, (hereafter cited as *Enchiridion*).

[16] Canon 12.

the former bond contracted in infidelity. St. Paul is the authority for this doctrine:

> "For to the rest I say, not the Lord: If any brother has an unbelieving wife and she consents to live with him, let him not put her away. And if any woman has an unbelieving husband and he consents to live with her, let her not put away her husband. . . . But if the unbeliever departs, let him depart. For a brother or sister is not under bondage in such cases, but God has called us to peace."[17]

In the verses just preceding this text the Apostle addresses himself to two classes of Corinthians, the unmarried Christians and the married. He gives advice to the first, and then reminds the latter that Christ has so excoriated divorce that if perchance a separation does occur, no new marriage may be contracted. In the above quotation the Apostle directs his words to a third class called *"the rest,"* or those who were already married at the time of their conversion, but whose partner remained a pagan. There are no known words of Christ to substantiate St. Paul's teaching: "I say, not the Lord." This statement, however, is not to be understood as signifying that the Apostle's advice is to be regarded as merely human. He speaks with apostolic authority and under the guidance of inspiration.[18]

Exegetes are not agreed whether St. Paul commands or counsels the convert to continue living with the pagan consort if the latter refuses to be baptized but nevertheless is willing to abide in peace. St. Augustine held that perfection counsels the preserving of the marriage intact.[19] But what if the infidel spouse refuses to live with the consort, or shares such hostility to Christian faith and morals that common life is intolerable, if not altogether impossible? St. Paul meets this contingency when he states: "If the unbeliever departs,

[17] I Cor., VII:12-15.

[18] Gasparri, *Tractatus Canonicus de Matrimonio* (ed. nova ad mentem Codicis, 2 vols., Typis Polyglottis Vaticanis, 1932), nn. 1135, 1166, (hereafter this work will be cited as *De Matrim*). Wernz-Vidal, *Ius Canonicum ad Codicis normam exactum* (7 toms. in 8 vols., Romae: Apud Aedes Universitatis Gregorianae, 1923-1938), Vol. V (*Ius Matrimoniale,* 2. ed., 1928), n. 631, note 56, (henceforth this work will be cited as *Ius Matrimoniale*).

[19] *De Coniugiis Adulterinis,* lib. 1, cap. XIII, n. 14—*Corpus Scriptorum Ecclesiasticorum Latinorum* (68 vols., Vindobonae-Tempsky, 1866-1936), XLI (1890), 361, (hereafter this work will be cited as *CSEL*); Migne, *Patrologiae Cursus Completus, Series Latina* (221 vols., Parisiis, 1844-1855), XL, 459, (hereafter this work will be cited as *MPL*).

let him depart."[20] If the unbeliever departs, then the Christian is not bound to oppose the separation or seek a reconciliation. The departure may be either physical or moral, depending on whether the unbeliever actually deserts his spouse, refusing to live under the same roof,[21] or on whether the unbeliever, by hostility to religion or by the refusal to live in peace, renders common life intolerable, or by constant persuasion attempts to lead the convert into apostasy or serious sin.[22]

The problem was undoubtedly acute in the infant Church, inasmuch as the subsequent tragedy of an unbearable life or of desertion often faced the convert. Had St. Paul merely intended to justify the separation, he would have granted nothing that was not already allowed. His words were directed to the solution of a perplexing problem. Their meaning is that the Christian who is thus ill-treated or abandoned is given the right to contract another marriage. The Apostle definitely states in the earlier verses of I Cor., Chapter XV, that a Christian marriage which had subsequently ended in separation brooks no new nuptials; and likewise he holds the convert to celibacy should a separation occur, if the pagan spouse is willing to continue the common life in peace. Here, however, he states that "a brother or sister is not under bondage in such cases." If another marriage was not allowed, the Christian law would involve a very real bondage for the convert, who would be confronted with a life of enforced celibacy. That the convert has a right under such conditions to enter a new marriage, naturally with a Christian, is the meaning which Catholic tradition attaches to St. Paul's epistle, and this is what is signified by the Pauline privilege.[23]

In the actual application of the privilege four conditions must be

[20] I Cor., VII:15.

[21] Feije (*De Impedimentis et Dispensationibus Matrimonialibus* [3. ed., Lovanii: Typis Caroli Peeters, 1885], nn. 495, 496, 602 [hereafter cited as *De Imped. et dispens. Matrim.*]) states that according to the Pauline privilege a convert is not held to such slavery as to be bound to one who is *de facto* absent. Cf. S.C.S. Off. (Natal), 11 iul. 1866, ad 2—*Fontes,* n. 996; (Siam), 22 nov. 1871—*Fontes,* n. 1019; (Victoriae Nyanzae), 8 iul. 1891—*Fontes,* n. 1140.

[22] S.C.S. Off. (Natal), 11 iul. 1866, ad 2, 3, 4—*Fontes,* n. 996.

[23] Innocent III, "*Quanto te magis,*" 1 maii 1199—c. 7, X, *de divortiis,* IV, 19; *Regesta Pontificum Romanorum,* ed. Augustus Potthast (2 vols., Berolini, 1874-75), n. 684, (hereafter this work will be cited at Potthast); cf. also Benedictus XIV, *De Synodo Dioecesana* (2 vols., Romae, 1806), lib. VI, c. 4; Sanchez, *De Matrim.,* lib. VII, disp. LXXIV; Schmalzgrueber, *Ius Eccles. Universum,* lib. IV, tit. XIX, n. 24.

fulfilled: (1) A legitimate marriage must exist between the non-baptized parties,[24] for if no valid marriage exists, then rather a declaration of nullity must be sought; (2) one of the parties must be converted and validly baptized, the other spouse remaining in infidelity;[25] (3) there must be a departure or a *discessus* on the part of the unbeliever;[25a] (4) the unbeliever must be interpellated.[26]

[24] Can. 1120, § 2; S.C.S. Off. (Siouxormen.), 19 maii 1892, ad 2—*Collectanea S. Congregationis de Propaganda Fide* (2 vols., Romae, 1907), n. 1796, (hereafter this work will be cited as *Coll.*); S.C.S. Off. (Niger), 17 aug. 1898—*Coll.*, n. 2017; De Smet, *De Spons. et Matrim.*, n. 543.

[25] S. C. de Prop. Fide, (C. P. pro Sin.), 16 ian. 1803, ad 1—*Coll.*, n. 665; *Acta Sanctae Sedis* (41 vols., Romae: Ex Typographia Polyglotta, 1865-1908), XXXIII (1900-1901), 549-550, (in the future this work will be cited *ASS*).

[25a] "Ambrosiaster," *Commentaria in Epistolam ad Corinthios Primam*—*MPL*, XVII, 219; for an appreciation of the entire topic cf. Souter, *A Study of Ambrosiaster* (Cambridge Texts and Studies, VII, 4); "Ambrosiaster,"—*Catholic Encyclopedia* (15 vols., New York, 1907-1912), I, 406; Innocent III, "*Quanto te magis,*" 1 maii 1199—c. 7, X, *de divortiis*, IV, 19; Potthast, n. 684; Wernz, *Ius Decretalium* (2. ed., 6 vols. in 10 toms., Romae et Prati, 1905-1913), IV, pars II, n. 702, note 62; De Smet, *De Spons. et Matrim.*, n. 347; Vermeersch, *De Casu Apostoli seu De Fidei Privilegio* (Brugis, 1911), n. 51, (hereafter this work will be cited as *De Casu Apostoli*).

[26] Cf. next article within this chapter.

§2. *The Interpellations Defined*

Baptism confers on the convert partner of a marriage which was entered in infidelity a *right* under certain conditions to contract a new marriage with a Christian, but of itself baptism does not dissolve the infidel marriage.[27] Before the convert may invoke the Pauline privilege there must be a departure for which the unbelieving spouse is accountable. The certified revelation of this kind of departure is to be determined by the interpellations.[28]

The term interpellations denotes the act by which the convert seeks a declaration from the unbeliever on two vital questions: (1) whether he wishes to be converted and to receive baptism, and (2) in case the unbeliever be unwilling to become a Christian, whether he will continue conjugal life in peace, without offense to Almighty God.[29]

The expression "offense to Almighty God" in relation to the Pauline privilege is understood in accordance with the meaning attached to it by tradition. It signifies blasphemy of the Divine Name or, in a more general sense, obstinacy in serious sin on the part of the infidel.[30]

Only as long as at least one of the alternatives is not complied with may the convert proceed to a new marriage. But this negative will of the infidel may not be presumed,[31] nor can it be definitely known under normal circumstances unless he is interpellated. Consequently, since the words of the Apostle presuppose either a physical or a moral departure on the part of the unbelieving spouse, there normally follows the necessity of making the interpellations if the certainty of such a departure is to stand fully established.

[27] S.C.S. Off. (Cochinchin.), 1 aug. 1759, ad 5—*Fontes,* n. 810.

[28] Vermeersch, *De Casu Apostoli,* n. 51.

[29] Innocent III, "*Quanto te magis,*" I maii 1199—Potthast, n. 684; Pallottini, *Collectio Omnium Conclusionum et Resolutionum Quae in causis propositis apud Sacram Congregationem Cardinalium S. Concilii Tridentini interpretum Prodierunt ad eius institutione anno MDLXIV ad MDCCCLX, distinctis titulis alphabetico ordine per materias digestas, cura et studio* Salvatoris Pallottini (18 vols., Romae, 1868-1895), s.v. "Matrimonium," § XIV, n. 2, (hereafter cited as *Collectio Resolutionum S.C.C.*); Benedictus XIV, *De Synodo Dioecesana,* lib. XIII, c. 21, n. 1; S. C. de Prop. Fide (ad C. P. pro Sin.), 16 iun, 1796— *Coll.,* n. 634; (C. P. pro Sin. Tunk. Occid.), 5 mart. 1816, ad 2—*Coll.,* n. 704.

[30] Innocent III, "*Quanto te magis,*" 1 maii 1199—Potthast, n. 684; Gasparri, *De Matrim.,* n. 1139, note 3.

[31] Vermeersch, *De Casu Apostoli,* n. 51.

PART ONE—HISTORICAL CONSPECTUS

CHAPTER I

DEVELOPMENT REGARDING THE INTERPELLATIONS IN EARLY HISTORY

ARTICLE I. WRITINGS OF THE FATHERS AND ANCIENT ECCLESIASTICAL AUTHORS

As already mentioned, an understanding of the interpellations is impossible without an appreciation of the doctrine of the Pauline privilege. The interpellations are an integral part of that doctrine. Treated by themselves they would be quite meaningless. Their history, therefore, coincides with the history of the privilege itself, but prior to the seventeenth century this history stands little revealed inasmuch as the earlier sources are not explicit on how knowledge of the infidel's departure was attained, though the condition of departure was in the main always demanded as a prerequisite for the use of the privilege, at least in the Western Church.

The knowledge of the doctrine on the Pauline privilege as crystalized in modern thought was somewhat vague until the eighth century. Prior to that time no practical example of the Pauline privilege procedure can be cited. The works of the Fathers and writers of that early period lack definite conclusions, though frequent references are found that justify the surmise that they refer to the Pauline privilege.[1] Indicative of this is the statement of Wernz who says that unless they are discussing the Pauline privilege their writings in frequent instances are unintelligible.[2] They make no direct reference to any interpellations.

The author of the Commentary on the Thirteen Epistles of St. Paul

[1] St. John Chrysostom, *Hom.* 19 *in I. Cor.*—Migne, *Patrologiae Cursus, Completus, Series Graeca* (161 vols., Parisiis, 1856-1866), LXI, 155, (in the future this work will be cited as *MPG*); Tertullian, *Ad Uxorem*, lib. II, cap. 2—*MPL*, I, 1290-1292; St. Augustine, *De Coniugiis Adulterinis*, lib. I, cap. XIII, n. 14—*CSEL* XLI (1890), 361; St. Jerome, *Adversus Iovinianum*, lib. 1, cap. 10—*MPL*, XXIII, 223-224.

[2] Wernz, *Ius Decretalium*, IV, Pars II, n. 702, note 61.

called the "Ambrosiaster," who lived toward the end of the fourth century, is the first to speak rather plainly of the privilege. He gives an unqualified statement of the right of the convert to remarry, and he establishes the juridic principle on which it is allowed to take advantage of the privilege, "contumelia Creatoris solvit ius matrimonii."[3] Like the Fathers, the author of the "Ambrosiaster" mentions nothing of the obligation to admonish the unbeliever. His statement seems to imply, however, a summary extrajudicial knowledge of the departure, and it is of considerable importance because of its influence on the future legislation concerning the interpellations.[4] The prevalent opinion upheld the indissolubility of the marriage bond, and on the conversion of one of the infidel parties permitted only a separation if the unbeliever refused to cohabit peacefully. The "Ambrosiaster," contrary to contemporaneous thought, held for the right of remarriage, given the condition of departure. It would seem that one can safely presume that some extrajudicial procedure was in vogue in order to determine the presence of this *sine qua non* condition.[5]

[3] " 'Quod si infidelis discedit, discedat.' Propositum religionis custodit, praecipiendo ne Christiani relinquent coniugia; sed si infidelis odio Dei discedit, fidelis non erit reus dissoluti matrimonii; maior enim causa Dei est, quam matrimonii, 'non est enim frater aut soror servituti subiectus in huiusmodi.' Hoc est, non debetur reverentia coniugii ei, qui horret auctorem coniugii; non enim ratum est matrimonium, quod sine Dei devotione est; ac per hoc non est peccatum ei, qui dimittitur propter Deum, si alii se coniunxerit. *Contumelia enim Creatoris solvit ius matrimonii circa eum qui relinquitur,* ne accusetur alii copulatus."—*Ad Omnia Opera Sancti Ambrosii Appendix, Commentaria in Epist. ad Corinthios Primam—MPL,* XVII, 219; c. 2, C. XXVIII, q. 2. Cf. Souter, *A Study of Ambrosiaster,* Cambridge Texts and Studies, VII, Serial 4; "Ambrosiaster,"—*Catholic Encyclopedia,* I, 406; Wernz, *Ius Decretalium,* IV, Pars II, n. 702, note 61.

[4] Gregory states that during the middle ages this writing was erroneously attributed to St. Ambrose, and that even now it is found appended to his works. —*The Pauline Privilege,* p. 17. The letter was also either falsely or incorrectly quoted by Gratian as having been written by St. Gregory. "Haec non sunt inventa apud B. Gregorium, sed apud B. Ambrosium ad c. VII: I Corinthiorum eadem fere leguntur melius atque aptius exposita."—Notationes Correctorum ad c. 2, C, XXVIII, q. 2.

[5] Lämmer, "Die Interpellatio coniugis infidelis und die päpstliche Dispens von derselben,"—*Archiv für katholisches Kirchenrecht,* XI (1864), 246, n. 3, (hereafter this periodical will be cited as *AKKR,* and the article as "Die Interpellatio").

Article II. Local Conciliar References

Some authors think that the first piece of legislation on the interpellations is to be found in the acts of the IV Provincial Council of Toledo (633) in canon 63 which reads as follows:

> "Iudaei qui Christianas mulieres in coniugio habent, admoneantur ab episcopo civitatis ipsius, ut si cum eis permanere cupiunt, Christiani efficiantur. *Quod si admoniti noluerint, separentur:* quia non potest infidelis in eius permanere coniugio, quae iam in Christianam translata est fidem. Filii autem qui ex talibus nati existunt, fidem atque conditionem matris sequantur. Similiter et hi qui procreati sunt de infidelibus mulieribus et infidelibus viris, Christianam sequantur religionem, non Iudaeicam superstitionem."[6]

Opinion, however, is divided as to whether this canon deals with the possible use of the Pauline privilege or refers to a declaration of nullity relative to attempted marriages entered into between Christians and Jews in spite of the diriment impediment of disparity of worship. If the latter is the subject under discussion, there would be no reference to the interpellations in the warning there expressed. Those who hold that it involves the privilege understand this canon as a direction to Jewish converts to discontinue cohabitation with their unbelieving partners if, after admonishing them, the latter refuse to be converted and baptized. Acosta asserts:

> "Separationem autem illam Concilii Toletani ego non solum quoad torum intelligo, sed etiam quoad vinculum. Itaque licebit, ut graves quoque auctores confirmant, fideli iam tunc alias nuptias conciliare sibi. Contumelia enim Creatoris et periculum fidei intelligitur, cum animus coniugis infidelis adeo est in sua superstitione obstinatus."[7]

Santi agrees with Acosta:

> "Verum ex Conciliis Toletanis habemus primam faciendam esse interrogationem parti infideli, ita ut pars conversa

[6] Mansi, *Sacrorum Conciliorum Nova et Amplissima Collectio* (53 vols., in 59, Paris-Arnhem-Leipzig, 1901-1927), X, 634, (hereafter this work will be cited as Mansi).

[7] Acosta, *De Natura Novi Orbis et de Promulgatione Evangelii apud Barbaros sive De Procuranda Indorum Saluti Libri Sex* (Salmanticae, 1589), lib. VI, cap. XXI, (hereafter cited as *De Procuranda Salute Indorum Libri Sex*).

> possit post primam interpellationem reiectam ab infideli ad alia vota transire."[8]

Wernz, with other authorities of weight, on the contrary asserts:

> "Vix quidquam de privilegio Paulini colligi potest ex can. 63 Concilii Toletani IV . . . qui secundum sensum obvium potius explicandus est de matrimonio *inito* cum disparitate cultus . . ."[9]

Though it seems that the obvious interpretation supports Wernz the question, however, remains unsolved because of a lack of any known contemporaneous commentary on the definite meaning of the canon. The matter is treated here solely because of the influence the canon had on later writers who supported the view that it involved the use of the privilege. Of itself the IV Council of Toledo was local to seventh century Spain and its enactments were intended to meet pressing conditions there. The acts of the Council were never accepted as a source of law for the universal Church.

The next important reference is furnished by St. Theodore of Canterbury (+690).[10] According to him it seems that an interpellation was necessarily expected, for Theodore allowed not merely a divorce when the unbeliever departed, but held that the marriage should be dissolved whenever the infidel refused to accept the faith. Here, however, the English Archbishop of Eastern origin and culture erred on the side of laxity, as he did on other matrimonial matters. His teaching is worthy of note, however, since it affords a picture of how the privilege was regarded by those of Oriental training.[11]

The Council of Trullo (692) made an attempt to check the lax matrimonial practice of the Eastern Church as subscribed to by Theodore, decreeing that there could be no divorce if the infidel was

[8] Santi, *Praelectiones Iuris Canonici* (4 vols., Ratisbonae-Neo Eboraci-Cincinnati: Pustet, 1886), II, p. 174, n. 10; Sanchez, *De Matrim.*, lib. VII, disp. LXXIV, n. 12.

[9] Wernz, *Ius Decretalium,* IV, pars II, n. 702, note 61; Fahrner, *Geschichte des Unauflöslichkeitsprinzips und der vollkommenen Scheidung der Ehe im kanonischen Recht* (Freiburg im Breisgau, 1903), p. 162.

[10] *Concilium sub Theodoro,* can. 63; "Cuius uxor est infidelis et gentilis et non potest eam convertere, dimittat eam."—Mansi, XII, 30.

[11] *Poenitentiales Theodori,* lib. II, c. 12, n. 18—Mansi, XI, 53; cf. Ott, "Card. C. Tarquini über das paulinische Privileg,"—*AKKR,* L (1883), 229-230.

willing to abide in peace.[12] Later, however, the Oriental Church returned to the laxities in vogue prior to the Trullan Council.[13]

Article III. The Penitentials

Almost two centuries after the Trullan Synod, Hincmar of Rheims (+882) recognized the Pauline privilege in accordance with Christian tradition. Though always an invincible defender of the marriage bond, Hincmar permitted this exception and quoted the "Ambrosiaster" as his authority.[14] Burchard of Worms (+1025) and Ivo of Chartres (+1117) included Theodore's canon in their collections,[15] but credited it to Pope St. Eutychian (275-283) rather than to Archbishop Theodore of Canterbury (669-690).[16] It is doubtful how far Ivo of Chartres held the privilege to be in force in his time. In a letter of the Bishop of Sens, which dealt with the case of a convert Jewess who wished to break the marriage which she had contracted in infidelity, he suggested no way out of the difficulty, except to investigate the possibility of an impediment of consanguinity.[17]

Hugh of St. Victor (+1141) quoted the "Ambrosiaster," crediting the statement in it to Pope St. Gregory the Great (+604). Hugh held that the convert was free to repudiate the unbelieving consort even if the latter, though declining to be converted, was willing to live without offense to Almighty God.[18]

[12] Conc. in Trullo, can. 72: ". . . cum fideli autem cohabitare velit infidelis, vel cum infideli rursus fidelis, ne a se invicem separentur (I Cor., VII: 12). Si quis frater uxorem habet infidelem, et haec consentit habitare cum illo, non dimittat illam . . ."—Mansi, XII, 53. Cf. Wernz, *Ius Decretalium,* IV, pars II, n. 702, note 61.

[13] Theodotus, *Ius Canonicum,—MPG,* CXIX, 767.

[14] *De Divortio Lotharii,* Interrog. XIX—*MPL,* CXXV, 730; Interrog. XXI—*MPL,* CXXV, 732.

[15] Buchardus, *Decretum,* lib. IX, c. 60—*MPL,* CXL, 825; Ivo, *Decretum,* lib. VIII, cc. 195-196—*MPL,* CLXI, 625; *Panormia,* lib. VI, c. 97—*MPL,* CLXI, 1265; Cf. Jemolo, "Il Privilegio Paolino dal Principio del secolo XI agli albori del XV," *Studi Sassaresi,* II (1923), 267; Gregory, *The Pauline Privilege,* p. 15, note 13.

[16] Cf. Gregory, *The Pauline Privilege,* p, 15, for an explanation of the letter ascribed to Pope St. Eutychian.

[17] Ivo, *Epistola CCXXX—MPL,* CLXII, 233.

[18] *De Sacramentis,* lib. II, pars XI, c. 13—*MPL,* CLXXVI, 506, 508.

Robert Cardinal Pullen (+1146) treated of the privilege, but erred in his explanation. He held that only Christian marriage was indissoluble and that unions of infidels and Jews admitted of divorce. Regarding the *Casus Apostoli* he taught that even if the unbeliever desired to abide in peace, the convert was free to depart and to contract another marriage on the assumption that obstinacy in infidelity was a kind of spiritual adultery.[19] The influence of Oriental thought on the English Church, through the Penitentials of Theodore of Canterbury, probably colored the views of Pullen.

Article IV. The Decree of Gratian

The fundamental idea common to all writers up to the twelfth century with regard to the Pauline privilege and the conditions on which it could be invoked lacked the quality of well defined doctrine. The Fathers left us no definite conclusions. Of the other writers on the subject some were lax,[20] others orthodox,[21] and at least Ivo of Chartres too exacting.[22]

Gratian took a decisive stand regarding many points of doctrine hitherto indefinite. His *Decretum* was compiled about the year 1140. The work as a whole, being edited by private authority and composed of spurious as well as authentic canons, had no authentic legislative value; however, its authentic parts enjoyed legal force.[23] Its chief value was the profound influence it exercised on subsequent practice, science and legislation. Regarding the Pauline privilege, Gratian was not guilty of the error of those who subscribed to the teaching of Theodore of Canterbury. Theodore held that the marriage should

[19] Robertus Pullen, *Sententiarum Libri Octo,* lib. VII, c. 29—*MPL,* CLXXXVI, 947.

[20] Theodore of Canterbury, *Concilium sub Theodoro,* can. 63—Mansi, XII, 30; Theodotus, *Ius Canonicum—MPG,* CXIX, 767; Pullen, *Sententiarum Libri Octo,* lib. VII, c. 29—*MPL,* CLXXXVI, 947; Hugh of St. Victor, *De Sacramentis,* lib. II, pars XI, c. 13—*MPL,* CLXXVI, 506, 508.

[21] "Ambrosiaster," in *Ad Opera Sancti Ambrosii Appendix, Commentaria in Epist. ad Corinthios Primam—MPL,* XVII, 219; c. 2, C. XXVIII, q. 2; Council in Trullo (692), can. 72—Mansi, XII, 53; Hincmar of Rheims, *De Divortio Lotharii,* Interrog. XIX—*MPL,* CXXV, 730; Interrog. XXI—*MPL,* CXXV, 732.

[22] Ivo, *Decretum,* lib. VIII, cc. 195, 196—*MPL,* CLXI, 625; *Panormia,* lib. VI, c. 97—*MPL,* CLXI, 1265; *Epistola CCXXX—MPL,* CLXII, 233.

[23] Kuttner, "The Father of the Science of Canon Law,"—*The Jurist* (Catholic University of America, Washington, D. C.), I (1941), 15, n. V.

be dissolved if the infidel refused baptism, even though willing to abide in peace with the Christian convert. Gratian held that the convert by baptism was given the right to contract a new marriage only in the event that the unbeliever departed; that new nuptials were possible for the convert only if the infidel effected a separation.[24] The same thought was expressed by Peter Lombard (+c. 1160).[25] The insistence both of Gratian and of Peter Lombard on the necessity of the departure by the unbelieving spouse presumes knowledge of the intention to that effect and seems to indicate at least the acknowledged need of a summary interpellation.

Article V. The Decretals of Pope Innocent III

Interest in the possibilities of the Pauline privilege notably increased in the twelfth century. The doctrine furnished much cause for debate. As a consequence there followed a more accurate determination of the scope of the privilege. Finally, at the end of the century, Pope Innocent III introduced the privilege into the canonical legislation of the Church in two decretals addressed respectively to the Bishop of Ferrara and to the Bishop of Tiberias in Palestine. Here we have the first official sanction of the doctrine by the Church and a declaration that its application depends upon the departure of the unbeliever. Innocent restated the interpretation of the term "depart" in accordance with Catholic tradition. He applied the principle of the "Ambrosiaster," *"contumelia Creatoris solvit ius matrimonii,"*[26] which he understood in the sense not only of the unbeliever's actual but also moral departure. The latter was recognized as obtaining when continued cohabitation was rendered morally impossible in view of the unbeliever's manifest disrespect for the Divine Name, or also in view of the unbeliever's effort to induce the convert to commit serious sin. These decretals constitute an important link in the development of the doctrine on the privilege and the interpellations. Because of their influence on the future legislation of the Church they deserve to be quoted in their pertinent parts:

> ". . . Si enim alter infidelium coniugum ad fidem catholicam convertatur, altero vel nullo modo, vel saltem non sine blasphemia divini nominis, vel ut eum pertrahat ad mortale peccatum, ei cohabitare volente: qui relinquitur, ad secunda,

[24] *Dictum* ad c. 2, C. XXVIII, q. 2.

[25] *Sententiarum, Libri Quatuor,* lib. LV, dist. 39, c. 4, n. 358.

[26] *Ad Opera St. Ambrosii Appendix, Commentaria in Epist. ad Corinthios Primam—MPL,* XVII, 219; c. C. XXVIII, q. 2; *Supra,* p. 9.

si voluerit, vota transibit. Et in hoc casu intelligimus quod ait Apostolus: 'Si infidelis discedit, discedat. Frater enim vel soror non est servituti subiectus in huiusmodi,' et canonem etiam, in quo dicitur, quod 'contumelia Creatoris solvit ius matrimonii circa eum, qui relinquitur.' "[27] ". . . Qui autem secundum ritum suum legitimam repudiavit uxorem cum tale repudium veritas in evangelio reprobaverit, numquam ea vivente licite poterit aliam, etiam ad fidem Christi conversus, habere nisi post conversionem ipsius illa renuat cohabitare cum ipso, aut etiamsi consentiat, non tamen absque contumelia Creatoris, vel ut eum pertrahat ad mortale peccatum. In quo casu restitutionem petenti, quamvis de iniusta spoliatione constaret, restitutio negaretur, quia secundum Apostolum frater aut soror non est in huiusmodi subiectus servituti."[28]

Innocent here crystalized the orthodox thought of the foregoing centuries. His principle became the norm for future speculation. In these decretals, however, there is as yet no hint of the procedure to be followed in admonishing the unbelieving spouse. Since the letters were directed to episcopal ordinaries, it is evident that they were constituted the competent judges, who were presumed to obtain at least extrajudicial knowledge of the mind of the infidel. The cycle of the next three centuries, with conditions demanding the practical use of the Pauline privilege, was to see further developments.

Article VI. The Commentators from the Thirteenth to the Seventeenth Centuries

The issuance of these decretals by Pope Innocent III inspired interest in the privilege on the part of theologians and canonists. The decretals were originally issued as letters to certain bishops. The *promulgation* did not come until the year 1234 in the Gregorian Collection, except perhaps in the *Compilatio III*, which was an authentic collection promulgated by the Bull *"Devotioni vestrae,"* December 28, 1210, and which contained the decretals of the first twelve years of Innocent's reign (1198-1210). Innocent's statements, inserted in the official collection of the decretals of Pope Gregory IX, were adopted as authoritative, and practice was thenceforth based on the principles enunciated by him relative to the Pauline privilege. Thus Panormitanus (1386-

[27] Innocent III, *"Quanto te magis,"* 1 maii 1199—c. 7, X, *de divortiis*, IV, 19; Denzinger, *Enchiridion*, n. 406; Potthast, n. 684.

[28] Innocent III, *"Gaudemus in Domino,"* 22 apr. 1201—c. 8, X, *de divortiis*, IV, 19; Denzinger, *Enchiridion*, n. 407; Potthast, 1325.

1453) tells us that in his day the conversion of Jews was a matter of almost daily occurrence and that the Jewish converts retained their non-converted Jewish consorts, provided that the latter were willing to dwell in peace with them, but that they could contract a new marriage if their non-converted consorts either refused to live with them, or in cohabiting with them practiced a life of sin.[29] In his teaching on the privilege, St. Thomas Aquinas was consistently orthodox and traditional.

> ". . . Quia si infidelis vult cohabitare sine contumelia Creatoris, vel sine hoc quod ad infidelitatem inducat, potest fidelis libere discedere; sed discedens non potest alteri nubere."[30]

The commentators from the thirteenth to the seventeenth centuries were especially interested in the implications of the principle *"contumelia Creatoris solvit ius matrimonii."* Speculation on what this principle permitted in its application to a particular case undoubtedly gave rise to the forthcoming legislation on the Pauline privilege and on the necessity of the accompanying interpellations.

It was argued whether this principle was the intrinsic element that dissolved the bond which was contracted in infidelity. Some held that the refusal to consent to the partner's conversion and the subsequent failure of the unbeliever to abide in peace severed the bond.[31] The common opinion, however, stated that the bond was broken by the second marriage; that Christian nuptials were the immediate annulling cause of the previous union.[32] Great weight was added to this view by Pope Innocent's decretals in which it was stated that, if the unbeliever was converted before the second marriage of the convert, the parties had to resume conjugal life. The Pope made no mention of the need of renewing matrimonial consent; he presumed, rather, that the marriage had perdured.[33]

[29] Panormitanus (Nicolaus de Tudeschis), *Commentaria in Quinque Libros Decretalium* (5 vols. in 7, Venetiis, 1588), c. 7, X. *De Divortiis*, IV, 19.

[30] IV Sent., dist. XXXIX, q. un., art. 5.

[31] Hostiensis (Henricus de Segusio) stated: "Notabis etiam quod hic solvitur matrimonium, non per sententiam sed ipso iure propter contumeliam Creatoris."—*Commentaria in Libros V Decretalium* (5 vols. in 3, Venetiis, 1581), IV, *De Divortiis*, cap. 7, n. 3.

[32] Pontius, *De Sacramento Matrimonii Tractatus cum Appendice de Matrimonio Catholici cum Haeretico* (2. ed., Bruxellis, 1627), lib. IX, c. 4, n. 16, (hereafter cited as *De Sacram. Matrim.)*; Sanchez, *De Matrim.*, lib. VII, disp. LXXIV, nn. 2, 3, 4; Schmalzgrueber, *Ius Eccles, Universum*, lib. IV, tit. XIX, n. 27.

[33] *"Gaudemus in Domino,"* 22 apr. 1201—c. 8, X. *de divortiis*, IV, 19; Denzinger, *Enchiridion*, n. 407; Potthast, n. 1325.

CHAPTER II

FROM THE COUNCIL OF TRENT UP TO THE CODE

ARTICLE I. THE CONSTITUTIONS OF POPES PAUL III, ST. PIUS V AND GREGORY XIII

While the foregoing historical résumé is concerned almost directly with the Pauline privilege, there is evident in the gradual expansion of the argument a growing insistence on the fulfillment of the condition demanded by the interpellations, namely, that of certifying with a definite knowledge the departure of the unbeliever, so that subsequent legislation on this particular point was morally inevitable. A combination of circumstances in the fifteenth and sixteenth centuries furnished the occasions for the achieving of this effect.

The voyages and geographical discoveries of the Spanish and Portuguese explorers revived a practical interest in the Pauline privilege. With the finding of the Americas and their colonization, a new field of labor was opened to the Church, for missionary activity was simultaneous with secular expansion. The Spanish sovereigns, Ferdinand and Isabella, in subsidizing Columbus, declared in several documents that the chief end of conquest was the conversion of the natives. An excerpt from the will of Queen Isabella entreats her successors to work unceasingly for the conversion of the Indians.[1] But in their work the missionaries found themselves confronted not only with matrimonial problems similar to those which had arisen in the Church at Corinth and had been solved by St. Paul, but also with unfamiliar situations such as had never been experienced in Europe. There were involved and complicated polygamous unions the status of which demanded a solution if mass conversions were to be made. It could not be presumed that all of these marriages were invalid in order to allow the natives after baptism to take new Christian wives, for, as has been mentioned previously, the Church has consistently regarded infidel unions as valid, provided that they were not rendered null and void by any impediment deriving from the natural and positive divine laws.[2] On the contrary, the presumption at least favored the validity of the first marriage of a polygamist.

[1] Cf. Burton, *A Commentary on Canon 1125*, p. 15, note 6.

[2] *Supra*, pp. 1-6.

Up to the period of the Protestant revolution (c. 1517) the debate regarding the dissolubility of infidel marriages was confined to the case in which the Pauline privilege was operative.[3] Canonists and theologians agreed that such marriages lacked the firmness that attended a sacramental marital union, but that the bond could be broken in no other way than by the remarriage of the convert after the departure of the unbeliever. With new and unprecedented conditions demanding an answer, theologians and canonists were led to reconsider the questions involved, and in this manner the doctrine on marriage, so far as it applied to pagans, underwent fresh developments. The principle which theology had reached, namely, that there is a distinction between extrinsic and intrinsic indissolubility, was recalled. All valid marriages, whether of Christians or of infidels, were intrinsically indissoluble and could not be dissolved by the will of the contracting parties. Once, however, infidel unions came under the jurisdiction of the Church through the baptism of one of the parties of such a union, they were no longer absolutely indissoluble; they could be broken in certain circumstances by papal authority.[4] From this canonists began to realize that the *privilegium fidei* included more than just the *Casus Apostoli.*

In 1537 mission conditions forced Pope Paul III to act. He issued his Constitution "*Altitudo,*"[5] which presupposes simultaneous or successive polygamy or polyandry.[6] In this decretal Pope Paul III allowed a convert polygamist who could not recall which woman he first married to choose and marry any one of the several women with whom he had attempted marriage, whether she was baptized or not. However, if the convert remembered whom he first married, he had to retain her and dismiss the others. A renewal of consent was required but not the interpellations. This grant exceeded the limits of the Pauline privilege, for the constitution made no mention of the necessity of the conversion of the partner so chosen. If the convert's legitimate wife refused to live in peace, then the Pauline privilege could be invoked.

[3] Joyce, *Christian Marriage,* pp. 490, 492, 493.

[4] Gregory XIII, const. "*Populis,*" 25 ian. 1585—*Appendix ad Bullarium Pontificium Sacrae Congregationis de Propaganda Fide* (2 vols., Romae: Typis Collegii Urbani, no date given on title page), I, 103; *C.I.C.*, Documentum VIII; cf., Cappello, *Tractatus Canonico-Moralis de Sacramentis* (3 vols. in 6, Taurini: Marietti, 1932-1939, Vol. I, 3. ed., 1938; Vol. II, pars 1, 3. ed., 1938; Vol. II, pars II, 1932; Vol. II, pars III, 1935; Vol. III, partes I et II, 4. ed., *De Matrimonio,* 1939), n. 45, (hereafter cited as *De Matrim.).*

[5] 1 iun. 1537—*Appendix ad Bullarium Pontificium S.C.P.F.*, I, 25; *C.I.C.*, Documentum VI.

[6] Burton, *A Commentary on Canon 1125,* pp. 139-140.

Pope St. Pius V later sustained in his constitution "*Romani Pontificis*" [7] by still wider grants the privileges accorded by his predecessor Paul III. This constitution also presumes cases of polygamy. In countries where polygamy was practiced and where a man had married and dismissed several wives, and finally he desired to embrace the faith, Pius V allowed him to retain any one of the several women he had married, if the one of his choice was likewise willing to be converted and baptized. No renewal of consent was demanded nor were the interpellations required. Here again the Sovereign Pontiff was in many cases dissolving legitimate marriages in favor of the faith, and he was dissolving a marriage *ratum,* not one *ratum et consummatum,* in case the separated party had already been baptized and had not yet used the Pauline privilege to break the former bond.[8] If the convert wished to marry a Catholic woman who was not one of his former consorts, then he had to determine the first wife and apply the Pauline privilege, for the option granted by this constitution did not embrace this particular case.

Neither of these two constitutions required that the interpellations be proposed to the unbelieving spouse. As long as no attention was paid to the first spouse's disposition of will, either relative to embracing the faith or relative to abiding at least peacefully with the converted party, the Pauline privilege did not become operative, rather the Pontiff dissolved the bond "ex . . . apostolicae potestatis plenitudine," as Pius V expressed it. Authors concluded from this that the Pope was exercising his apostolic power with no thought of applying or extending the Pauline privilege.[9] While these two constitutions are silent on the matter of the interpellations, this brief summary of their contents was necessary for an appreciation of the further extension of the principles as later granted in the constitution "*Populis*" of Gregory XIII, in which the necessity of admonishing the unbeliever was for the first time, at least by negative implication, incorporated in an official document.

This most extraordinary constitution appeared under date of January 25, 1585. It did not mention polygamy, but supposed the captivity of

[7] 2 aug. 1571—*Appendix ad Bullarium Pontificium S.C.P.F.,* I, 45; *C.I.C.,* Documentum VII.

[8] Payen, *De Matrimonio in Missionibus ac Potissimum in Sinis Tractatus Practicus et Casu* (2. ed., vols., Zi-ka-wei: Typographia T'ou-Sè-Wè, 1935-1936), n. 2406, (hereafter cited as *De Matrimonio.)*

[9]. Mansella, *De Impedimentis Matrimonium Dirimentibus ac de Processu Iudiciali in Causis Matrimonialibus* (Romae: Typographia S.C. de Prop. Fide, 1861), pp. 114, 115, note 1, (hereafter cited as *De Imped. Matrim.);* De Smet, *De Spons. et Matrim.,* n. 355.

the infidel party, and enabled the convert to contract a Catholic marriage, though the pagan consort was known to be still alive, without asking the latter's consent or expecting an answer. The constitution was issued to meet a grave situation. The African slave trade was carrying on its destructive activities unchecked, tearing thousands from their homes and transporting them to distant lands, chiefly to other parts of Africa and to the Americas. The constitution was addressed to Angola, Ethiopia, Brazil and certain Indian regions, and was granted in favor of all persons who had been captured and transported away. It also allowed the persons remaining in the original territory, on conversion, to make use of the concession.[10] It further allowed infidel married couples who had become separated—one party or perchance both of whom had been carried off in slavery or by an enemy in time of war—to marry upon their conversion any Catholic without the previous making of interpellations, provided that the party did not know where the unbelieving consort was or, if such knowledge was had, that the party could not without grave danger or serious difficulty approach the infidel or send messengers to make the interpellations.

On these conditions ordinaries and pastors were declared competent to dispense from the bond of the infidel marriage and to allow remarriage with a Catholic, provided that summary extrajudicial evidence was produced to show that the unbeliever could not be interpellated, or, if interpellated, that he could not give an answer within a specified time.

> ". . . dummodo constet etiam summarie et extrajudicialiter, coniugem, ut praefertur, absentem moneri legitime non posse, aut monitum intra tempus in eadem monitione praefixum suam voluntatem non significasse . . ."[11]

Aside from the conclusion of Gregory's constitution, which declares the later marriage valid even when it becomes known after its celebration that the former partner was also converted when this marriage was contracted, the constitution is more concerned with the Pauline privilege than the constitutions of his predecessors, for it presupposes the neces-

[10] Woods, *The Constitutions of Canon 1125 and Their Application in the United States* (Milwaukee: Bruce, 1935), p. 64, (hereafter cited as *The Constitutions of Canon 1125).*

[11] Gregorius XIII, "*Populis,*" 25 ian. 1585—*Appendix ad Bullarium Pontificium S.C.P.F.*, I, 103; *C.I.C.*, Documentum VIII; cf. Augustine, *A Commentary on the New Code of Canon Law* (8 vols., St. Louis: Herder, 1925-1938, Vol. V, 5. revised ed. 1935), V. pp. 361-363, (hereafter cited as *A Commentary on Canon Law.)*

sity of admonishing the unbeliever, since the Pontiff here dispenses with the admonition for the reasons alleged. It is an important step in the development that led to the legislation on the interpellations which was soon to be enacted.

Article II. The First Explicit Act of Legislation on the Necessity of the Interpellations

The first piece of definite legislation which in a positive way demanded the interpellations is found in a response of the Sacred Congregation of the Council, January 23, 1603. It stated:

> "Sacra Congregatio censuit ita respondendum, minime posse praedictos ad veram Fidem conversos accipere alias fideles uxores, nisi prius constiterit, utrum primae voluerint cum eis permanere, vel non. Quod si noluerint cohabitare, vel si voluerint, non tamen absque contumelia Creatoris, vel ut conversos ad mortale peccatum pertrahant, tunc posse eos alias fideles accipere uxores. Si cohabitare absque Creatoris contumelia velint, et absque eo quod conversos ad mortale peccatum pertrahant, quamvis veram agnoscere Fidem noluerint, non posse conversos alias fideles accipere uxores. Non sufficere ea, quae proponuntur, nempe loci distantiam, difficultatem, ac praesumptionem, quum constare debeat de voluntate ipsarum uxorum infidelium."[12]

On the following day the Sacred Congregation of the Council further declared:

> ". . . distantiam, difficultatem, et praesumptionem, quod Uxores Infideles nolint cohabitare cum Viris conversis ad veram fidem, vel volentes cohabitare, non tamen absque contumelia Creatoris, vel absque eo, quod ipsos pertrahant ad mortale peccatum, non sufficere ad hoc, ut praefati Viri conversi possint Fideles ducere Uxores, sed constare debere de voluntate ipsarum Uxorum Infidelium."[13]

In these two responses the policy of the Church was established.

[12] Cf. Benedictus XIV, *De Synodo Dioecesana,* lib. XIII, c. 21, n. 1; S.C. de Prop. Fide, (ad C.P. pro Sin.), 16 iunii 1797—*Coll.,* n. 634; Feije, *De Imped. et Dispens. Matrim.,* n. 475.

[13] S.C.C., *Dubium* die 24 ianuarii 1603 lib. 10 Decretorum pag. 54, Pallottini, *Collectio Resolutionum S.C.C.,* s.v. "Matrimonium," § XIV, n. 2.

The interpellations were officially recognized as the ordinary means of determining the departure of the unbeliever. They set the standard for all future canonical legislation. While this is the first enunciation of the law, Catholic tradition back to the "Ambrosiaster" always held that for its validity the new marriage of the convert depended on the infidel's departure.[14] Merely in view of the silence of history on the procedure of proving the fact one cannot conclude that the proof of the fact was not always necessary for the application of the privilege. It is important to remember the distinction between the judicial, the summary extrajudicial, and the private interpellations. The latter under given conditions sufficed, as it now suffices, for the valid use of the Pauline privilege and undoubtedly this procedure, at least, was demanded whenever it was possible.[15]

It is true, the interpellations by their very nature do not constitute the essence of the Pauline privilege, but they are the medium ordinarily necessary to prove the fact of the unbeliever's departure, just as proof is needed of the fact of death in the event of a contemplated second marriage by a widower or a widow. Here the validity of the second marriage does not depend on the proof of death being made or neglected, but on the objective fact of the death of the first husband or wife. The essential element of the privilege is the physical or moral departure of the infidel for which the convert is not accountable. Under certain conditions the Church recognizes summary knowledge to this effect and for a grave cause may dispense from the interpellations. Normally, however, the interpellations must be made,[16] and this rule has been definitely maintained since the appearance of the responses issued in the year 1603.

Article III. Subsequent Development of the Doctrine by Reason of Direct Legislation

Since the time when the Sacred Congregation of the Council gave its response in 1603 all canonists have admitted the necessity of the interpellations, but at the same time have debated over the question of procedure when ecclesiastical authority was faced with an impasse.

[14] Ballerini-Palmieri, *Opus Theologicum Morale* (3 ed., 7 vols., Prati, 1898-1901), VI, n. 691; cf. also Vermeersch who stated: ". . . valorem novarum nuptiarum ab interna infidelis dispositione pendere."—*De Casu Apostoli,* n. 52.

[15] Wernz, *Ius Decretalium,* IV, pars II, n. 703, note 72.

[16] Wernz-Vidal, *Ius Matrimoniale,* n. 632, note 68; Mansella, *De Imped. Matrim.,* pp. 105-106, nn. 15, 16.

Canonists further have asked if the interpellations might on occasion be omitted. In the seventeenth century the doctrine concerning the need of a papal dispensation, or of a declaration with like effect, was not yet clearly developed; in fact, it was not definitely legislated until the Code that if the interpellations were to be omitted such a dispensation or declaration was necessary for the valid use of the Pauline privilege.[17]

For some time authors held that if the fact of the departure was established by means other than the interpellations, then the second marriage was both valid and licit. The School of Salamanca asserted:

> ". . . necessaria est admonitio infidelis, et illius interrogatio, an velit ad fidem converti? Quia novum matrimonium contrahi non potest, nisi ipse nolit converti; et sic necesse est eius voluntatem explorare; nisi aliunde constet de obstinatione infidelis; quia tunc non est necessaria admonitio: et nisi adeo distet, ut commode nequeat admoneri."[18]

Vasquez (1549-1604) likewise held that the interpellations were not required when it was apparent that it was impossible or useless to make them. Whether Vasquez was acquainted with the response of the Sacred Congregation of the Council of the year 1603 is not known as he died a few months after the decree was issued.[19] Sanchez (1550-1610) was of the opinion that when there was moral certitude of the obstinacy of the unbeliever, or when it was morally impossible to make the interpellations, as happens when the infidel cannot be contacted—and this fact in itself Sanchez considered as betokening a form of obstinacy—then his mind on the matter could be presumed and the obligation to make any interpellations ceased. "Non ergo necessaria est monitio, ubi moraliter est certa obstinatio." He quoted as his authority Vasquez. If, however, there was any doubt about the obstinacy of the unbeliever, then Sanchez held that the interpellations had to be

[17] Canon 1121; cf. also Mansella, *De Imped. Matrim.*, pp. 105, 106, nn. 15, 16; Vermeersch stated: "Si constet de discessu post baptismum, novae nuptiae *validae* sine interpellatione fient; *licitae* tamen non erunt, nisi legitime dispensetur."—*De Casu Apostoli,* n. 52.

[18] Salmanticenses, *Cursus Theologiae Moralis* (6 vols. in 4, Venetiis, 1728, Vol. I, Tract. IX, *De Matrimonio),* cap. IV, punctum II, n. 48, (hereafter cited as *Cursus Theol. Moralis.*)

[19] Vazquez, *Commentarium ac Disputationum in Primum Secundae Sancti Thomae Tomus Primus* (2 vols., Lugduni, 1620), q. XIX, art. VI, disp. LXVI, cap. V, nn. 25, 26.

made, or a dispensation to omit them had to be obtained from the Holy See.[20]

The School of Salamanca also held that if there was doubt about the will of the infidel to become converted or to live in the prescribed manner, it was not possible for the convert to remarry until that doubt was settled. But for the determination of this question this school of thought stated: "Non autem requiritur Ecclesiae declaratio ad hoc, sed sufficit prudens iudicium . . ."[21]

A conclusion of the Sacred Congregation of the Council in 1722 acknowledged these opinions as probable, but concluded that it was better to seek a dispensation from the Sovereign Pontiff. By reason of this answer there appeared evident the gradual insistence on a papal dispensation when conditions prevented the making of the interpellations. Authors consequently began to hold the opinion that the second marriage was illicit if the interpellations were neglected. The response was soon confirmed by the legislation of Pope Benedict XIV.[22]

An instruction of the Holy Office in 1757 recalled the statements of Benedict XIV, and declared that opinion not sufficiently safe which in practice allowed the judicial interpellations to be omitted simply because it appeared impossible to make them, or when it was foreseen that they would be useless, and maintained that in these circumstances a dispensation from the Supreme Pontiff was necessary, for it concluded that it pertained to the Holy Father alone to decide when and under what circumstances the interpellations could be or were to be omitted.[23]

[20] Sanchez, *De Matrim.*, lib. VII, disp. LXXIV, nn. 13, 15; cf. also Mansella, *De Imped. Matrim.*, P. 105, n. 16.

[21] Salmanticenses, *Cursus Theol. Moralis,* I, tract. IX, *De Matrim.*, cap. IV, punctum II, n. 46.

[22] Const. "*Apostolici ministerii,*" 16 sept. 1747—*Fontes*, n. 381. Pope Benedict stated: "Matrimonium ab infidelibus in statu infidelitate initum, et consummatum Divina lex solvit . . . iuxta praeceptum Apostoli in Epistola I, ad Cor., cap. 7. Ex hoc principio alterum veluti consequens deductum fuit ut coniux conversus coniugem infidelem requirere ac interpellare debeat, ut mentem suam super hac re aperte declaret . . ."—*De Synodo Dioecesana,* lib. XIII, c. 21, n. 4; lib. VI, c. 4, n. 3.

[23] Benedictus XIV, *De Synodo Dioecesana,* lib. VI, c. 4, n. 3; S.C.S. Off. (ex Litter. S.C. de Prop. Fide ad N. Mission. Pondicher.), 5 ian. 1757, ad 5—*Collectanea Constitutionum, Decretorum, Indultorum ac Instructionum S. Sedis ad usum Societatis Missionum ad exteros* (2 ed., Hongkong, 1905), n. 1428, (henceforth this work will be cited as *Coll. Hong.*) Cf. De Becker, *De Sponsalibus et Matrimonio Praelectiones Canonicae* (2. ed., Lovanii, 1903), p. 445, n. 3°, (hereafter cited as *De Spons. et Matrim.).*

This response established the norm for the subsequent instructions issued by the Sacred Congregations, excepting always the concessions granted by the papal constitutions previously mentioned.[24]

When the interpellations had been omitted and no dispensation had been secured, the Holy Office held specifically for the invalidity of the second marriage and refused to grant a *sanatio in radice*.[25] In response to an individual case the Congregation for the Propagation of the Faith informed the petitioners that a dispensation from the interpellations was thereby granted and that they were to seek a renewal of consent from the interested parties.[26]

The Holy Office, bearing in mind the statement of Benedict XIV, construed the omission of even one of the interpellations as affecting the validity, for when the Congregation was questioned about the practice of certain missionaries who failed to interpellate the unbelieving spouse regarding his possible desire for baptism, asking only if he would be willing to abide in peace with his convert partner, it responded that it did not consider this interrogation as fulfilling the precept of the interpellations. It appears, however, that in the following century Pope Gregory XVI was more indulgent relative to the posing of the questions, for he granted radical sanations for all the marriages which had been contracted after the proposing of but one of the two prescribed questions.[27]

A decree on the necessity of the interpellations is given in the Chinese Synod of Suchow.[28] The decree admirably demonstrates the official attitude of the Church. Though it was only a local synod, nevertheless the synod of Suchow had far-reaching authority because of its papal approbation. In the year 1803 the Sacred Congregation for the Propagation of the Faith undertook studies for the revision of

[24] S.C.S. Off. (ad Superiorem Mission. Peguan.), 11 iun. 1760—*Coll.*, n. 430; (Chen-si et Chan-si), 23 nov. 1769—*Coll.*, n. 475; instr. (ad Archiep. Quebecen.), 16 sept. 1824, ad 1, 3—*Coll.*, 784; (Cochinchin, Occid.), 12 iun. 1850, ad 1—*Fontes*, n. 910; (Pondicher.), 20 iun. 1855—*Coll.*, n. 1162; S.C. de Prop. Fide (C.P. pro Sin. Tunk. Occid.), 6 mart. 1816, ad 1—*Coll.*, n. 704; (Sutchuen.), 17 iun. 1836—*Coll.*, n. 845.

[25] S.C.S. Off. (Coreae), 11 sept. 1878, ad 1—*Coll.*, n. 1499.

[26] S.C. de Prop. Fide (C.P. pro Sin. Tunk. Occid.), 5 mart., 1816—*Coll.*, n. 706. The query is about the validity of a marriage prior to which the interpellations were omitted. The reply indicated that the marriage between Julius and Martha had been contracted as a null and void union.

[27] S.C. de Prop. Fide (Sutchuen), 17 ian. 1836—*Coll.*, n. 845.

[28] Synodus Sutchuensis, 2 sept. 1803—Mansi, XXXIX, 43.

the original synodal prescriptions. Due to the Napoleonic persecution the work was interrupted, but it was continued later, with the Holy See putting its stamp of approval on the acts of the Synod, June 29, 1822. Some years later these prescriptions were extended to all of China and the bordering empires. From the text of the synodal acts there is recognizable a rescript of the Roman Pontiff regarding the interpellations. The rescript states that always and in all cases the interpellations are to be made, except when it appears morally impossible or exceedingly difficult, in which contingency a dispensation is to be sought from the Holy See. The text is insistent that nothing can excuse from the securing of a dispensation,[29] and that the Divine law of making the interpellations has the character of such a grave positive obligation that apart from a papal dispensation the interpellations may not be omitted. They may not be omitted, the synodal acts state, even if in the effort to make them the physical safety of the convert is jeopardized, as, for example, when it is known that the infidel under subterfuge desires a reunion with his convert spouse in order to sell her into slavery.[30] And as if to strengthen an already impregnable canon, the acts further declare that not even a danger to an entire Christian community would suffice to omit them. However, in this event recourse should be had to the Holy See, or to the Vicar Apostolic as the representative of the Holy See, for the proper dispensation. The Synod concludes that the norms guiding such requests are to be found in the constitution of Pope Gregory XIII.[31] From the tenor of the Suchow synodal acts and of the responses of the Holy Office it is evident that the Church was committed to the policy of demanding the interpellations for the valid use of the Pauline privilege.

Because of the lack of uniformity in practice as well as in canonical legislation, and because the Church does not intend the responses of the Sacred Congregations to have the force of *ex cathedra* pronouncements, some authors prior to the Code[32] held that the necessity of making the interpellations ceased when there was moral certitude of the unbeliever's departure. All agreed that, according to St. Paul's doctrine, there had to be a departure effected by the infidel, but opinion

[29] S.C. de Prop. Fide (Sutchuen.), 17 ian. 1836—Coll., n. 845.

[30] S.C. de Prop. Fide (ad Vic. Ap. Sutchuen.), 17 ian. 1836, ad 2—*Coll.*, n. 845; cf. also S.C.S. Off. (Portland), 18 iun. 1884—*Fontes*, n. 1088.

[31] "*Populis*," 25 ian. 1585—*C.I.C.*, Documentum VIII; Synodus Sutchuensis, 2 sept. 1803—Mansi, XXXIX, 43; cf. also S.C.S. Off. (Chen-si et Chan-si), 23 nov. 1769, ad 1, 4—*Coll.*, *n.* 475; Lämmer, "Die Interpellatio," *AKKR*, XI (1864), 249-251, nn. 7-10.

[32]. E.g., Vermeersch, *De Casu Apostoli*, nn. 52, 56.

was divided regarding the specific proof necessary to establish that fact. All likewise admitted that the Sovereign Pontiff had reserved judgment of the fact to himself. It was contended,[33] however, that if the departure of the unbeliever was definitely known by means other than those afforded by the interpellations, and the interpellations were omitted, the second marriage of the convert might be presumed valid unless the Holy See decreed otherwise.

On the contrary, others[34] were of the opinion that the privilege could not be invoked apart from the supreme authority of the Sovereign Pontiff, but only when its use was subjected to his authority, so that in the cases wherein the Pauline privilege was not applicable for use in accordance with the expressly stipulated conditions requisite for its certified operation, the Pope alone could supply, in favor of the faith, for what was lacking.

This latter opinion—that for the validity of the convert's second marriage the interpellations had to be made, unless the Holy See declared otherwise—was, even prior to the Code, more in harmony with the mind of the Church as is shown by the decrees of the Pontiffs and the responses of the Sacred Congregations issued up to the promulgation of the Code. However, the former viewpoint, prior to the Code, was probably tenable at least theoretically, namely, that a second marriage, if it was contracted by a convert without having interpellated the unbelieving spouse, was valid when certified knowledge of the infidel's departure was had through means other than that afforded by the interpellations.[35]

Since the Code the question has been definitely settled for not only is departure a condition for the valid use of the privilege, but it is also enacted in ecclesiastical law[36] that proof of the infidel's desertion is likewise a condition. Hence, the interpellations must always be made,[37] or the proper dispensation must be obtained.[38]

[33] Vermeersch, *loc. cit.*

[34] Cf. Arendt, "Quomodo in favorem fidei solvatur a S. Pontifice matrimonium in infidelitate contractum," *Ephemerides Theologicae Lovanienses,* I (1924), 174-184, and especially page 177.

[35] Payen, *De Matrimonio,* n. 2351; Vermeersch, *De Casu Apostoli,* n. 53; Ojetti, *Synopsis Rerum Moralium et Iuris Pontificii* (Romae, 1899), s.v. "Casus Apostoli," (hereafter cited as *Synopsis Rerum Moralium);* Mansella, *De Imped. Matrim.,* p. 109, n. 19.

[36] Canon 1121.

[37] Petrovits, *The New Church Law on Matrimony* (2. ed., Philadelphia: McVey, 1926), n. 562, (hereafter cited as *The New Church Law);* De Smet, *De Spons. et Matrim.,* n. 352; Wernz-Vidal, Ius *Matrimoniale,* n. 632, note 68.

[38] Wernz, *Ius Decretalium,* IV, pars II, n. 704.

Article IV. Historical Development of the Dispensation from the Interpellations

When for a just cause it is impossible to make the interpellations the Sovereign Pontiff or his delegate may dispense from them. The Holy Father reserves to himself the right of adjudicating the merits of each case,[39] unless circumstances allow the application of the concessions to omit the interpellations accorded in the Constitutions referred to in the Code of Canon Law.[40]

Concomitant with the development of the doctrine of the necessity of the interpellations in the seventeenth century were the opinions of canonists on when and under what circumstances the interpellations might be omitted. Revived practical interest in the Pauline privilege occasioned by the sixteenth century conditions in missionary countries, together with the growing opinion as to the absolute necessity of the interpellations, inspired these discussions. The Constitutions of Popes Paul III, Pius V and Gregory XIII had solved problems for certain restricted missionary areas, but this particular legislation did not answer for the application of the Pauline privilege, possibly available in new regions. The seventeenth century authors concluded that the omission of the interpellations was lawful when certain circumstances were verified, but held that if there was any doubt about the unbeliever's mind they either had to be made or a papal dispensation had to be sought.[41] This gave rise to the opinion that not only in doubtful cases but in any event a dispensation was necessary whenever it was impossible to propose the interpellations. As a result, a definite policy began to shape itself as early as the year 1722, when the Sacred Congregation of the Council issued its conclusions on the disputed question. The issued document stated the opinion of authors of note,[42] who taught that the interpellations could be omitted under difficult or impossible situations, and stated the arguments for and against with regard to the necessity of recourse to the Holy See under the circumstances. After weighing the opinions, the instruction concluded that a dispensation from the Roman Pontiff should be sought in all cases. Because of the importance of this decision and its influence on subsequent legislation it is herewith quoted:

> "Concurrentibus autem consimilibus circumstantiis, nonnulli putant, posse iure suo Coniugem Fidelem, omissa interpel-

[39] Canons 1121, § 2; 1123.

[40] Canon 1125.

[41] *Supra*, pp. 22-26.

[42] Cf. Sanchez, *De Matrim.*, lib. VII, disp. LXXIV, nn. 14-15.

latione Viri Infidelis, transire ad alia vota, *Sanchez, de matrim., lib.* 7, *disp.* 74, *n.* 14 *et* 15; sicque fuisse in Curia Archiepiscopali Neapolitana decisum, referunt *Genuensis in praxi dictae Curiae cap.* 27, *n.* 20, *Riccius in praxi par.* I, *resolut.* 241; et haec opinio tamquam probabilis admittitur *a Diana in Oper. Coord. tom.* 2, *tract.* 6, *resolut.* 124, et in terminis Mulieris Hebraeae ad Fidem conversae, et hic in Italia degentis, quod, stante latitatione Viri in infidelitate permanentis, posset, omissa interpellatione, aliud Matrimonium contrahere, docuerunt *Comitol. lib.* I, *quaest.* 124, *Clericat. de Sacram. Matrim. decis.* II, *num.* 29.

"E contra alii censent, quod, etiam concurrentibus circumstantiis, de iure sit locus interpellationi, sed quod si graves sint, haberi debeat recursus ad Summum Pontificem, cuius est, in eo rerum statu indulgere, ut, omissa interpellatione, Coniux Fidelis ad alia vota transire possit, *Pontius, de Matrim, lib.* 7, *cap.* 48, *n.* 22, concordat *Nicolaus Lucubr. civil. lib.* I, *tit.* 10, *de Nuptiis num.* 43, ubi dicit sic resolutum fuisse ab hac Sacra Congregatione, et faciunt Apostolicae litterae Gregorii XIII apud *Pignatell. consult.* 93, *tom.* 8, *versus fin.*, in quibus singulis locorum Ordinariis, Parochis, et Presbyteris Missionariis Societatis Iesu in Angola, Ethiopia, et Brasilia degentibus concessit, ut, si aliquis ex Coniugibus ad Fidem convertatur, et alius in infidelitate remaneat, quoties sibi summarie, et extraiudicialiter constiterit, Coniugem Infidelem abesse, et legitime moneri non posse, dispensare valeant, ut Coniux Fidelis, omissa interpellatione, aliud contrahat Matrimonium."

"His stantibus, dignabuntur EE. VV. decernere:

I. An de iure necessaria sit interpellatio in casu et cetera et quatenus affirmative.

II. An, stantibus circumstantiis, indulgenda sit dispensatio ab interpellatione in casu etcetera.
Ad utrumque affirmative."[43]

"Unde licet Vir Hebraeus Mulieri pariter Hebraeae ab annis undecim dedisset libellum repudii, conceptum verbis adeo iniuriosis, ut nullum spei vestigium superesset reditus Viri ad

[43] *Thesaurus Resolutionum Sacrae Congregationis Concilii* (167 vols., Romae 1718-1908), tom. I, pp. 116-119; cf. also S.C.C., *Florentina,* die 17 ian. 1722 —Pallottini, *Collectio Resolutionum S.C.C., s.v.* "*Matrimonium,*" § XIV, n. 3.

> Uxorem, isque ad ignotas Regiones perrexerit, quin unquam ipsam ac filios requisiverit, nihilominus Sacra Congregatio, haud etiam obstante quod periculum esset in mora, declaravit, de iure necessariam esse interpellationem, dum praefata Mulier, iam ad fidem conversa, transire exoptaret ad secunda vota, stantibus tamen huiusmodi circumstantiis, censuit, indulgendam ei esse dispensationem a praedicta interpellatione."[44]

Benedict XIV as Cardinal Lambertini always championed the prerogative of the Sovereign Pontiff to declare that a dispensation was applicable in a given case. With his advent to the papacy a relatively short time after this decision of the Congregation of the Council, it is noticeable that the official attitude of the Church more and more adopted this as a principle in practice. The opinion of authors and the responses of the Congregations, under his direction, began to stress the need of such a dispensation when it was determined that the interpellations could not be made.

Guided by the principles of his predecessor, Gregory XIII, as expressed in the constitution *"Populis,"* [45] as well as by the response of the Sacred Congregation of the Council of January 23, 1603, Benedict XIV issued two documents that have a direct bearing on the question.[46] In the earlier one he granted the faculty to dispense from the interpellations in all cases contained in Pope Gregory XIII's constitution. In Benedict's *De Synodo Dioecesana* the same thought is found expressed as in these documents.[47] After stating cases which involved the inability of certain Jewish converts to propose the interpellations, he quoted the opinion of Sanchez[48] and agreed with him that the interpellations could be omitted, but, that in these instances a dispensation from the Supreme Pontiff should be obtained, because it was for him to declare when and in what circumstances the interpellations could be omitted. He here quoted also Pontius [49] as additional authority for his doctrine.

[44] Pallottini, *ibid.*, n. 5.

[45] 25 ian. 1585—*Appendix ad Bullarium Pontificium S.C.P.F.*, I, 103; *C.I.C.*, Documentum VIII.

[46] Ep. *"In suprema,"* 16 ian. 1745—*Fontes*, n. 353; Const. *"Apostolici ministerii,"* 16 sept. 1747—*Fontes*, n. 381.

[47] Lib. VI, c. IV, n. 3.

[48] *De Matrim.*, lib. VII, disp. LXXIV, n. 14.

[49] *De Sacram. Matrim.*, lib. VII, c. XLVIII, n. 22.

It seems that this opinion of Benedict XIV established the principle which Rome as the "*magistra veritatis*" desired to see followed in practice, for subsequent responses of the Sacred Congregations with few exceptions [60] emphasized the fact that the Roman Pontiff alone was the competent authority to declare whether the interpellations in a given case could be omitted. The Sovereign Pontiff alone possessed the power of dispensing from the interpellations. Only with his authorized dispensation could the convert licitly or even validly enter a new marriage, as a study of the papal documents and the replies of the Holy Office show.[61]

As a corollary to the recognition of the papal authority to dispense from both interpellations, it follows *a fortiori* that he may for a cause dispense from one or the other of them. This is established by the early precedent set by the Sacred Congregations,[62] when they allowed the convert to omit the second interpellation.

When necessity urged, the Holy Office allowed ordinaries, acting as delegates of the Supreme Pontiff, to dispense from the interpellations if time prevented recourse and the departure of the unbeliever was certain.[63] But while permitting this in practice, the Holy Office advised the ordinaries that they should be prepared to meet these emergencies by securing faculties to dispense in a determined number of cases.[64] The decrees of the Synod of Suchow admonished missionaries who had received faculties for this purpose to use them seldom and only in cases of grave and urgent necessity: "*ut non dispensetur nisi . . . in casu urgentissimae necessitatis.*" As in the constitution of Pope Gregory XIII and according to the norms of the responses of the Holy Office,

[60] S.C. de Prop. Fide (C.P. pro Sin. Sutchuen.), 5 mart. 1787, ad 2—*Fontes*, n. 4615.

[61] Gregory XIII, const. "*Populis*," 25 ian. 1585—*Appendix ad Bullarium S.C.P.F.*, I, 103; Benedictus XIV, ep. "*In suprema*," 16 ian. 1745, ad 2—*Fontes*, n. 353; const. "*Apostolici ministerii*," 16 sept. 1747—*Fontes*, n 381; S.C.S. Off. (Cochinchin.), 1 aug. 1759, ad 5—*Fontes*, n. 810; *S.C.* de Prop. Fide, (ad C. P. pro Sin.), 3 ian. 1777—*Coll.*, n. 517; cf. *De Synodo Dioecesana*, lib. XIII, c. 21, n. 4; Lämmer, "Die Interpellatio,"—*AKKR*, XI (1864), p. 250, n. 9.

[62] S.C.S. Off. (Cochinchin.), 1 aug. 1759, ad 3—*Fontes*, n. 810; 8 iun. 1836—*Fontes*, n. 874; (Siam), 4 iul. 1855—*Fontes*, n. 931; instr. (pro Vic. Ap. ad Gallas), 20 iun. 1866—*Fontes*, n. 994; cf. Wernz, *Ius Decretalium*, IV, pars II, n. 704; Cappello, *De Matrim.*, n. 781.

[63] S.C.S. Off., 11 aug. 1859—*Fontes*, n. 954.

[64] S.C.S. Off. (Portland), 18 iun. 1884—*Fontes*, n. 1088.

the Synod prescribed previous extrajudicial procedure to determine the impossibility of making the interpellations.[55]

A study of the responses of the Holy Office to petitions for dispensations from the interpellations reveals that there had to be grave reasons prompting the request. The impossibility was not to be presumed, but had to be demonstrated by a summary and extrajudicial examination, from which it was morally certain that the interpellations could not be made, that the effort would be futile, or that there was present the factor of grave harm accruing either to the individual or to the Christian community.[56]

Among the causes generally admitted were the following: (1) if the unbeliever lived in a hostile country or in a district overrun with outlaws, so that he could not be approached either personally or by means of a messenger;[57] (2) if, to make the interpellations, a long and arduous journey was necessary, involving heavy expenses or serious inconvenience;[58] (3) if the unbeliever's domicile was unknown;[59] (4) if, by reason of the interpellations, a wave of bigotry or persecution was feared by a Christian community;[60] (5) if a polygamous convert could not remember who was his first legitimate wife;[61] or, if indeed he knew this, but nevertheless could not locate her;[62] or, if there was a probable doubt whether the polygamous convert had given true matrimonial consent to any of his wives;[63] (6) if the unbeliever could respond but

[55] Synodus Sutchuensis, 2 sept, 1803—Mansi, XXXIX, 43; Lämmer, "Die Interpellatio,"—*AKKR,* XI (1864), p. 250, n. 9.

[56] "Iustae autem huiusmodi causae tunc aderunt cum ex processu saltem summario et extraiudicialiter moraliter constet coniugem infidelem interpellari non posse, aut interpellationem vel inutilem vel graviter periculosam futuram esse."—S.C.S. Off. (ad Vic. Ap. Iaponiae Merid.), 4 febr. 1891—*Fontes,* n. 1130.

[57] Gregorius XIII, const. *"Populis,"* 25 ian. 1585—*C.I.C.,* Documentum VIII; S.C.S. Off. (Mongoliae), 29 nov. 1882—*Fontes,* n. 1075.

[58] Synodus Sutchuensis, cap. IX, n. 8—Mansi, XXXIX, 43; Mansella, *De Imped. Matrim.,* p. 118, note 4.

[59] Synodus Sutchuensis, cap. IX, n. 8—Mansi, *loc. cit;* Mansella, *loc. cit.*

[60] S.C.S. Off. (Chen-si et Chan-si), 23 nov. 1769, ad 4—*Fontes,* n. 825.

[61] Paul III, const. *"Altitudo,"* 1 iun. 1537—*C.I.C.,* Documentum VI; S.C.S. Off. 8 iun. 1836—*Fontes,* n. 874; (Siouxormen.), 18 maii 1892—*Fontes,* n. 1155.

[62] Pius V, const. *"Romani Pontificis,"* 2 aug. 1571—*C.I.C.,* Documentum VII; S.C.S. Off. (Siam), 22 nov. 1871—*Fontes,* n. 1019.

[63] Paul III, const. *"Altitudo,"* 1 iun. 1537—*C.I.C.,* Documentum VI; S.C.S. Off. 8 iun. 1836—*Fontes,* n. 874.

failed to do so within the peremptory period of time;[64] (7) if the unbeliever was perpetually insane.[65]

The Holy Office did not accept as sufficiently grave the following proposed causes: (1) that the unbelieving woman might possibly suffer in reputation; (2) that indignation might result on the part of the unbelieving spouse, or that threats might be made against the person of the messenger attempting to secure the interpellations; (3) that the infidel had secured a civil divorce and had remarried and could not by law return to his former spouse because the civil law stood in his way to effect such a return.[66]

In granting faculties to ordinaries to dispense from the interpellations in a certain number of cases, the Holy Office usually included a list of legitimate causes on which it was safe to act. They were generally taken from the acts of the Synod of Suchow, which again were founded on the norms established by Gregory XIII in his constitution "*Populis.*" The causes were enumerated thus:

> "Noverint missionarii, quibus concessa est facultas dispensandi ab interpellatione, ea non uti, nisi ad normam brevis Gregorii XIII, scilicet, ut non dispensetur, nisi quando fidelis coniugem infidelem absentem, an sine contumelia Creatoris secum habitare velit, ut par est, monere nequit, vel quia interdum ad hostiles et barbaras provincias ne nuntiis quidem accessus pateat, vel quia prorsus ignoratur in quas regiones fuerit transactus, vel quia itineris longitudo magnam affert difficultatem; et praeterea rarissime, et in casu urgentis necessitatis. Extra hos casus omnino fieri debet interpellatio, etiamsi inutilis aut periculosa videatur, si fidelis velit ad alias nuptias transire, nec ab ea dispensari potest, sive timeatur ne infidelis interpellatus, sicut prima vice uxorem vendidit, eamdem recuperatam iterum vendat; sive praesumatur cum fundamento vel ex dissentionibus coniugum in praecedenti cohabitatione, vel ex

[64] S.C.S. Off. 1 aug. 1859—*Fontes,* n. 954; (Mongoliae), 29 nov. 1882, ad 2, 3—*Fontes,* n. 1075; S.C. de Prop. Fide (ad C.P. pro Sin.), 5 mart. 1816, ad 1, 3—*Coll.,* n. 704.

[65] S.C. de Prop. Fide (C.P. pro Sin.), 5 mart. 1787, ad 1—*Coll.,* n. 589.

[66] La mente è che nè il divorzio, nè il secondo matrimonio civile sono sufficienti per esimere dall'obbligo dell'interpellazione.—Quatenus vero saltem summarie et extraiudicialiter constet interpellationem vel impossibilem vel inutilem fore, utetur (Episcopus) facultate dispensandi, si ea polleat: . . ."—S. C. S. Off. (Portland), 18 iun. 1884, *ad mentem*—*Fontes,* n. 1088; (Chen-si et Chan-si), 23 nov. 1769—*Fontes,* n. 825.

> alia quavis circumstantia, partem infidelem nolle redire. Quodsi periculum adsit, ne facta interpellatione exinde oriatur molestia seu persecutio contra christianos, huiusmodi casus deferatur ad Vicarium Apostolicum, ut S. Sedes consulatur, prout olim responsum est in Congregatione S. Officii anno 1769."[67]

Aside from these causes, excepting always extraordinary faculties to dispense, missionaries were not to use their faculties but were to appeal to the Holy Office.[68]

An example of extraordinary faculties which acknowledged extensive causes for the granting of a dispensation is found in a response of the Holy Office directed to the Archbishop of Quebec, wherein it was permitted him to dispense at his discretion for any serious cause. The usual list of causes is omitted,[69] but this is most uncommon. However, another somewhat isolated example is found in the *Acta Sanctae Sedis*,[70] in which the Archbishop of Vrhbosna (Sarajevo) was conceded similar privileges, but the majority of replies indicated the mind of the Sovereign Pontiff, namely, that he insisted upon the verification of one or the other of the delineated causes before the faculty could be employed. In the event of any contingency concerning which no specific mention was made in the granted faculties recourse was to be made to the Holy See.

The constitution of Gregory XIII, the statements of Benedict XIV and the responses of the Holy Office announced the far-reaching effects of a dispensation from the interpellations. Not only did the dispensation permit the convert to enter another marriage validly and licitly without contacting the unbelieving partner, but by reason of it the new marriage was regarded as valid even if it later developed that the former consort was already baptized at the time. Usually, of course, a dispensation allowed the Pauline privilege to take its course,

[67] Synodus Vicariatus Sutchuensis (1803), cap. IX, n. 8—*Acta et Decreta Sacrorum Conciliorum Recentiorum, Collectio Lacensis* (7 vols., Friburigi Brisgoviae, 1870-1890), VI, 623, (hereafter cited as *Coll. Lac.)*.

[68] S.C.C. Off. (Siam), 4 iul 1855—*Fontes*, n. 931; (Mongoliae), 29 nov. 1882—*Fontes*, n. 1075.

[69] "Iudicio autem remittitur Episcoporum in illis Missionibus versantium, quibus facta sit facultas huiusmodi concedendae dispensationis, decernere in casibus particularibus, an concurrant urgentes eae circumstantiae ob quas dispensandum sit ab interpellationis obligatione."—S. C. S. Off. (ad Archiep. Quebecen.), 16 sept. 1824, ad 3—*Fontes*, n. 866.

[70] 16 aug. 1895—*ASS*, XXIX (1896-97), 565.

but in the event of the deserting infidel's baptism in the interim the Roman Pontiff dissolved the ratified but non-consummated marriage in consideration of the favor and benefit which was to be derived by the parties from their newly found faith.[71]

Unlike the interpellations concerning which, when once made, there was no need of repeating them,[72] the Sacred Congregation for the Propagation of the Faith required a convert to secure a renewal of the dispensation from the making of the interpellations if he failed to avail himself of the privilege within a year from the date the dispensation was granted. The response did not state, however, whether the renewal of the dispensation was required for the valid or simply for the licit use of the Pauline privilege.[73]

[71] Gregorius XIII, const. "*Populis,*" 25 ian. 1585—*Appendix ad Bullarium S.C.P.F.*, I, 103; *C.I.C.*, Documentum VIII; Benedictus XIV, ep. "*In Suprema,*" 16 ian. 1745—*Fontes,* n. 353; S.C.S. Off. (ad Vic. Ap. Iaponiae Merid.), 4 febr. 1891—*Fontes,* n. 1130; Benedictus XIV, *De Synodo Dioecesana,* lib. XIII, c. 21, n. 5; Cf. also De Becker, *De Spons. et Matrim.*, p. 456; Wernz, *Ius Decretalium,* IV, pars II, n. 704.

[72] Wernz, *Ius Decretalium,* IV, pars II, n. 703.

[73] S.C. de Prop. Fide (C.P. pro Sin. Sutchuen.), 26 iun. 1820—*Coll.,* n. 743.

CANONICAL COMMENTARY

PART TWO. THE LEGISLATION OF THE CODE ON THE INTERPELLATIONS

CHAPTER III

THE OBJECT AND NECESSITY OF THE INTERPELLATIONS

ARTICLE I. THE OBJECT IN MAKING THE INTERPELLATIONS

In the present chapter it needs to be recalled that the application of the Pauline privilege, with which the interpellations are all but inseparably connected, obtains exclusively in the case of valid marriages originally contracted by the unbaptized, and always entails the dissolution of a true matrimonial bond. The marriages of infidels are presumed to be valid whenever it is shown, in a specific case, that the marriage was really entered upon with some external ceremony or other action signifying marital consent. For although infidels are not bound by laws merely ecclesiastical,[1] the Church, when called upon to judge their marriages, applies the presumptions which the natural and positive divine law and correct jurisprudence establish in the case.

The dissolution of marriages which were contracted in infidelity, whenever such marriages create a serious obstacle for the newly embraced faith of one of the parties, has been practiced from the beginning of the Church. It has been noted how inviolable the marriage contract has always been regarded by right minded people, and particularly by Christ and His Church. Hence the severance of this bond under any conditions is indeed a grave matter.

As has been seen previously, a consummated marriage between baptized Christians, Catholic or non-Catholic, is both intrinsically and extrinsically indissoluble; death alone can dissolve the bond.[2] But the marriages between two infidels, or the marriages between a baptized and an unbaptized party, when the question involved is one that favors the true faith, are not similarly indissoluble. The subject of this treatise does not propose to deal with the latter of these two possibilities but rather the former, that is, with the dissolution of

[1] Canon 12.

[2] Canon 1118.

the validly contracted marriages, be they consummated or unconsummated, between two unbelievers, when one of them has become converted and has received the sacrament of baptism.

Prior to any discussion of the legislation of the Code on the interpellations, a briefly restated definition of the Pauline privilege will not be amiss. This privilege denotes a special concession granted on the apostolic authority of St. Paul, by virtue of which a converted infidel, whose consort remains in infidelity and declines to cohabit peacefully, is given the right to contract a Christian marriage, by the use of which right there is effected a dissolution of the first marriage, even though it was consummated.

Four conditions must be fulfilled for the licit and valid use of the Pauline privilege: (1) the first supposition is that a legitimate marriage exists between the unbaptized parties;[3] (2) the second assumption is that one of the parties has validly received the sacrament of baptism. The necessary presence of this condition is but a consequence of the doctrine enunciated by the Apostle.[4] For this reason catechumens cannot avail themselves of the concession, for the foundation of the Pauline privilege is not simply the possession of the true faith, but the reception of the sacrament of faith;[5] (3) the third postulate is the actual departure, either physical or moral, of the unbelieving spouse because of hatred of the faith or because of any of the other recognized reasons;[6] and (4) the fourth requirement is the evidence which is necessary for proving the fact of departure. The fact of the infidel's contumacy must be established in the external forum. This is accomplished by means of the interpellations.

If for some legitimate reason it is impossible to make the interpellations, and if the concessions of canon 1125 cannot be applied, then a papal dispensation from the interpellations must always be secured. This leads to the specific consideration of canon 1121.[7]

[3] Canon 1120, § 1; S.C.S. Off. (Siouxormen.), 18 maii 1892, ad 2—*Fontes*, n. 1155; (Niger), 17 aug. 1898—*Fontes*, n. 1205; De Smet, *De Spons. et Matrim.*, n. 343; Cappello, *De Matrim.*, n. 769.

[4] I Cor., VII: 12-16.

[5] Canon 1121, §1; ". . . matrimonium non solvitur nisi per baptismum."—S.C. de Prop. Fide (ad C.P. pro Sin.), 16 ian. 1803, ad 1—*Fontes*, n. 4671; De Smet, *De Spons. et Matrim.*, n. 345; Vermeersch, *De Casu Apostoli*, n. 37; Wernz-Vidal, *Ius Matrimoniale*, n. 631, note 55; Gasparri, *De Matrim.*, nn. 1137, 1138.

[6] Cf. p. 43ff.

[7] On these general notions the reader may confer: Wernz-Vidal, *Ius Matrimoniale*, n. 631; De Smet, *De Spons. et Matrim.*, n. 341; Gasparri, *De Matrim.*,

Canon 1121

Can. 1121. § 1. *Antequam coniux conversus et baptizatus novum matrimonium valide contrahat, debet, salvo praescripto can. 1125, partem non baptizatam interpellare:*

1°. *An velit et ipsa converti ac baptismum suscipere;*

2° *An saltem velit secum cohabitare pacifice sine contumelia Creatoris.*

2. *Hae interpellationes fieri semper debent, nisi Sedes Apostolica aliud declaraverit.*

The primary object or purpose for making the interpellations is to ascertain the desire of the unbeliever regarding his possible conversion to the faith. But the questions in the interpellations are not alone concerned with obtaining the manifestation and certification of this desire, whether it reveals a positive wish to embrace the faith or whether, on the contrary, it reflects a negative will in this regard. In the event of a negative will the second of these questions seeks to establish assurance and certainty regarding the unbeliever's willingness or unwillingness to abide in peaceful cohabitation with the converted partner and to allow the unrestricted practice of the new faith postulated by the conversion. If the answer of the unbeliever is again negative in its import, then the convert becomes free to leave the infidel partner and may in addition contract a new Christian marriage.

In granting this privilege in favor of the faith St. Paul was inspired to remove the relatively insuperable burden of enforced celibacy inevitably facing many converts. There are circumstances in which the road to heaven would present extreme difficulty to converts if the dissolution of their earlier marriage in infidelity were not possible. In an instance wherein these unfavorable conditions are truly extant and are ascertained as such by a negative reply to both of the questions addressed to the unbeliever in the interpellations, a new avenue lies open for the neophyte's achievement of peace of conscience in the new faith.[8] "But if the unbeliever depart, let him depart. For a

n. 1132; Cappello, *De Matrim.*, n. 767; Vermeersch-Creusen, *Epitome Iuris Canonici* (5 ed., 3 vols., Mechliniae-Romae: Dessain, 1934—1937), II, n. 427, (hereafter cited as *Epitome*); Blat, *Commentarium Textus Codicis Iuris Canonici* (5 vols. in 7, Romae: Collegio Angelico, 1921-1938, Vol. III, pars I, *De Sacramentis*, Romae, 1924), III, pars I, nn. 526, 530, (hereafter this volume of Blat's Commentarium will be cited as *De Sacramentis*).

[8] Vermeersch, *De Casu Apostoli*, n. 54.

brother or sister is not under bondage in such cases, but God has called us to peace." [9]

However, if the unbelieving spouse is willing to accept the situation caused by the conversion of his partner, then a new marriage is not permitted to the convert. On the other hand, if the unbeliever is not willing to abide peacefully, or if he has already actually abandoned the converted party, a new marriage is permitted to the convert, provided that the interpellations have established proof for the fact of the infidel's departure, a matter which may not be presumed, or, provided that a papal dispensation from the making of the interpellations has been secured.[10]

St. John Chrysostom held that the condition of departure was fulfilled not merely if the unbeliever had already separated, but also if he endeavored to induce the convert to join in pagan or false worship or to become an accomplice in some grave sin.[11] This interpretation of the passage of St. Paul's Epistle [12] renders it probable that St. John Chrysostom understood "depart" in this sense: "If the unbeliever is the cause of the separation, let him cause separation." The words thus rendered have a much wider scope in their meaning than when translated: "If the unbeliever departs, let him depart." The unbeliever brings about the separation no less by making the practice of the Christian religion difficult or impossible for the convert, than by forsaking him. One is safe in accepting Chrysostom's explanation of St. Paul's words.

The decretals of Pope Innocent III [13] reach the same results. The Pope enumerates three cases in which separation is justified: (1) when the unbelieving spouse refuses cohabitation; (2) when he will not refrain from blasphemy against the Divine Name; and (3) when he endeavors to lead the convert into mortal sin. The introduction of the last two suppositions was due, as has been noted in the historical conspectus,[14] to the general recognition of the principle estab-

[9] I Cor., VII:15.

[10] Canon 1121.

[11] *In Epistolam I ad Corinthios, Homilia XIX*, n. 3—*MPG,* LXI, 155.

[12] I Cor., VII: 15.

[13] *"Quanto te magis,"* 1 maii 1199—c. 7, X, *de divortiis,* IV, 19; *"Gaudemus in Domino,"* 22 apr. 1201—c. 8, X, *de divortiis,* IV, 19; cf. also Denzinger, *Enchiridion,* nn. 406, 407; Potthast, nn. 684, 1325.

[14] Cf. pp. 9-23, and especially p. 15.

lished by the "Ambrosiaster," *"contumelia Creatoris solvit ius matrimonii."* [15] Hence the term "depart" must be acknowledged to include not only a physical but also a moral separation.[16]

It is likewise evident from a study of the Scriptural text and of the interpretation attached to it by tradition that the word "depart" refers only to a separation effected by the unbeliever: "But if the *unbeliever* depart, let him depart." [17] This separation may be culpable, or it may be a separation over which the convert has no control precisely because he has not brought it about through any fault of his own, or for any reason that is attributable to him as its cause.[18]

It is quite evident that malicious desertion allows the use of the Pauline privilege by the convert, but it is equally true that the privilege may be used when the separation effected by the unbelieving spouse is not due to any hostility towards the Christian faith, but to some obstacle he is powerless to remove. A case occurred in which the convert had at some previous time divorced his wife, who later entered another marital union. It appeared on inquiry that she would have been willing, both to return to her first husband and even to accept Christianity, but that it was impossible for her to alter the present situation. Again, it has happened that the convert's pagan wife has been carried off during a raid by some hostile tribe, so that it was beyond his power even to communicate with her. The Holy Office[19] in these and similar cases has decided liberally. Hence, notwithstanding the good will of the unbelieving party, the existing factor of his or her non-return was acknowledged as sufficing for the use of the Pauline privilege.

§ 1. *The Factor of Physical Departure*

Physical departure or desertion is effected primarily if the unbeliever leaves his convert consort because of hatred for the faith; if he has already departed and has actually attempted another marriage; if, as may readily happen in pagan countries, the unbeliever

[15] *Ad Omnia Opera Sancti Ambrosii Appendix, Commentaria in Epist. ad Corinthios Primam—MPL,* XVII, 219; cf. also c. 2, C. XXVIII, q. 2.

[16] Wernz-Vidal, *Ius Matrimoniale,* n. 631, note 58; Cappello, *De Matrim.,* n. 770; Vermeersch, *De Casu Apostoli,* n. 43, Augustine, *A Commentary on Canon Law,* V, 350; Gregory, *The Pauline Privilege,* p. 58.

[17] I Cor., VII:15.

[18] Cappello, *De Matrim.,* n. 770; Gregory, *The Pauline Privilege,* p. 58; De Smet, *De Spons. et Matrim.,* n. 347.

[19] S.C.S. Off. (Cochinchin. Occident.), 12 iun. 1850, ad 1—*Fontes,* n. 910.

is held in a condition of slavery or quasi-slavery by a creditor because of unpaid debts; and if he has unjustly left the convert who has given him no cause for desertion.[20] Cappello[21] particularizes some of the causes which, as he deems, constitute physical desertion. He states without qualification that, if the unbeliever contracts a venereal disease, leprosy or some other infectious malady which prevents common conjugal life over an extended period of time, then the convert may avail himself of the privilege.

This probably would be true in regard to leprosy, though today even this disease is at times arrested in its early stages and the victim is allowed to return to society. It appears to the writer, however, that a distinction should be made in regard to the manner in which venereal disease is contracted. If the infection is contracted as the result of a licentious life, the disease would be mute evidence of serious marital infidelity, which in itself constitutes an offense to Almighty God, and a sufficient reason to construe the infidel's actions as having caused a moral separation. Moreover, the prolonged period of hospitalization and medical treatment, interfering with normal conjugal relations, would constitute a physical departure. But, if the social disease is contracted innocently and the unbeliever is taking all the means at his disposal to effect a cure, it appears that the convert could not construe the temporary suspension of marital relations as implying the fact of departure. It is acknowledged today that venereal diseases once contracted can with the proper medical treatment be normally controlled or arrested, if not entirely cured, so that after a reasonable period of time there is little or no danger of infection to others.[22]

Other factors constituting physical departure and which prove sufficient for the use of the Pauline privilege are had if the unbeliever becomes hopelessly insane, or is justly imprisoned for life or for an extended period of time.[23]

It may be concluded, therefore, that for the possible application of the privilege it is not essential that the separation should be due to the

[20] S.C.S. Off. (Cochinchin.), 1 aug. 1759, ad 2—*Fontes,* n. 810; (Cochinchin.), 12 iun. 1850, ad 1—*Fontes,* n. 910; S.C. de Prop. Fide (ad Vic. Ap. Sutchuen.) 30 ian. 1807—*Fontes,* n. 4690; Cf. also Augustine, *A Commentary on Canon Law,* V, 350, Lämmer, "Die Interpellatio,"—*AKKR,* XI (1864), 246.

[21] *De Matrim.,* n. 771, 13°

[22] Stokes, *Dermatology and Syphilology for Nurses* (2 ed., Philadelphia and London: W. B. Saunders Company, 1937) p. 227; Cecil, *A Text Book of Medicine by American Authors* (3. ed., Philadelphia and London: W. B. Saunders Company, 1934), p. 457.

[23] Cappello, *De Matrim.,* n. 771, 13°.

stubborn infidelity of the non-Christian; but that it suffices that the unbeliever, even through no fault of his own, cannot in fact resume conjugal life with the converted spouse.[24]

§ 2. *The Factor of Moral Departure*

The doctrine concerning moral departure is founded on the principles enunciated by Pope Innocent III, which presuppose as present a contempt of God or an effort to lead the convert into grievous sin. Thus departure results not only from real desertion, but from actions which are contrary or prejudical to faith or morals on the part of the unbelieving spouse. Such a departure is effected by one or more of the following actions: blasphemous language and the attempt to lead the convert to apostasy;[25] the refusal of the unbelieving partner to give up a life of concubinage;[26] the refusal of the unbeliever to allow the children of the union to be baptised and reared as Catholics;[27] and any attempt of the infidel to lead the convert into grave sins of any description, but especially sins against marital chastity, as for example, onanism, birth control, abortion, adultery.[28]

The solicitation to sin, however, must come from the unbelieving spouse personally. In a decision of the Sacred Congregation for the Propagation of the Faith it is stated that if the infidel partner is not personally accountable for the occasion of sin, but rather that the enticement comes from others who live in the same house, for example, from relatives such as the father-in-law or the mother-in-law, the convert may withdraw from the home if other means fail to remedy the situation, but may not contemplate another marriage.[29]

[24] S.C.S. Off. (Cochinchin, Occident.), 12 iun, 1850, ad 1—*Fontes*, n. 910; (Siam), 4 iul, 1855—*Fontes*, n. 931; S.C. de Prop. Fide (ad Vic. Ap. Sutchuen.), 30 ian. 1807—*Fontes*, n. 4690; cf. also Gregory, *The Pauline Privilege*, p. 58; Lämmer, "Die Interpellatio,"—*AKKR*, XI (1864), 246.

[25] S.C.S. Off. (Cochinchin.), I aug. 1759—*Fontes*, n. 810; cf. also Cappello, *De Matrim.*, n. 770, 4°; Gasparri, *De Matrim.*, n. 1139.

[26] S.C.S. Off. (Siam), 4 iul. 1855—*Fontes*, n. 931; (Natal), 11 iul. 1866, ad 2—*Fontes*, n. 996; cf. also Vermeersch, *De Casu Apostoli*, n. 54.

[27] S.C.S. Off. (Tunkin. Occident.), 14 dec. 1848, ad 2—*Fontes*, n. 908; (Natal), 11 iul. 1866, ad 1—*Fontes*, n. 996; cf. also Vermeersch, *loc. cit*; Gasparri, *De Matrim*, n. 1139; Cappello, *De Matrim.*, n. 770, 6°. Augustine, *A Commentary on Canon Law*, V, 350; Feije, *De Imped. et Dispens. Matrim.* n. 487.

[28] S.C. de Prop. Fide, 5 mart. 1816, ad 6—*Coll.*, n. 704; Cappello, *De Matrim.*, n. 770, 4°; Augustine, *A Commentary on Canon Law*, V, 350.

[29] S.C. de Prop. Fide, 5 mart. 1816, ad 6—*Coll.*, n. 704.

Finally, moral departure is effected by the leading of a scandalous life which reflects infamy upon the conduct of the convert, or by any practice provoked by the infidel partner which may prove a menace to the virtuous life of the convert, even prolonged and continued quarreling and strife which leads to very unhappy if not altogether intolerable home conditions, provided, of course, that these untoward conditions are not occasioned by overt acts of the convert after the reception of baptism.[80]

The departure of the unbelieving spouse, therefore, need not necessarily be occasioned by hatred of religion, nor does it have to be a malicious departure. If the convert after baptism is blameless and in no way gives cause for the separation, be it physical or moral, then any just reason suffices to invoke the Pauline privilege. The words "*contumelia Creatoris*" are verified when the intention on the part of the unbeliever to jeopardize the faith or morals of the converted partner is manifested. However, the departure which is the condition for the use of the privilege may not be presumed but must be demonstrated. Hence, there appears the need of the interpellations.[81]

Article II. The Necessity of Making the Interpellations

In the procedure attending the use of the Pauline privilege the party remaining in infidelity must be interpellated. This is of necessary importance to the valid use of the privilege and is the ordinary means of determining the unbeliever's will and intention. It is to be recalled that the interpellations are made not simply with a view of establishing proof of the unbeliever's departure, but also for the sake of ascertaining his possible will of conversion and, lacking that, his possible desire to live peaceably with the new convert, so that the existing legitimate marriage may be preserved intact. Hence there arises from the doctrine of St. Paul the natural corollary of the need of the interpellations in all ordinary cases, as asserted by Pope Innocent

[80] S.C.S. Off. (Cochinchin.), 1 aug. 1759, ad 2—Quaeritur: An id [privilegium ab Apostolo promulgatum] solum habeat locum quando infidelis discedit odio fidei, an etiam quando discedit propter discordis, vel aliam causam a fide diversam." Ad. 2. "Cum militet ex parte coniugis conversi favor fidei, eo potest uti quacumque ex causa, dommodo iusta sit, nimirum si non dederit iustam ac rationabile motivum alteri coniugi discedendi . . ."—*Fontes*, n. 810; cf. also S.C.S. Off., 26 apr. 1899—*Fontes*, n. 1222.

[81] Gasparri, *De Matrim.*, n. 1140; Petrovits, *The New Church Law*, p. 398; Gregory, *The Pauline Privilege*, p. 59.

III in his decretal "*Gaudemus in Domino*,"[32] and as now restated in the Code.[33]

However, regardless of the decision of the Sacred Congregation of the Council,[34] wherein the interpellations are for the first time officially legislated as the ordinary means of determining the departure and the intentions of the infidel, it has been seen in the study of the development regarding the interpellations in history that prior to the Code canonists were not unanimous in their opinions about the necessity of making them if the fact of the desertion of the unbelieving spouse along with the underlying motives prompting it was established by other means. Some authors[35] held that a second marriage by the convert apart from the making of the interpellations could be not only validly but also licitly undertaken. Though a decision of the Sacred Congregation of the Council of the year 1722[36] acknowledged these opinions as probable, it concluded that it was better to seek a dispensation from the Sovereign Pontiff. This decision was soon followed by a pontifical decree demanding that the interpellations be made or that they be dispensed by the Pope.[37] Thus from this time forward there is evident the gradual insistence on the necessity of proposing the interpellations for the licit and valid use of the privilege regardless of any presumption favoring the infidel's departure. It was asked by the Bishop of Portland (Me.) whether the interpellations are necessary when the unbelieving wife has obtained a civil divorce from the now converted husband and has married another, and when it is plain that both the infidel party and the new husband would resent the interpellations and possibly

[32] 22 aug. 1201—c. 8, X, *de divortiis*, IV, 19; Potthast, n. 1325; cf. also Benedictus XIV, *De Synodo Dioecesana*, lib. XIII, c. 21, n. 1; Mansella, *De Imped. Matrim.*, p. 105; Wernz, *Ius Decretalium*, IV, pars II, n. 703, note 72; Vermeersch, *De Casu Apostoli*, n. 51; Wernz-Vidal, *Ius Matrimoniale*, n. 632 note 68; Augustine, *A Commentary on Canon Law*, V. 353.

[33] Canon 1121, §2.

[34] Cf. Benedictus XIV, *De Synodo Dioecesana, lib.* XIII, c. 21, n. 1; S.C. de Prop. Fide (ad C.P. pro Sin.), 16 iun. 1797—*Coll.*, n. 634; Feije, *De Imped. et Dispens. Matrim.*, n. 475.

[35] Salmanticenses, *Cursus Theol. Moralis*, I, tract. IX, cap. IV, punctum II, n. 48; Vazquez, *Commentrarium ac Disputationum in Primum Secundae Sancti Thomae Tomus Primus*, q. XIX, art. VI, disp. LXIV, cap. V, nn. 25, 26.

[36] S.C.C., *Florentina*, die 17 ian. 1722—Pallottini, *Collectio Resolutionum S.C.C.*, s.v. "Matrimonium," § XIV, n. 3.

[37] Benedictus XIV, const. "*Apostolici ministerii*," 16 sept. 1747—*Fontes*, n. 381; cf. also Benedictus XIV, *De Synodo Dioecesana*, lib. XIII, c. 21, n. 4; lib. VI, c. 4, n. 3.

injure the interpellating messenger, and in any case the former wife would not return to the first husband because the civil law prohibited it. The Holy Office[38] answered that all this was not sufficient of itself to justify the omission of the interpellations, but that the bishop might in such instances use or obtain faculties wherewith to dispense from the making of the interpellations.

In another case the Congregation for the Propagation of the Faith[39] declared that without the interpellations "non esse locum dissolutioni matrimonii;" and in a very interesting case from India the Holy Office[40] decided that a convert who had married a Catholic woman without interpellating his infidel wife had the obligation, even after three children had already been born to the second union, to leave the Catholic wife and to return to the formerly pagan but now converted first wife.

Regardless of this official attitude of the Church on the necessity of the interpellations as late as the year 1911, however, Vermeersch[41] held that in a case wherein the unbeliever, *after* the baptism of his wife, showed intense displeasure at her conversion and demonstrated it by cursing both the woman and Christianity, no further interpellation was necessary, because his attitude was manifested by his actions. He considered the two responses of the Sacred Congregation for the Propagation of the Faith,[42] which required a dispensation from the interpellations even though the unbeliever's departure was patent, to be not applicable in his conjectured situation, since in the cases to which the decisions applied the desertion had taken place *prior* to the baptism of the neophyte. In pre-Code times Vermeersch's opinion was probably tenable,[43] and a second marriage contracted by a convert under these conditions might then have been presumed valid unless the validity had been attacked and a decisive answer had been given by the Holy See to establish the nullity of this marriage.[44]

[38] S.C.S. Off. (Portland), 18 iun. 1884—*Fontes,* n. 1088.

[39] (Tunk. Occident.), 5 mart. 1816, ad 1—*Coll.,* n. 704.

[40] S.C.S. Off. (Pondichery), 20 iun. 1858—*Fontes,* n. 947; cf. also S.C.S. Off. (Coreae), 11 sept. 1878—*Fontes,* n. 1057.

[41] *De Casu Apostoli,* n. 53.

[42] (C.P. pro Sin.), 5 mart. 1816—*Coll.,* n. 705; (Portland), 18 iun. 1884—*Fontes,* n. 1088.

[43] Sanchez, *De Matrim.,* lib. VII, disp. LXXIV, n. 13; Lämmer, "Die Interpellatio,"—*AKKR,* XI (1864), 247.

[44] Wernz, *Ius Decretalium,* IV, pars II, n. 703, note 72; Vermeersch, *De Casu Apostoli,* nn. 52, 56.

With the promulgation of the Code, however, the doctrine regarding the necessity of proposing the interpellations to the unbeliever, "unless the Holy See has declared otherwise," [45] was formally incorporated into the law of the Church. Since then canonists generally have held that the interpellations are always necessary, if not by Divine law at least by ecclesiastical law, for the licit and valid use of the Pauline privilege, with the exceptions granted by the law itself in canon 1125.

This requirement of the Code is reasonable and in accordance with the norms established by St. Paul. The Apostle gave a privilege to those whose conversion to the faith becomes a cause of oppression or undue hardship to them. But it is necessary to ascertain whether, in a given case, that oppression or hardship has actually resulted. To this end the questioning of the unbeliever is but a natural and proper means. Furthermore, the unbelieving partner, as the legitimate spouse of the convert, cannot on private authority be deprived of his legally acquired right without his own unequivocal consent. He must knowingly and willingly either accept or reject the situation caused by the conversion of his spouse.

In conclusion, therefore, it may be said that by reason of the prescriptions of the sacred canons either the interpellations are always necessary for the licit and valid use of the Pauline privilege or a dispensation from them must be obtained from the Sovereign Pontiff.

§1. *Opinions Regarding the Origin of This Necessity*

Whether the interpellations are necessary by Divine or ecclesiastical law cannot be ascertained from any uniform view of the authors, for no such uniformity of opinion exists. There are two opinions regarding the origin of the Pauline privilege. Names of real weight may be cited for each of the two opposing views. The viewpoint regarding the origin which gives rise to the need of the interpellations is naturally conditioned upon the opinion which any given author holds relative to the source from which the Pauline privilege itself derives.

A. *First Opinion: Origin from Divine Law*

Some authorities hold that the Pauline privilege is of immediate Divine origin. They state that the privilege was directly instituted by Christ, promulgated by St. Paul and extended to the universal

[45] Canon 1121, §2.

Church by St. Peter.[46] They contend that, though there are no known words of Christ to substantiate their claim, consummated marriages are absolutely indissoluble. Indissolubility, they say, is not merely a precept of the natural law, but is a commandment given by God to our first parents, and promulgated anew by our Lord. From that law none save God can dispense; and the sole exception which He has given in the new dispensation is the Pauline privilege. According tc them, not even the Sovereign Pontiff can do more than interpret the terms of that concession; he has no authority to extend its scope. Canonists and theologians supporting this opinion claim, therefore, that the convert is bound to interpellate the unbelieving partner by divine precept.[47]

Cornelius a Lapide (1567-1637) gives an exegesis that strongly favors this opinion. He refers the sentence, "For to the rest I say, not the Lord," [48] to the preceding verses eight to eleven, not to the verses which follow. In verses ten and eleven the Apostle had given instructions to the married; in verses eight and nine he had given advice to the widows and the unmarried. "For to the rest I say, not the Lord," is referred by this explanation to verses eight and nine and the meaning conveyed is that the commandment to the married is given by Christ, but that it is St. Paul who addresses the widows and the unmarried. If the passage is thus rendered, then the succeeding verse in which the Pauline privilege is mentioned would not be governed by the sentence, "For to the rest I say, not the Lord." [49]

Apparently partial to the view that the privilege is of immediate divine origin and that the interpellations are demanded by divine precept are also many of the responses of the Sacred Congregations

[46] Gasparri, *De Matrim.*, n. 1135; Sanchez, *De Matrim.*, lib. VII, disp. LXXIV, n. 4; Wernz-Vidal, *Ius Matrimoniale,* n. 631, note 56, Vermeersch-Creusen, *Epitome,* II, n. 427.

[47] Benedictus XIV, *De Synodo Dioecesana,* lib. VI, c. 4, n. 3: Pontius *De Sacram. Matrim.,* lib. IX, c. 2, n. 8; Sanchez in subscribing to this opinion stated that the infidel marriage is not dissolved "ex iure aliquo Pontificio, quamvis in infidelitate initum sit . . . sed dissolvitur ex privilegio Christi id in fidei favore concedentis: quod privilegium D. Paulus explicuit I. Cor., VII, in verbis allegatis, ita intellectus ab Ecclesia."—*De Matrim.,* lib. VII, disp. LXXIV, n. 4; Feije, *De Imped. et Dispens. Matrim.,* n. 602; Lämmer, "Die Interpellatio,"—*AKKR,* XI (1864), 245; Petrovits, *The New Church Law,* n. 553.

[48] I Cor., VII: 12.

[49] Cornelius a Lapide, *Commentaria in Scripturam Sacram* (ed. A. Crampon, Parisiis, 1866), XVIII, *In Epistolas Divi Pauli,* 306.

in which the Roman Curia in a customary style speaks of the Pauline privilege as being a divine grant. Two instructions of the Holy Office are very specific concerning the origin of the privilege, and there are other instructions which are equally specific concerning the necessity of the interpellations: ". . . *privilegio in favorem fidei a Christo Domino concesso et a Paulo Apostolo promulgato,*"[50] ". . . *virtute privilegii in favorem fidei a Christo Domino concessi, et per Apostolum Paulum promulgati.*"[51] "*Affirmative: nempe conversum de quo agitur, si non est legitime ab Apostolica Sede dispensatus, teneri ex divino praecepto ad faciendam in praesenti casu una vice interpellationem alteri coniugi: . . .*"[52]

Also indicative of the attitude of the Sacred Congregations in regard to the origin of the privilege is their custom of using the term "declaraverit," and not the normally expected "dispensaverit," when granting permission to omit the interpellations. Partisans of the opinion that the privilege was divinely instituted assert that this custom indicates the necessity of making the interpellations by divine precept, for since the Pope does not possess the power of dispensing from that law, the Holy See has logically adopted the term *declare,* and not *dispense.* It is true that the Holy See cannot dispense from an obligation the existence of which rests exclusively on the will of God. If the interpellations are demanded by divine precept then they must be judged in the same manner as the prenuptial guarantees demanded in mixed marriages. In these cases the Holy See cannot dispense in a constitutive sense, for it can only declare as the authentic interpreter of the divine law that in the particular case the obligation of making the interpellations does not exist.[53]

The fact that the Sacred Congregations are wont to use this terminology generally in their formal responses does unquestionably lend

[50] S.C.S. Off., instr. (Pro Vic. Ap. ad Gallas), 20 iun. 1866, "*Prima dubiorum classis.*"—*Fontes,* n. 994.

[51] S.C.S. Off. (Natal), 11 iul. 1866, ad 8—*Fontes,* n. 996

[52] S.C.S. Off. (Cochinchin. Occident.), 12 iun. 1850, ad 1—*Fontes,* n. 910; cf. also instr. (ad Archiep Quebecen.), 16 sept. 1924, and 3—*Fontes,* n. 866; S.C. de Prop. Fide, instr. (Tunkin.), 5 mart. 1816, ad 1—*Coll.,* n. 704; Wernz, *Ius Decretalium,* IV, Pars II, n. 704; Augustine, *A Commentary on Canon Law,* V, 353; Vermeersch-Creusen, *Epitome,* II, n. 434.

[53] Benedictus XIV, *De Synodo Dioecesana,* lib. VI, c. 4, n. 3; ". . . Summi Pontificis cuius est declarare, in quibusnam circumstantiis desinat obligare praeceptum divinum." Cf. also Triebs, *Praktisches Handbuch des geltenden kanonischen Eherechts in Vergleichung mit dem deutschen staatlichen Eherecht* (I-IV in one volume, Breslau; Ostdeutsche Verlagsanstalt, 1933), p. 715, (in the future this work will be cited as *Praktisches Handbuch*).

weight to this side of the debate, but the practice does not give conclusive proof for the immediate divine origin of the Pauline privilege or for the necessity of proposing the interpellations by divine precept, for it is plain that the Sacred Congregations do not here answer *ex professo* the question of the origin of the law requiring the interpellations.[54] When in 1816 the Congregation for the Propagation of the Faith, at that time fully commissioned to negotiate in matters respecting the Pauline privilege,[55] was directly asked "utrum . . . interpellatio partis . . . sit de iure divino . . . ," the Congregation gave a practical answer which entirely avoided the problem of whether interpellations were or were not of divine origin.[56] Furthermore, the terminology of the responses of the Congregation bears the interpretation that the privilege has divine authority because St. Paul wrote his Epistle under the guidance of the Holy Spirit and in the exercise of his apostolic ministry to which he was commissioned by our Lord.[57] A close examination of the canons inclines one to conclude that the Church has continued in the Code the policy of declining to effect a forthright settlement of the question.

Up to the period of the Protestant revolution the debate regarding the dissolution of non-Christian marriages, when those marriages were an impediment to embracing the faith, had been confined entirely to the question of the Pauline privilege.[58] But in the sixteenth century, so rich in missionary expansion, this power to dissolve legitimate marriages received various interpretations and adaptations.

The dispensations accorded in the papal concessions [59] of that time

[54] On the authority of Pope Clement X (1676) it was decreed that resolutions of doubts made by the Holy Office and the Congregation for the Propagation of the Faith were not given as definitions, but as simple instructions, by which those concerned could and should be governed.—19 sept. 1671—*Coll. Hong.*, n. 6; cf. also S.C.S. Off. (Cochinchin. Occident.), 12 iun. 1850—*Fontes*, n. 910.

[55] Wanenmacher, *Canonical Evidence in Marriage Cases* (Philadelphia: Dolphin Press, 1935), n. 95.

[56] S.C. Prop. Fide (Tunk. Occident.), 5 mart. 1816, ad 1—*Coll.*, n. 704.

[57] MacRory, *The Epistles of St. Paul to the Corinthians* (St. Louis: Herder, 1915), pp. 94-95; Vermeersch, *De Casu Apostoli, n.* 2; Gregory, *The Pauline Privilege*, p. 49.

[58] Cf. *supra*, p. 19.

[59] Paulus III, const. "*Altitudo*," 1 iun. 1537—*Fontes*, n. 81; cf. also *Appendix ad Bullarium Pontificium S.C.P.F.*, I, 25; *C.I.C.*, Documentum VI; S. Pius V, const. "*Romani Pontificis*," 2 aug. 1571; Gregorius XIII, const. "*Populis*," 25 ian. 1585, *Appendix ad Bullarium Pontificium S.C.P.F.*, I, 45 and 103; *C.I.C.*, Documenta VII, VIII.

gave unlooked for developments to the doctrine of marriage and sharply divided theological opinion. As to the nature of the concessions made by the constitutions, two explanations were offered. Some authors, especially those who adhered rigidly to the opinion that the privilege is of divine origin, contended that the provisions contained in the constitutions were merely applications of the Pauline privilege. Benedict XIV [60] always supported the opinion that the constitutions merely relaxed the discipline of the judicial interpellations.

On the other hand, it was contended by many canonists that the concessions of the constitutions cannot be brought under the provisions of the Pauline privilege as they go immensely farther in the favors they grant than anything conceded by the privilege.[61]

A few authors [62] who admit that the constitutions in their grants are broader in scope than the Pauline privilege, and still wish to maintain that the privilege is of immediate divine origin, assert that to the Sovereign Pontiff as the Vicar of Christ on earth was given further power over marriage contracted in infidelity, that is, a general apostolic power conferred on St. Peter and his successors, to be exercised with the authority of Christ, and to supply for those cases which do not fulfill the conditions necessary for the use of the Pauline privilege. These propositions are not mutually exclusive and there is no contradiction in subscribing to this theory. The opinion, however, admits of two distinct sources of power over infidel marriages: the one immediately divine; the other contained in the general apostolic grants to the Popes. Unless the argument is reduced to a mere matter of words there appears to be no reason for the existence of this dual

[60] Benedict mentions that Vericellus interpreted the constitutions as dissolving the marital bond, but contrary to this Benedict himself always held that the constitutions merely relaxed the rigor of the judicial interpellation.—*De Synodo Dioecesana,* lib. VII, c. 21, n. 5; cf. also *ibid.,* lib. XIII, c. 21, nn. 4, 5, 6; Payen, *De Matrimonio,* n. 2447.

[61] " . . . The marriages contracted between unbelievers, though they are true marriages, are yet not reckoned as being so confirmed that, in case of necessity, they cannot be dissolved. . . . We decree that, though it should hereafter appear that the former partners were hindered by a just cause, and could not declare their will, and even that at the time of the second marriage they were converted to the faith, these marriages shall never have to be rescinded, but shall be valid and firm and that the children born of them shall be legitimate. . . ."—const. Gregorii XIII, "*Populis,*" 25 ian. 1585—*Appendix ad Bullarium Pontificium S.C.P.F.,* I, 103; *C.I.C.,* Documentum VIII; cf. Burton, *A Commentary on Canon 1125,* pp. 164, 165.

[62] E. g., Sanchez, *De Matrim.,* lib. II, disp. XVII, n. 2; lib. VII, disp. LXXIV, n. 4.

source of power. The opinion seems to be a compromise between that of the immediate divine origin and that which is to be discussed, namely, the opinion that the privilege, together with its formalities, is of apostolic origin.[63]

B. *Second Opinion: Origin from Ecclesiastical Law*

That the Pauline privilege is of mediate divine origin, that is, that St. Paul both instituted and promulgated the doctrine and that the interpellations are demanded for this reason by ecclesiastical law only, appears to have the stronger arguments in its favor and is upheld by the majority of modern canonists.[64] This opinion holds that Christ gave complete power to His Vicar to dissolve for a weighty and just cause all lawful marriages that come under his jurisdiction by baptism, except the valid and consummated marriages between Christians. According to this view the Pauline privilege is merely a special case of the exercise of a more general power,[65] and is not to be considered as a unique exception to the law of indissolubility beyond the strict limits of which the Pope may not go.

Writers inclined to this view consider St. Paul's statement, "For to the rest I say, not the Lord," as an introductory phrase which establishes his exact purpose in writing what is to follow, rather than a conclusion to what went before. They assert that the obvious sense of the words should be accepted, since this interpretation does not exclude the necessary divine basis for the privilege.[66] Though it is

[63] Vromant, *Facultates Apostolicae Quas S.C. de Prop. Fide delegare solet Ordinariis Missionum, Commentaria in Formulam Tertiam* (Louvain, 1926), n. 271.

[64] Sanchez, *De Matrim.*, lib. II, disp. XVII, n. 2; Wernz, *Ius Decretalium*, IV, pars. II, n. 705; Wernz-Vidal, *Ius Matrimoniale*, n. 636; Vermeersch-Creusen, *Epitome*, II, n. 434; Cappello, *De Matrim.*, n. 791; Woods, *The Constitutions of Canon 1125*, p. 18; Payen, *De Matrimonio*, n. 2446; Burton, *A Commentary on Canon 1125*, pp. 75-89; Ayrinhac-Lydon, *Marriage Legislation in the New Code of Canon Law* (revised ed., New York: Benziger Brothers, 1935), n. 300 (hereafter cited as *Marriage Legislation*).

[65] Joyce, *Christian Marriage*, p. 493; Burton, *A Commentary on Canon 1125*, p. 85.

[66] MacRory, *The Epistles of St. Paul to the Corinthians*, pp. 94-95; Cornely, *Commentarius in Primam Epistolam ad Cor.*, p. 181; Lehmkuhl, *Theologia Moralis* (5. ed., 2 vols., Friburgi Brisgoviae, 1888), II, n. 709; De Smet, *De Spons., et Matrim.*, n. 341; Gasparri, *De Matrim.*, n. 1166; Cappello, *De Matrim.*, n. 767.

to be admitted that this text is open to another interpretation,[66a] the exegesis favoring the apostolic institution of the privilege seems strengthened by the exegesis of another text of Scripture. Authorities [67] assert that through the "bill of divorce" or *libellus repudii* the marriage bond of the Jews was dissolved; but this bill of divorce by which consummated marriages were dissolved was not directly instituted by God, but by Moses, as supreme head of the synagogue and interpreter of God. They quote our Lord for authority that the practice was not directly instituted by God. In Matthew XIX:8, Christ says: "Because Moses, by reason of the hardness of your heart, permitted you to put away your wives," not "Because God, by reason of the hardness of your heart, permitted you to put away your wives." Zitelli, who cites this exegesis, concludes that if Moses could dissolve the consummated marriages of the Jews by reason of his supreme and exalted position in the synagogue, then surely the Roman Pontiff, whose authority far exceeds that of Moses, may for a just cause dissolve the marriage bond under certain specified conditions, without any immediate divine intervention.

Writers, therefore, who stand for the apostolic origin of the Pauline concession hold that the necessity of making the interpellations is founded purely on ecclesiastical law,[68] and as the author of this requirement the Church may dispense with one or both of the interpellations as she deems necessary.[69] This argument seems to be more consonant with the *de facto* actions of the Popes. The opinion also is considered to be more in harmony with Christ's plan of giving a broad general spiritual authority to the Church, and leaving to it the details of discipline.[70]

[66] a Cf. p. 50.

[67] Cf. Zitelli, *De Dispensationibus Matrimonialibus iuxta Recentissimas Sac. Urbis Congreg. Resolutiones Commentarii* (Romae: Ex Typis Soc. Edit. Rom., 1887), p. 190. Hereafter this work will be cited as *De Dispens. Matrim.*

[68] Cappello, *De Matrim.*, n. 777; Scherer, *Handbuch des Kirchenrechts* (2 vols., Graz, 1886-1898), II, 563; Lehmkuhl, *Theologia Moralis*, II, nn. 929-932.

[69] De Smet, *De Spons. et Matrim.*, n. 555; Wernz-Vidal, *Ius Matrimoniale*, n. 632, note 70.

[70] Gregory, *The Pauline Privilege*, p. 67; Fahrner, *Geschichte des Unauflöslichkeitsprinzips und der vollkommenen Scheidung der Ehe im kanonischen Recht* (Freiburg im Breisgau, 1903), p. 284; Ojetti, *Synopsis Rerum Moralium et Iuris Pontificii* (Romae, 1899), v. "Casus Apostoli:" Wernz, *Ius Decretalium*, IV, pars II, n. 702, note 60.

§ 2. *Appraisal of the Proposed Opinions*

The discussion whether the Pauline privilege has its origin from an immediate divine source or whether it derives from apostolic authority is of long standing. Both sides of the question are represented by solid arguments proposed by eminent minds. The common opinion undoubtedly favors the divine authorship of the privilege and the necessity of proposing the interpellations by divine precept. It appears to the writer, however, that those who advance this theory and who admit of no other power in the Church to dissolve legitimate marriages must meet with insuperable difficulties in their effort to explain the actions of the Popes in dissolving such unions on the conversion of one or of both of the parties, and yet this power has long been conceded to the Sovereign Pontiff.[71]

To assert that in these cases the Pontiff merely relaxes the discipline of the judicial interpellations does not solve the problem for, as mentioned previously, the dissolution of these marriages cannot readily be brought under the Pauline privilege and the effort made to include within its limited scope all the concessions granted by the constitutions seems forced and without justification. Taken in their obvious sense, the constitutions are not applications of the privilege but dispensations granted through papal authority by which marriages contracted between unbaptized persons are dissolved. If Christ had provided no other means by which the bond of consummated legitimate marriage could be dissolved except the Pauline privilege, then the Popes in these constitutions were giving only a declarative interpretation of the privilege. But an extensive interpretation would be impossible, for the Pope was unable then, as he is unable now, to extend or restrict divine law by his interpretation. The privilege would have to be interpreted strictly. Moreover, if the Popes intended to give merely an interpretation of the privilege, that interpretation would be valid everywhere. It would be as universal as the privilege itself. But they limited their concessions to apply only to certain regions. It is improbable, then, that they considered themselves to be only interpreting the Pauline privilege.

The opinion that the Pauline privilege is of apostolic origin, instituted and promulgated by St. Paul in virtue of his participation in apostolic authority, solves these difficulties quite simply. Proponents

[71] Paulus III, const. "*Altitudo,*" 1 iun. 1537; S. Pius V, const. "*Romani Pontificis,*" 2 aug. 1571; Gregorius XIII, const. "*Populis,*" 25 ian. 1535—*Appendix ad Bullarium Pontificium S.C.P.F.*, I, 25, 45, 103; *C.I.C.*, Documenta VI, VII, VIII.

of this viewpoint stress the fact that the privilege is but a specific entity within the more comprehensive *privilegium fidei.* The same purpose as that for which St. Paul used his participation in apostolic authority to grant the privilege, could be considered also as a just cause for the Popes to exercise their authority to the same end.

Though this opinion is broad, it must not be imagined that it claims for the Popes an unrestricted and absolute power in regard to infidel marriages. The indissolubility of marriage reflects a divine law: and it is open to the Sovereign Pontiff to dissolve a union only when he has grounds for judging that God would wish him to grant an exception in a certain case.[72]

ARTICLE III. THE QUESTION OF OMITTING THE INTERPELLATIONS

Canon 1121 states that before a convert may validly contract a new marriage the interpellations must always be made unless the concessions of canon 1125 can be applied or unless the Holy See has declared otherwise.

All authors are in agreement that a departure effected by the infidel party, either as a physical or as a moral departure, is a necessary condition for the use of the Pauline privilege.[73] Also the authors prior to the Code were in agreement that either an interpellation or a dispensation from the interpellations was demanded by ecclesiastical law for the licit use of the privilege.[74]

However, regardless of the apparently clear diction of the text of the canon there is a lack of unanimity of opinion among the recent authors, not to speak of the older ones, as to whether the illegitimate omission of the interpellations always and under all circumstances militates against the use of the Pauline privilege and invalidates the ensuing marriage of the convert.[75]

[72] Joyce, *Christian Marriage,* p. 497; Burton, *A Commentary on Canon 1125,* p. 85.

[73] Wernz-Vidal, *Ius Matrimoniale,* n. 631, note 58; De Smet, *De Spons. et Matrim.,* n. 346; Vermeersch-Creusen, *Epitome,* II, n. 433; Gasparri, *De Matrim,.* n. 1142; Gregory, *The Pauline Privilege,* p. 58.

[74] Vermeersch, *De Casu Apostoli,* n. 52; Payen, *De Matrimonio,* n. 2351; Wernz, *Ius Decretalium,* IV, pars II, n. 705, note 92; Cappello, *De Matrim.,* n. 776; Gasparri, *De Matrim.,* n. 1142; Lämmer, "Die Interpellatio,"—*AKKR,* XI (1864), 247-250; Vito, "Il Privilegio Paolino,"—*Perfice Munus,* XI (1936), 97.

[75] Jone, "Wie müssen die Interpellationen bei Anwendung des Paulinischen Privilegs gemacht werden,"—*Theologisch-praktische Quartalschrift,* LXXX (1927), 345, 348. In the future this periodical will be cited as *LQS (Linzer Quartalschrift).*

To investigate the question more thoroughly a study of the compelling force of the law will be in order. Does the law which demands that the unbeliever be interpellated always urge for the licit and valid use of the Pauline privilege?

§ 1. *Regarding the Licit Use of the Privilege*

By reason of ecclesiastical law the interpellations are always necessary for the licit use of the Pauline privilege, unless for a just cause a papal dispensation from them is granted.[76] Whence, even if the interpellations are useless, as for instance when the convert is morally certain of the unbeliever's aversion to be baptized and is equally certain of his unwillingness to live without offense to Almighty God, the omission of the interpellations would not be licit without a dispensation from the Holy See.

Payen[77] states that the reason for this broad extension of the law which admits of no exceptions is intended for the purpose of avoiding any possible error in a matter of such grave moment. Furthermore, he states that an interested party cannot be a judge in his own case. Wernz[78] likewise taught that the obligation of questioning the unbeliever always urged and that if such questioning was not possible it was only proper that the judgment as to the merits of the individual case was to be rendered by the supreme authority of the Church. He asserted that authorities subordinate to the Holy See might either mistakenly or too easily conclude that the infidel party had manifested the will to separate.

Gasparri[79] also confirmed these opinions. He stated that regardless of any seeming futility, the procedure of making the interpellations or of securing a papal dispensation from them was always necessary for the licit use of the privilege, and alleged as a reason the avoidance of possible abuse or error.

[76] Vermeersch states: "Si constet de discessu post baptismum, novae nuptiae *validae* sine interpellatione fient; *licitae* tamen non erunt, nisi legitime dispensetur."—*De Casu Apostoli,* n. 52; cf. also Payen, *De Matrimonio,* n. 2351; Cappello, *De Matrim.,* n. 776; Lämmer, "Die Interpellatio,"—*AKKR,* XI (1864), 247-250.

[77] *De Matrimonio,* n. 2351.

[78] *Ius Decretalium,* IV, pars II, n. 705, note 92; cf. also Wernz-Vidal, *Ius Matrimoniale,* n. 632, note 68; Cappello, *De Matrim.,* n. 776.

[79] *De Matrim.,* n. 1142.

Prescinding from the exceptions to this obligation as granted in the common law (can. 1125) one may state, therefore, that even if there is a presumption born of facts which affords moral certainty of departure,[80] as for example when there exists a civil divorce procured by the unbeliever and a second attempted marriage already effected by him, the interpellations must nevertheless always be made for the licit use of the Pauline privilege, or a dispensation from them must be obtained.[81]

§ 2. *Regarding the Valid Use of the Privilege*

While it is clear that the Church always considers the use of the Pauline privilege illicit when the interpellations have been omitted without a papal dispensation, it is not so clear that it always considers such a procedure invalid. There is a diversity of thought on this point even among post-Code authors. Opinion ranges from that which holds that the interpellations are never required by divine law for the valid use of the privilege to that which contends that they are always required. Likewise not all are agreed that the ecclesiastical law as given in canon 1121 is so rigid as to admit of no exception.[82]

Wernz[83] held that the interpellations are never required by divine law if the condition of departure truly exists. He asserted that St. Paul demanded this one condition only for the valid use of the privilege and the subsequent valid marriage of the convert. According to those holding this opinion, the valid use of the Pauline privilege does not depend by reason of divine law upon the proof of the infidel's departure but on the actual fact of departure. For the licit use of the privilege, however, it is admitted that the interpellations must always be made.

Other authors[84] think that the interpellations are *regularly* but not

80 Clement XIV warned against indulging frivolous presumptions to the end that the interpellations might be omitted.—S.C.S. Off. (Chen-si et Chan-si), 23 nov. 1769—*Fontes*, n. 825.

81 Burton, *A Commentary on Canon 1125*, p. 97.

82 Payen, *De Matrimonio*, n. 2332.

83 *Ius Decretalium*, IV, pars II, n. 702, note 72; cf. also Wernz-Vidal, *Ius Matrimoniale*, n. 632, note 68.

84 Sanchez, *De Matrim.*, lib. VII, disp. LXXIV, nn. 12, 13; Vermeersch, *De Casu Apostoli*, nn. 40, 51, 52; De Smet, *De Spons. et Matrim.*, n. 351.

always required by divine law for the valid use of the privilege. These writers distinguish between a departure regarding which there is *certainty* and a departure concerning which there is *doubt.*[85] They glean from the words of St. Paul, "But if the unbeliever depart, let him depart," [86] that the Apostle did not intend to grant a convert the right of entering a new marriage unless the departure of the unbelieving spouse was certain. If, therefore, this certainty concerning the departure is established by means other than the interpellations, they hold that the obligation to make them by reason of divine law ceases. According to this opinion divine law demands that, if there is any doubt about the fact of departure, the interpellations must be proposed, and any illegitimate omission under such conditions would invalidate the use of the privilege and the ensuing marriage.[87]

Still other authorities [88] hold that the interpellations are *always* required by divine law. These are among the authors who assert that the Pauline privilege is of immediate divine origin. Hence they subscribe to the opinion that not only the departure, but also proof of the departure by means of the interpellations is a condition required by divine law. They likewise allege the terminology of the responses of the Sacred Congregations [89] to substantiate their assertion but, as already noted, these official documents do not treat of this question *ex professo.*[90]

[85] Cf. Cappello, *De Matrim., nn.* 776, 777.

[86] I Cor., VII: 15; Payen, *De Matrimonio,* n. 2353.

[87] Gasparri states: "Ex verbis Apostoli evidens est fidei privilegium esse *condicionatum*: coniux enim conversus potest ad alias transire nuptias *si* coniux infidelis renuat converti ad fidem aut saltem pacifice cohabitare. . . . De impleta igitur condicione constare debet, ut coniux conversus possit ad alia vota convolare. Cum autem de hoc ordinarie constare nequeat, nisi . . . interpellando . . ., inducta est disciplina interpellationum."—*De Matrim.,* n. 1140; and he later states: "Nonnulli magnae auctoritatis canonistae putaverunt legem interpellationum non urgere, si iam *constet* de discessu infidelis . . . eorumque sententiam Benedictus XIV [*De Synodo Dioecesana,* lib. XII, cap. 21, n. 4] dicit communiorem. Licet haec sententia speculative vera videatur, tamen Ecclesia, ne abusus irreperent in re tanti momenti, eam numquam probavit, imo expresse declaravit etiam hoc in casu interpellationes esse faciendas, aut dispensationem ab eisdem petendam esse."—*Ibid.,* n. 1142.

[88] Cf. Pesch, *Praelectiones Dogmaticae* (3. ed. Vol. VII, Pars II, Friburgi Brisgoviae, 1909), Vol. VII, Pars II, *(De Sacramentis),* n. 793. In the future this work will be cited as *De Sacramentis.*

[89] S.C.S. Off. (Ex Litter. S.C. de Prop. Fide ad N. Mission. Pondicher.), 5 ian. 1757, ad 5—*Coll. Hong.* n. 1428; instr. (Ad Archiep. Quebecen.), 16 sept. 1824, ad 3—*Fontes,* n. 866; (Siam, 4 iul. 1855—*Fontes,* n. 931; 11 aug. 1859—*Fontes,* n. 954; (Portland), 18 iun. 1884—*Fontes,* n. 1088.

[90] Cf. *supra,* pp. 27, 51.

In another sense, however, the tenor of the responses of the Congregations appears to indicate the official mind of the Church on this question. For the most part the Congregations are consistent in stating indirectly, but more or less as a general principle, that the interpellations are of obligation by divine law. This principle has been applied in the solution of practical cases by the refusal of the Congregations to grant radical sanations for marriages in which the interpellations or a dispensation from them had been omitted,[91] the reason alleged being that the marriage contracted in infidelity was an impediment to a new valid marriage until the interpellations had been provided for. The petitioners were instructed to dispense from the interpellations and to procure a renewal of consent from the interested parties.[92]

This summary statement of the lack of harmony existing among contemporaneous authors as to whether or not the interpellations are demanded by divine law demonstrates that the Church has not as yet definitely settled the controversy. Though authors of distinction are found subscribing to either of the opposing views, today the weight of opinion among canonists is on the side of those who hold that the interpellations are required not by divine but rather by canonical or ecclesiastical law for the valid use of the privilege.[93]

Those who hold the view that the interpellations are demanded for validity only by reason of ecclesiastical law base their opinion on the following argument. Canon 1121 reads: "*Antequam* coniux conversus . . . *valide* contrahat matrimonium debet . . . partem non baptizatam interpellare;" canon 1123 states: "Si interpellationes ex declaratione Sanctae Sedis omissae fuerint aut si infidelis negative responderit expresse vel tacite, pars baptizata *ius habet* novas nuptias . . . contrahendi." From the text of these two canons, the right to remarry, and not simply the permission therefore, is granted only when the interpellations have been made or when a dispensation has been obtained. Thus it appears that canon law not only considers the unbeliever's departure as a condition for the valid use of the privilege but also the manner of proof.[94] But, however clear the text of the

[91] S.C.S. Off., resp. (Coreae), 11 sept. 1878, ad 1—*Fontes*, n. 1057; resp. (Curatus Dioecesis N.), 19 ian. 1900—*Coll. Hong.*, n. 2288.

[92] Payen, *De Matrimonio*, n. 2354; Burton, *A Commentary on Canon 1125*, p. 96.

[93] Vermeersch-Creusen, *Epitome*, II, n. 430; Cappello, *De Matrim.*, n. 776; Ayrinhac-Lydon, *Marriage Legislation*, p. 311.

[94] Gasparri, *De Matrim.*, n. 1140; Noldin-Schmitt, *Summa Theologiae Moralis iuxta Codicem Iuris Canonici* (31. ed., 3. vols., Oeniponte: Pustet,

canons appears to be, the wording is not so explicit that all authors are willing to hold it as indisputable that every marriage contrary to the prescriptions of the canons is invalid. They object to the interpellation which allows of no exception. They assert that in canons 1121 and 1123 the condition that the interpellations be made is always understood unless the fact of desertion be established and that, though canon 1121 says "*Hae interpellationes semper fieri debent . . . ,*" it does not add an annulling clause and, finally that it seems that the legislator purposely omitted such a clause.[95]

Because of these divergent opinions regarding the compelling force of the law on interpellations, it is apparently the mind of the Church to urge the necessity of always proposing them to the unbeliever or of petitioning a dispensation from them, but at the same time not to close the door to all speculation on the question of necessity.[96]

Regardless of this lack of unanimity of opinion, it may be said by way of conclusion that the interpellations may not be omitted on private authority no matter what the presumption may be in favor of the unbeliever's departure. In practice they are regularly necessary if not by divine law, at least by ecclesiastical law, and must be made unless a dispensation from them is secured from the Holy See.[97]

If an actual case of the illegitimate omission of the interpellations should arise, immediate recourse should be had to the Holy Office, which is the designated competent agency to investigate questions involving the Pauline privilege. In the interim the second alliance contracted by the convert may be presumed valid by reason of the principle incorporated in canons 1014 and 1127, namely, that the favor of the faith secures the presumption of validity for the Christian marriage.[98]

1932), III, n. 523. (In the future this work will be cited as *Summa Theologiae Moralis*); Sabetti-Barrett, *Compendium Theologiae Moralis* (33. ed,, New York: Pustet, 1931), n. 859, q. 14; Nau, *Manual on the Marriage Laws of the Code of Canon Law* (2. ed., New York: Pustet, 1934), n. 141; Gregory, *The Pauline Privilege,* p. 71; Vito, "Il Privilegio Paolino,"—*Perfice Munus,* XI (1936), 97-102; S.R.R., Nullitatis matrimonii, 5 dec. 1925, coram Rmo. P.D. Maximo Massimi, dec. XLIX—*S. Romanae Rotae Decisiones seu Sententiae,* XVII (1925), 396-399, (hereafter this Collection will be cited *Decisiones*). Cf. also Bouscaren, *Canon Law Digest* (2 vols., and Supplement-1941, Milwaukee: Bruce Publishing Company, 1934-1941), II, 156.

[95] Cappello, *De Matrim.,* nn. 776, 777; Vermeersch-Creusen, *Epitome,* III, n. 430; Wernz-Vidal, *Ius Matrimoniale,* n. 632, note 68; De Smet inclines to this opinion but is hesitant—*De Spons. et Matrim.,* n. 353.

[96] Cf., Gasparri, *De Matrim.,* n. 1142; Payen, *De Matrimonio,* n. 2355.

[97] Payen, *De Matrimonio,* n. 2348.

[98] Wanenmacher, *Canonical Evidence in Marriage Cases,* n. 488; Cappello, *De Matrim.,* n. 777; Payen, *De Matrimonio,* n. 2358.

CHAPTER IV

FACTORS ATTENDING THE INTERPELLATIONS

Canon 1122, §1. *Interpellationes fiant regulariter, forma saltem summaria et extraiudiciali, de auctoritate Ordinarii coniugis conversi, a quo Ordinario concedendae sunt quoque coniugi infideli, si quidem eas petierit, induciae ad deliberandum, eo tamen monito, fore ut, induciis inutiliter praeterlapsis, responsio praesumatur negativa.*

§2. *Interpellationes etiam privatim factae ab ipsa parte conversa, valent, imo sunt etiam licitae, si forma superius praescripta servari nequeat; hoc tamen in casu de ipsis, pro foro externo, constare debet duobus saltem testibus vel alio legitimo probationis modo.*

ARTICLE I. THE INITIAL ACTION OF THE ORDINARY OR HIS DELEGATE

As a general rule, the initial action in making the interpellations is to be instituted by the ordinary of the convert, or by someone delegated with the ordinary's power who can act in his name and in the name of the convert.[1]

The ordinary is to be here understood according to the meaning attached to the term in canon 198, namely, within their respective territories, the residential bishop, the abbot and the prelate *nullius* (and their vicars general), the administrator, the vicar and the prefect apostolic, as well as those who during the vacancy of these offices succeed in the government of the respective territories according to the provisions of the law.

In exempt clerical religious organizations the major superiors are ordinaries over their own subjects. But by the term "local ordinary" as used in canon 198, §2, are meant all persons enumerated, with the exception of religious superiors. From the nature of the case, it is only the local ordinary who could be involved in the obligation of canon 1122. Therefore, these ordinaries, religious excepted, may take the initial action in making the interpellations in behalf of their con-

[1] Payen, *De Matrimonio*, n. 2362; Putzer, *Commentarium in Facultates Apostolicas* (Ilchester College, Maryland: Typis Cong. Sanctissimi Redemptoris, 1893), n. 129; Cappello, *De Matrim.*, n. 779.

vert subject. This action should be taken at the request of the convert personally after the reception of baptism.[2]

Who is one's proper ordinary? Canon 94 states that through domicile or quasi-domicile each of the faithful acquires his or her proper pastor or ordinary. Canon 92 further states that a domicile is acquired by continued residence in a parish or diocese extending over a period of ten years, or by a residence which is established with the intention to stay in a definite place permanently; quasi-domicile is acquired by a residence which is established in a parish or a diocese with the intention to remain there for the greater part of the year, or by continued residence there for that period. From the texts of these canons it is evident that a person acquires a domicile in a new place from the moment he arrives if he has the intention to stay there permanently. However, it is the common opinion of canonists that to comply with this phase of the law the intention to remain permanently, or at least indefinitely, must be unconditional.[3] Unforeseen circumstances which cause a change of mind later on are not conditions in the strict sense of the word, and do not invalidate the acquisition of a domicile.[4]

As regards married couples, a wife necessarily shares the domicile of her husband. But if she is legitimately separated from him,[5] she can obtain a domicile as well as a quasi-domicile of her own and thus can also acquire her own proper pastor or ordinary.[6] Since a convert wife, who has been deserted either morally or physically by her unbelieving husband, is legitimately separated from him, she acquires a domicile in the diocese where she happens to be at the time of the desertion is she has actual residence there, or the intention of staying there always unless something unforseen occurs. Hence the local ordinary, or one delegated with his authority, should institute proceedings

[2] Canon 1122, § 1.

[3] For an appreciation of the concepts of domicile and quasi-domicile consult Costello, *Domicile and Quasi-Domicile,* The Catholic University of America Canon Law Studies, n. 60 (Washington, D. C.: The Catholic University of America, 1930). Cf. also Vermeersch-Creusen, *Epitome,* I, n. 212; Coronata, *Institutiones Iuris Canonici* (5 vols., Taurini: Marietti; Vols. I-II, 2 ed., 1939; Vols. III-V, 1933-1936), I, nn. 124, 126; Cicognani, *Canon Law* (2. ed., Philadelphia: Dolphin Press, 1935), p. 574.

[4] Woywod, *A Practical Commentary on the Code of Canon Law* (2 vols., New York: Wagner, 1925), I, n. 69.

[5] Canon 93.

[6] Canon 94.

to secure the necessary interpellations in her behalf if she requests the favor.

The principles given in Canon Law for the acquisition of domicile likewise apply to a convert husband, though he acquires a domicile or quasi-domicile in his own right apart from the factor of a legitimate separation.

§ 1. *The Questions Proposed*

The subject matter of the interpellations is found in canon 1121, §1, 1° and 2°. There the questions to be proposed to the unbelieving party are succinctly given.

> Canon 1121. § 1. *Antequam coniux conversus et baptizatus novum matrimonium valide contrahat, debet, salvo praescripto can. 1125, partem non baptizatam interpellare:*
>
> 1°. *An velit et ipsa converti ac baptismum suscipere;*
>
> 2°. *An saltem velit secum cohabitare pacifice sine contumelia Creatoris.*

Whenever it is possible, as it will be in the normal cases of the Pauline privilege, to propose the interpellations to the unbelieving consort it is scarcely necessary to state that there should be explained to the infidel the full meaning of the doctrine of the privilege and the effect his answers may have on the existing marriage between himself and his convert spouse. It is true, the nature of the infidel's response—be it affirmative or be it negative—will do nothing to change the valid status of the marriage. It is only the subsequent use of the privilege that will disrupt the union.[7] The immediate effect of a negative answer to the interpellations will be at most a separation of the spouses. However, the infidel must appreciate that, though separation may be the only immediate effect, nevertheless a negative answer to both questions confers a right upon the convert to contract another valid marriage with a Catholic.

[7] Canon 1126; Benedictus XIV, ep. "*Postremo mense,*" 28 febr. 1747, ad 58—*Fontes,* n. 377; const. "*Apostolici Ministerii,*" 16 sept. 1747, ad 4—*Fontes,* n. 381; S.C.S. Off. (Cochinchin.), 1 aug. 1759, ad 2, 5—*Fontes,* n. 810; S.C. de Prop. Fide, instr. (ad Vic. Ap. Sutchuen.), 30 ian. 1807—*Coll.,* n. 690; Sanchez, *De Matrim.,* lib. VII, disp. LXXV; Feije, *De Imped. et Dispens. Matrim.,* n. 498; Wernz-Vidal, *Ius Matrimoniale,* n. 631; Gasparri, *De Matrim.,* n. 1153; Cappello, *De Matrim.,* n. 785.

After an elucidation of the doctrine of the Pauline privilege to the unbeliever, the significance of the first interpellation—whether the unbaptized party wishes to be converted and baptized—should be quite obvious. However, it should be made clear to the non-Christian that by conversion and baptism is meant conversion to and baptism in the Catholic Church.[8]

The exact sense of the second interpellation—if the unbeliever does not wish to be baptized, whether he be willing to live peacefully in marriage without offense to the Creator—should be explained in detail. One should recall that the full meaning of the phrase *"to cohabit in peace without offense to the Creator"* was the subject of discussions of major proportions among canonists and theologians for centuries,[9] and hence a non-Christian, in all probability totally ignorant of matters pertaining to faith, could scarcely be expected to have even a cursory knowledge of its import without explanation and amplification.

If the infidel is unwilling to embrace the faith he should be informed that he is to promise peaceful cohabitation; to allow the convert the unrestricted practice of religion; to refrain from any disrespect for the Holy Names of God and Christ; to allow the children of the union to be baptized and reared in the Catholic Church; and, as mentioned previously,[10] to avoid any practice that would prove dangerous to the faith or morals of the converted spouse.

It must be said, however, that this explanation is not necessary for the valid use of the Pauline privilege; it suffices merely to state the question. Furthermore, if the infidel spouse has already effected a departure for which the convert is not responsible and which is irremediable, for example a second attempted marriage, then a detailed explanation of the interpellation may be entirely omitted.

Finally, the unbeliever should be warned that, even though he now pledges himself to abide peacefully, any subsequent contumacy on his part will allow the convert to separate with the right to contract new nuptials with a Catholic if she desires to do so.[11]

[8] S.C.S. Off. (Mongoliae), 29 nov. 1882, ad 4—*Fontes,* n. 1075.

[9] Innocent III, *"Quanto te magis,"* 1 maii 1199; *"Gaudemus in Domino,"* 22 apr. 1201—c. 7, 8, X, *de divortiis,* IV, 19; Potthast, nn. 684, 1325; Denzinger, *Enchiridion,* nn. 406, 407; cf. also Panormitanus, *Commentaria in Quinque Libros Decretalium,* c. 7, X, *De Divortiis,* IV, 19; St. Thomas Aquinas, IV Sent., dist. XXXIX, q. un., art. 5; Schmalzgrueber, *Ius Eccles. Universum,* lib. IV, tit. XIX, n. 27.

[10] *Supra,* pp. 42ff.

[11] Canon 1124.

No subterfuge may be employed in proposing the interpellations to the unbeliever. They must be made direct and according to the form prescribed by the Church.[12]

The Holy Office[13] in answer to a query in which it was asked whether it sufficed merely to inform a polygamous infidel that his legitimate wife, whom he either deserted or dismissed, had joined a European religion, and then to ask him if he was willing to take her back, to live in peace with her and to dismiss his other wives, replied: ". . . . interpellationes esse omnino faciendas iuxta formas ab Ecclesiae praescriptas."[14]

The Congregation for the Propagation of the Faith was asked whether the second question is necessary for the licitness and the validity of the dissolution of the marriage. Without referring to the question of validity, it responded only that the second part of the interpellations must be observed.[15] In another case arising from the same vicariate it was asked whether the interpellations from which there was omitted the first question but in which there was contained a negative response to the second, were sufficient for the licit and valid contracting of a new marriage by the convert. The Congregation answered that the parties were not to be disquieted.[16] These responses, interpreting the mind of the Church, and now incorporated in their import by a specific and detailed indication of the questions in canon 1121, § 1, 1° and 2°, leave no alternative. Unless a dispensation has been granted, both interrogations as contained in the Code must be submitted to the unbeliever and he must substantially understand and grasp their meaning if his answer to them is to have any juridical value, and if, in particular, his negative answer is to open the way for the application of the Pauline privilege by the convert.

§ 2. *The Time of Their Proposal*

The interpellations regularly are to be made after all the conditions requisite for the use of the Pauline privilege have been fulfilled or,

[12] Wernz-Vidal, *Ius Matrimoniale,* n. 632; Cappello, *De Matrim.,* n. 779.

[13] S.C.S. Off. (Mongoliae), 29 nov. 1882, ad 4—*Fontes,* n. 1075.

[14] Suggested forms for proposing the interpellations will be found in the Appendix.

[15] S.C. de Prop. Fide (Tunkin. Occident.), 5 mart. 1816, ad 2—*Coll.,* n. 704.

[16] S.C. de Prop. Fide (Tunkin. Occident.), 21 iul, 1841—*Coll.,* n. 929.

in other words, in that period of time within which the use of the privilege is both licit and valid.[17]

The law as to the appointed time when the interpellations are to be proposed to the unbelieving spouse is clearly stated by the Code. Canon 1121, § 1, reads that they are to be made after the baptism of the convert *(coniux conversus et baptizatus)*,[18] before the proposed marriage can be validly contracted (*antequam . . . novum matrimonium valide contrahat*) [19] and, it may be added by way of commentary, before the use of the Pauline privilege is lost in perpetuity by reason of the conversion and baptism of the unbelieving spouse.[20] This is the general law of the Church, the compliance with which the Holy See always insists upon unless a papal dispensation from making the interpellations has been obtained.

For the licit use of the Pauline privilege the interpellations must be made after the convert's baptism. This law follows logically from the doctrine of the privilege itself, the foundation of which is the sacrament of faith, not merely the possession of faith alone.[21] A catechumen, not yet incorporated by baptism into the body of the Church, is incapable of making use of the Pauline privilege. And if he cannot enjoy the privilege, he is likewise barred, in ordinary circumstances, from placing the conditions which are necessary for its application. Only after the reception of baptism by him can the conditions demanded for the certified use of the privilege be truly fulfilled.

For the lawfulness of the interpellations, therefore, it is required that they be made after the baptism of the convert, though their

[17] Vermeersch-Creusen, *Epitome*, II, n. 431; Wernz-Vidal, *Ius Matrimoniale*, n. 632, note 70; Wernz, *Ius Decretalium*, IV, pars II, n. 703, note 74; Vermeersch, *De Casu Apostoli*, n. 55.

[18] S.C.S. Off. (Tchely Orient.), 13 apr. 1859—*Fontes*, n. 951; instr (ad Vic. Ap. Sutchuen. Orient.), 3 iun. 1874—*Fontes*, n. 1030; Cappello, *De Matrim.*, n. 775.

[19] S.C.S. Off. (Cochinchin. Orient), 6 aug. 1856—*Fontes*, *n.* 939; (Pondichery), 20 iun. 1858—*Fontes*, n. 947; Wernz-Vidal, *Ius Matrimoniale*, n. 632; De Smet, *De Spons. et Matrim.*, n. 349; Cappello. *De Matrim.*, n. 775.

[20] Payen, *De Matrimonio*, n. 2342.

[21] The baptism need not be in the Catholic Faith. By a valid baptism, no matter by whom or where conferred, the person is incorporated into the body of the faithful and thus the terms brother and sister, as used by St. Paul are verified. Cf., Wernz-Vidal, *Ius Matrimoniale*, n. 631; Sabetti-Barrett, *Compendium Theologiae Moralis*, n. 859, 1°; Nau, *Manual on the Marriage Laws of the Code*, n. 140; Gasparri, *De Matrim.*, n. 1136.

validity is not impaired should they be made without apostolic permission before the reception of the sacrament, provided only that the condition of departure existing at the time the interpellations were proposed to the unbeliever still exists after the convert's baptism,—"Dummodo, suscepto baptismo a parte fideli, constet infidelem in discessu perseverare." [22]

That making the interpellations prior to baptism without papal sanction does not vitiate them or invalidate the application of the privilege is evidenced by the fact that the Sacred Congregations have issued instructions to the effect that those persons who had so acted were not to be disturbed.[23] Yet, while the Holy Office has declared for the validity of marriages entered under these conditions, the licit application of the Pauline privilege demands that in practice the interpellations should be proposed after the convert's baptism or, if necessity demands, apostolic permission should be obtained either to make them during the catechumenate or to dispense with them entirely if the case warrants it.[24]

For a grave cause the Sacred Congregations will grant faculties to allow the proposing of the interpellations to the unbeliever before the baptism of the convert,[25] for example, when serious inconvenience is anticipated if the procedure of interrogating the unbelieving party is postponed until after the convert's reception of baptism; when it is foreseen that there may ensue obstacles of distance with resulting extraordinary delays, or difficulty in contacting the unbeliever at a later date; or when the party who wishes to invoke the privilege has already attempted a second marriage and cannot, for some grave reason, effect a temporary separation after receiving baptism while the interpellations are being made.[26]

[22] Payen, *De Matrimonio,* n. 2342; Gregory, *The Pauline Privilege,* p. 72; Vermeersch, *De Casu Apostoli,* n. 55; Vermeersch-Creusen, *Epitome,* II, n. 431.

[23] E. g., S.C.S. Off., instr. (ad Vic. Ap. Sutchuen. Orient.), 3 iun. 1874—*Fontes,* n. 1030.

[24] Wernz-Vidal, *Ius Matrimoniale,* n. 632, note 70; Vermeersch-Creusen, *Epitome,* II, n. 431; Vermeersch, *De Casu Apostoli,* n. 55.

[25] Permittendi ut, accedente gravi causa, interpellatio coniugis infidelis ante baptismum partis quae ad fidem convertitur fieri possit; necnon, gravi pariter de causa, ab eadem interpellatione ante baptismum partis quae convertitur dispensandi, dummodo, hoc in casu, ex processu saltem summario et extraiudiciali constet interpellationem fieri non posse, vel fore inutilem."—Faculty granted by the S.C. de Prop. Fide, Formula III, n. 26—*Periodica,* XI (1922), p. (140); cf. also, S.C.S. Off., instr. (ad Vic. Ap. Sutchuen. Orient.), 3 iun. 1874—*Fontes,* n. 1030.

[26] Payen, *De Matrimonio,* n. 2342; Vermeersch, "Commentaria de Formulis Facultatum Quas S.C. de Prop. Fide Concedere Solet,"—*Periodica,* XI (1922), n. 122, p. (140).

It seems almost superfluous to say that, unless a papal dispensation to omit the interpellations has been obtained, they must regularly be made prior to any attempt on the part of the convert to avail himself of the Pauline privilege. *"Antequam . . . novum matrimonium valide contrahat, debet . . . partem non baptizatam interpellare."* Otherwise the very purpose of the interpellations would be defeated, namely that of substantiating the fact of the unbeliever's departure.[27] Furthermore, they must naturally be made by the baptized party before the application of the privilege is lost through the conversion of the unbeliever, for in the event of the conversion of both parties to the faith there is no place for the use of the privilege, for then the original marriage stands as a ratified sacramental union.[28]

Article II. The Need of Repeating the Interpellations

The canons do not state how often the unbeliever should be interpellated, but the instructions and responses of the Congregations for the Propagation of the Faith and of the Holy Office direct that, if the interpellations are properly obtained after the baptism of the convert, they need be made only once.[29] Thus when the interpellations are once made and when proof exists that a negative answer, expressed or tacit, has been given, then the refusal of the unbeliever to accept the terms stated in the interpellations stands, even though the second marriage of the convert be deferred indefinitely. But if a dispensation from the interpellations was obtained and the interpellations were correspondingly omitted, then the dispensation is valid only for a year.

This discipline is based on a response of the Sacred Congregation for the Propagation of the Faith. It was asked and responded as follows about the need of repeating the interpellations or of securing a renewal of a dispensation:

> Quaeritur: "Utrum dilato ex parte fidelis per notabile tempus matrimonio post interpellationem factam, vel post

[27] Canon 1121, § 1; cf. also Cappello, *De Matrim.*, n. 775; Wernz-Vidal, *Ius Matrimoniale*, n. 632; Payen, *De Matrimonio*, n. 2342.

[28] ". . . patet . . . nullum huic privilegio esse posse lccum, si ambo simul legitimi coniuges ad fidem convertentur."—S.C.S. Off., instr. (pro Vic. Ap. ad Gallas), 20 iun. 1866—*Fontes*, n. 994; cf. also Payen, *De Matrimonio*, n. 2342; Gregory, *The Pauline Privilege*, p. 72; Vermeersch-Creusen, *Epitome*, II, n. 431; Vermeersch, *De Casu Apostoli*, nn. 55, 64; Woywod, *A Practical Commentary on the Code of Canon Law*, n. 1154; Feije, *De Imped. et Dispens. Matrim.*, n. 499; Cappello, *De Matrim.*, n. 773.

[29] The plural of the word "interpellations" as used in canon 1121, § 2, does not refer to the number of times that the interpellations are to be made but to the twofold question to be proposed to the unbelieving spouse; cf., Vermeersch-Creusen, *Epitome*, II, n. 431.

> obtentam ab ea dispensationem, nova interpellatio aut dispensatio nova necessaria sit? Et quatenus affirmative, quod temporis spatium intercedere debeat inter primam et secundam, aut interpellationem, aut ab ea dispensationem?" Resp: "Negative, quatenus fuerit facta interpellatio; affirmative, post annum, in casu dispensationis obtentae ab initio." [30]

It is lawful, therefore, to use a dispensation from the interpellations only within the space of one year from the date of granting. How is the year to be computed? The Code [31] declares that time must be computed in accordance with the norms established by the canons, unless a different method is explicitly provided. A month in law means a period of thirty days, and a year a period of three hundred and sixty-five days, unless the month and the year are said to be taken according to the calendar.[32]

The Code further states that if the month and the year is designated by its own proper name or its equivalent, for example, "in the month of February," of "the next following year"—they are to be taken as in the calendar.[33] Since the above mentioned response of the Sacred Congregation for the Propagation of the Faith simply states that after the lapse of a year a dispensation from the interpellations must be renewed if it has not been used, the year is to be reckoned according to the calendar. Hence the measurement of time is calculated from the date subscribed on the document of dispensation to midnight a year from that date.

There is no need of interpellating again an unbeliever who, when properly interpellated once, responded in the affirmative, at least to the second question, and for some time cohabited peaceably with the convert spouse, but subsequently and without a just cause effected either a physical or a moral departure.[34]

Charity, however, may prompt that the interpellations be repeated often, even though strictly this is not required by law.[35] This may

[30] S.C. de Prop. Fide, 26 iun. 1820—*Coll.*, n. 936; cf. also Feije, *De Imped. et Dispens. Matrim.*, n. 498.

[31] Canon 31.

[32] Canon 32.

[33] Canon 34.

[34] Canon 1124; Payen, *De Matrimonio*, n. 2344.

[35] S.C.S. Off. (Cochinchin. Occident.), 12 iun. 1850—*Fontes*, n. 910; S.C. de Prop. Fide, (Sutchuen.), 26 iun. 1820—*Coll.*, n. 743; Cappello, *De Matrim.*, n. 775; Vermeersch-Creusen, *Epitome*, II, n. 431; De Smet, *De Spons. et Matrim.*, n. 349; Nau, *Manual on the Marriage Laws of the Code*, n. 142.

be done in order to give the infidel party a chance with a favorable answer to preclude the potential use of the Pauline privilege.

An apparent exception to the rule that the interpellations need be made only once, if indeed it may be called an exception, is the case where the unbelieving party was hindered by a temporary obstacle from answering the interpellations when they were first proposed. In this event the interpellations are to be reiterated in order to give the unbeliever an opportunity in a knowing way to make his decision.[36] This second opportunity thus practically becomes the first opportunity for the infidel to answer with that possible deliberation with which he must be able to act. Hence, this exception, as it were, to making the interpellations only once is in reality not an exception to the rule at all.[37]

Though a repetition of the interpellations is regularly unnecessary no matter how long the second marriage of the convert is postponed, the convert must, if possible, be assured of the non-conversion of the unbelieving spouse at the time of applying for the privilege for, as has been noted previously, the privilege cannot be invoked if both parties are baptized.[38]

It may be recalled here that a second marriage contracted by a convert who has obtained a dispensation from the interpellations is valid even if subsequent investigation discloses either that the unbelieving consort had embraced the faith prior to or at the very time the convert contracted the second marriage, or that he was prevented from declaring his mind when an attempt was made to propose the interpellations.[39] The juridic effect of having made the interpellations is not so broad as that which is brought about by a dispensation, for should the unbeliever, after giving a negative answer to the interpellations, later undergo a change of heart and embrace the faith before the convert partner had contracted another marriage, the right to use the Pauline privilege is lost in perpetuity to both spouses, and regularly the couple must resume the common domestic life, unless the first convert partner has embraced a state of life incompatible with marriage, for example,

[36] Payen, *De Matrimonio,* n. 2344.

[37] Payen, *De Matrimonio,* n. 2344.

[38] Payen, *De Matrimonio,* n. 2342; Woywood, *A Practical Commentary on the Code of Canon Law,* n. 1154.

[39] Gregorius XIII, const. "*Populis,*" 25 ian. 1585—*C.I.C.,* Documentum VIII; Benedictus XIV, ep. "*In suprema,*" 16 ian, 1745—*Fontes,* n. 353; S.C.S. Off. (ad Vic. Ap. Iaponiae Merid.), 4 febr. 1891—*Fontes,* n. 1130.

the religious state, or if it is foreseen that on account of peculiar circumstances a common life is impossible.[40]

It may be asked, what would be the status of a second marriage contracted in good faith by a convert after having made the interpellations, when subsequently it is disclosed that the unbelieving spouse had likewise embraced the faith prior to the time of the marriage? On the principle that the Pauline privilege cannot be applied if both parties are converted, such a marriage would be invalid and the parties involved would be forced to separate immediately. "Cessat enim privilegium Paulinum, ubi primum coniuges legitimi sunt ambo baptizati."[41] However, there is a possible solution. The Holy See is wont for a grave cause to grant a dissolution of a Christian marriage which is *ratum sed non consummatum*.[42] If two legitimately wedded converts have never resumed conjugal relations since their marriage was sacramentally ratified by baptism, then for a serious reason the Sovereign Pontiff may grant a dissolution on the grounds, namely, that the marriage contracted in infidelity had not been consummated after both parties had embraced the faith.[43]

Article III. The Method of Proposing the Interpellations

Just as the Church legislates that the interpellations must regularly be made or dispensed from, so she also presents the canonical form or manner in which they must be executed in order to safeguard the licit and valid application of the Pauline privilege. Although in cases of the privilege the right to its use is self-executory, these formalities of procedure are prescribed for purposes of verification of the freedom to marry anew. Hence, according to the Code the interpellations must regularly be made, with at least summary extrajudicial formality, under the authority of the ordinary of the converted party. However, privately made interpellations are also admitted as valid and even licit if the summary methods of securing them cannot be observed.[44]

[40] S.C.S. Off., instr. (pro Vic. Ap. ad Gallas), 20 iun. 1866—*Fontes*, n. 994; Payen, *De Matrimonio*, n. 2342; Vermeersch-Creusen, *Epitome*, II, n. 431; Gregory, *The Pauline Privilege*, p. 72; Cappello, *De Matrim.*, n. 773; Vermeersch, *De Casu Apostoli*, n. 64.

[41] Payen, *De Matrimonio*, n. 2342.

[42] Canon 1119.

[43] Payen, *De Matrimonio*, n. 2197; Wernz, *Ius Decretalium*, IV, pars II, n. 699; Gasparri, *De Matrim.*, n. 1169; Cappello, *De Matrim.*, n. 773.

[44] Canon 1122, §§ 1-2.

If the summary method should be employed it may bear the aspect of a strictly judicial proceeding, lacking only the formalities of a solemn hearing; or it may be merely summary and extrajudicial, or administrative. Both methods are juridic. Ordinarily one of the juridic methods is demanded in order that the fact of the unbeliever's departure may be indisputably a matter of public knowledge and capable of proof in the external forum.

Some authors indicate that whenever feasible the summary judicial form should always be employed.[46] However, the Church does not seem to be insistent on a rigorous canonical procedure and allows the administrative or summary process in most instances.[47] Should it not be possible to execute the interpellations by means of either the judicial or extrajudicial process, the law admits of the use of the private interpellations. This type of procedure is valid, and if one or the other of the aforementioned formalities cannot be observed, it is also licit.[48]

When speaking of the tribunal competent to accept, hear and judge the merits of a case involving the Pauline privilege, one must make a distinction between the power of the ordinary and that of the Roman curia. A case of the privilege need not ordinarily become what is known in ecclesiastical procedure as a matrimonial cause. The latter involves a strictly judicial trial, whereas the privilege is merely the right granted to a convert to contract a second marriage. Hence, when all the conditions necessary for its application are verified, the ordinary or his delegate is competent to authorize the contracting of a new union for the convert. However, when a true matrimonial suit involving the Pauline privilege is instituted, the diocesan court is not capable of adjudication, but the case must be submitted to the Holy Office for a decision.[49] Canon 1962 specifically excludes from the judicial province of the ordinary all causes which directly or indirectly refer to the Pauline privilege. This fact is supported by canon 1964, which declares that in all other causes the competent judge is one of several possible ordinaries.

[46] E. g., Vlaming, *Praelectiones Iuris Matrimonii* (3. ed., 2 vols., Bussum in Hollandia, 1919-1921), n. 723, note 3; cf. also Payen, *De Matrimonio,* n. 2361.

[47] Cappello, *De Matrim.,* n. 779; Wernz, *Ius Decretalium,* IV, pars II, n. 703; Gasparri, *De Matrim.,* n. 1143; Vermeersch-Creusen, *Epitome,* II, n. 432.

[48] Canon 1122, § 2; De Smet, *De Spons, et Matrim.,* n. 350; Ayrinhac-Lydon, *Marriage Legislation,* n. 302.

[49] Canon 1962; Cappello, *De Matrim.,* n. 870; Wernz-Vidal, *Ius Matrimoniale,* n. 690; Gregory, *The Pauline Privilege,* p. 131.

The Holy See exercises its judicial power over marriage through the agency of the Sacred Congregations and Tribunals deputized for this purpose. Among these the Congregation of the Holy Office alone is competent to decide matrimonial causes which entail the Pauline privilege.[60] This Congregation must also be addressed in the seeking of a dispensation from the interpellations, or in the obtaining of a decision on any doubt which the ordinary feels is beyond his powers of solution.[61]

§ 1. *The Summary Judicial Form*

Wherever the formal judicial method of securing the interpellations is followed, the ordinary as an ecclesiastical judge,[62] either personally or through a priest delegated by him, hears the entire case according to the norms of the summary judicial process. It is called summary because the solemnities of law are omitted.[63] This type of procedure is composed of four elements: the citation; the interpellations; the sentence; and the composition of the acts of the case.

At the request of the convert *(actor)* the ordinary or his delegate will issue a written summons to the unbeliever *(reus)* to appear before the diocesan curia.[64] This citation is given in the vernacular, not in Latin. The Code does not prescribe the exact form in which the citation must be drawn up, but the essential elements of a valid summons are prescribed. First there is the act of writing a citation to appear and to answer to the matter of the trial, which is followed by the act of bringing this to the attention of the unbeliever.

The judge must call the unbeliever to court. Hence, the summons will bear the name of the diocesan curia that requires the unbeliever's presence at court. The name of the judge who will make the interpellations need not appear. However, if the judge is to sit by delegated jurisdiction, he should state by whom he has been delegated, but he need not furnish proof of his delegation in the act of citation.[65] The

60 Canons 247, § 3 and 1962; Pius X, const. "*Sapienti consilio,*" 29 iun. 1908, § I—*Fontes,* n. 682.

61 Cappello, *De Matrim.,* n. 781; Wernz-Vidal, *op. cit.,* n. 690.

62 Canon 1572, § 1.

63 Payen, *De Matrimonio,* n. 2361.

64 Canon 1711, § 1.

65 Schmalzgrueber, *Ius Eccles. Universum.,* lib. II, tit. III, n. 27.

citation will bear the full name and address of the unbeliever. If the unbelieving spouse is a wife who has resumed her maiden name, or who has taken a new name, and the judge is not able to ascertain under what name she is at present addressed, any summons that reaches her and makes it plain that precisely she is summoned will be valid.[56] If the unbeliever is insane the guardian should be summoned. It should be stated that though he (the guardian) is being summoned, it is not in his own name but in the name of the insane person, and this name should likewise be given.

This is followed by the request to appear. As the judicial power of the Church is not generally appreciated by laymen today, ecclesiastical judges should temper the categorical tone of the summons, lest the party cited become contumacious. The judge may attach a letter explaining the Church's duty in the affair and politely urge the unbeliever to appear,[57] or he may provide through the intervention of a friend of the unbeliever.[58]

The matter of the trial should be briefly stated. This includes notice of who the *actor* (convert) is, and what is asked of the court. The place and time (year, month, day and hour) for appearance should be given. The judge should appoint a date allowing a reasonable number of days before demanding appearance in order to give the unbeliever time for whatever preparation he desires to make. Finally, a peremptory period of time should be specified so that the infidel will realize that hesitation in heeding the citation is tantamount to his forfeiture of all later claims.[59] The written summons is then concluded with the signature of the judge and the notary and is authenticated by the seal of the curia.[60]

The citation will be made in duplicate, the original of which will be sent to the unbeliever, while the copy will be retained among the acts of the case in the curial archives, for a record.[61]

[56] Cf. canon 47.

[57] "Citatio parti et testi fit per litteras in modum invitationis, tamen praeceptive."—S.C. de Disciplina Sacramentorum, Instructio ad Rev. mos Ordinarios Locorum super Probatione Status Liberi ac Denuntiatione Initi Matrimonio, 7 maii 1923, n. 36—*AAS*, XV (1923), 399.

[58] *Ibid.*, n. 38, 2°—*AAS*, XV (1923), 400.

[59] Putzer, *Communtarium in Facultates Apostolicas*, nn. 129, 132; Augustine, *A Commentary on Canon Law*, V, 355.

[60] Canon 1715, § 2.

[61] Wanenmacher, *Canonical Evidence in Marriage Cases*, n. 46; Payen, *De Matrimonio*, n. 2361.

If the unbeliever answers the summons and appears *(in ius vocatus, in ius venerit)*, he is to be interpellated according to the norm of canon 1121, § 1, by the judge, in the name of the convert, and in the presence of two sworn witnesses. There is doubt as to whether the witnesses must be placed under oath inasmuch as they give no testimony. In practice, however, the oath should be administered to them in order to give every assurance of integrity to the proceedings.[62]

If no notary is present, one of the witnesses should act as a notary and record the exact answers made by the unbeliever. While not demanded by law, it is desirable to have the signature of the unbeliever affixed to the written record of his statements. If he refuses to do this, it suffices to have the document signed by the judge and the witnesses.[63]

Unless the unbeliever petitions and is granted time for reflection and deliberation, the interrogation is followed immediately by the sentence or pronouncement of the judge who, in accordance with the responses made by the unbelieving spouse, announces whether the convert may or may not apply the Pauline privilege and contract another matrimonial alliance with a Catholic.[64]

The sentence having been given, there remains the task of assembling all the authentic acts of the case. These are to be signed by the judge and the witnesses and filed in the episcopal archives for future reference.[65] Moreover, not only must the original acts pertaining to the interpellations be preserved in the chancery files but a decree of the Sacred Congregation for the Propagation of the Faith[66] further ordered that the fact of their having been made was to be noted in the chancery and parish vital statistic books, namely, in the convert's record of baptism and in the matrimonial register if the convert, by reason of the unbeliever's replies, availed himself of the privilege. This procedure was demanded in order that the validity of the subsequent marriage of the convert could

[62] Payen, *De Matrimonio*, n. 2361.

[63] Triebs, *Praktisches Handbuch*, p. 715.

[64] Canons 1060, 1874.

[65] Vermeersch-Creusen, *Epitome*, II, n. 432; Petrovits, *The New Church Law*, n. 563; Payen, *De Matrimonio*, n. 2361; Ayrinhac-Lydon, *Marriage Legislation*, n. 301; Putzer, *Commentarium in Facultates Apostolicas*, n. 129.

[66] Instr. n. 45 (a. 1883), which is found in the Appendix to the *Acta et Decreta Concilii Baltimorensis Tertii* (Baltimorae: Murphy, 1886), p. 278.

not later be contested on the grounds that the interpellations had been neglected, or, if the original documents were lost, that the fact that they had been made could be established in the external forum from the vital record books.[67]

Because of the formalities involved in the summary judicial interpellations, especially because of the necessity of the written summons, this form of procedure is not strictly demanded by the Church. In practice the less formal or summary extrajudicial process is more commonly adopted and suffices.

§ 2. *The Summary Extrajudicial Form*

The summary extrajudicial form for making the interpellations is juridic and therefore not only always valid but also licit. It may be employed any time that the summary judicial form is deemed not feasible.[68] For the licit use of the Pauline privilege this form at least

Here, as in the summary judicial interpellation, the unbeliever is questioned by the ordinary of the convert or by someone, delegated with his authority, who acts in the ordinary's name and in the name of the convert. In this procedure, however, the formal summons and the official sentence properly so-called are omitted. A letter signed by the ordinary and the chancellor is sent to the unbeliever requesting his presence before the ordinary or his delegate, in order to answer orally the two questions which constitute the interpellations; or, the delegate may omit the letter and personally or through authorized agents contact the unbeliever. It is most fitting that the actual process of making the interpellations should be witnessed by two trustworthy persons, although this does not seem to be demanded by law, for the priest delegated by the ordinary is a "*testis qualificatus qui deponit de rebus ex officio gestis.*"[70]

If for some grave reason the priest-delegate of the ordinary cannot interpellate the unbeliever personally, he may commission two responsible and trustworthy lay persons, who in his name, and in the

[67] Wanenmacher, *Canonical Evidence in Marriage Cases,* nn. 355, 372; Payen, *De Matrimonio,* n. 2361.

[68] Cappello, *De Matrim.,* n. 779; De Smet, *De Spons. et Matrim.,* n. 350.

is demanded, if without grave inconvenience it can be observed.[69]

[69] Payen, *De Matrimonio,* n. 2362.

[70] Canon 1791, § 1; cf. also Cappello, *De Matrim.,* n 779; Payen, *De Matrimonio,* n. 2362.

name of the ordinary and of the convert, may make the interpellations. Though somewhat informal, this method of interpellation still retains its juridic quality, since the unbeliever is interrogated *"de auctoritate Ordinarii,"* though neither of the witnesses is recognized as a *"testis qualificatus."* After having made the interpellations, the two authorized agents are to be put under oath and examined by the priest-delegate carefully and separately concerning the party interpellated and the responses given to the questions.[71]

Once the interpellations have been made, sentence is immediately passed either by the ordinary or his delegate, dependently upon who obtained them, as to whether the convert is free to apply the Pauline privilege contracting new nuptials. Then the written acts of the case are assembled, signed by the ordinary or his delegate and the witnesses, and filed in the episcopal archives. Again it may be noted that mention of the proceedings should be entered in the chancery and parish registers of baptism and of marriage if the convert is at liberty to invoke the privilege.

In both the summary judicial and the summary extrajudicial processes the ordinary is authorized by the Code to grant the unbeliever time for reflection and deliberation, if the latter requests it. Since this is a right accorded to the unbeliever by the law,[72] charity and justice demand that the petition always be granted whenever it is sought or whenever circumstances indicate the prudence or wisdom of a delay. Only the ordinary or his delegate is authorized to permit or to refuse this request for time. The grant of an extension of time may be refused if it is foreseen that the delay would seriously endanger the faith or morals of the convert, or if it is surmised that the unbeliever makes the request in bad faith.[73] Should the petition be granted, the case does not become adjudicated until the time allotted to the unbeliever for reflection has expired. The permission for delay must be accompanied with the admonition that, should the unbeliever neglect to declare his intentions before the expiration of the allotted time, his neglect will be considered as a tacit unwillingness to abide by even the minimum requirement, namely, to live peaceably with the converted spouse.[74]

[71] Payen, *De Matrimonio,* n. 2362.

[72] Canon 1122, § 1; cf. also S.C.S. Off. (Cochinchin, Occident.), 12 iun. 1850, ad 1—*Fontes,* n. 910.

[73] Petrovits, *The New Church Law,* n. 564; Blat, *Commentarium Codicis Iuris Canonici,* III, pars I, n. 533; Gregory, *The Pauline Privilege,* p. 93; Ayrinhac-Lydon, *Marriage Legislation,* n. 292; Cappello, *De Matrim.,* n. 779.

[74] Triebs, *Praktisches Handbuch,* p. 715.

The Code constitutes the ordinary or his delegate as the only person capable of defining the time to be allowed for consideration. As individual cases and circumstances may differ, they may use their own judgment, though a period of a month may be suggested as a sufficient extension.[75]

It appears reasonable that the period of time allotted be considered as *tempus utile,*[76] for unforeseen circumstances may prevent a well-meaning unbeliever from expressing his wishes within the unconditionally and absolutely indicated period of time.[77]

§ 3. *The Private Form*

The private form of interpellations allowed by the Code[78] is so called because the interpellations are not made with the authority of the ordinary but only in the name of the convert who has in mind a second marriage. The private interpellations are always valid but not always licit, for the Church regularly demands that one of the juridic methods of procedure be employed for the validity and licitness of the interpellations whenever that is possible. However, the Church recognizes the fact that the juridic interpellation may not be feasible in all cases. The unbeliever may erect a barrier by refusing to heed a legal summons or he may refuse to be interviewed by the ordinary or his auditor. In these contingencies the interpellations may be made validly and licitly in the private form, either by the convert personally or by proxy.[79]

There is no debate among authors about the fact that the Code permits a convert to interrogate the unbelieving spouse personally when the private method of interpellation is employed. But there is some discussion among authors as to whether the intervention of a proxy is permitted. The overwhelming weight of opinion, however, is that the employment of a responsible third party to make the interpellations for the convert is not only permissible but also preferable.

[75] Vermeersch, *De Casu Apostoli,* n. 59.

[76] Canon 35; Cappello, *De Matrim.,* n. 780; cf. p. 99.

[77] Gregory, *The Pauline Privilege,* p. 93.

[78] Canon 1122, § 2.

[79] Petrovits, *The New Church Law,* n. 565; Gregory, *The Pauline Privilege,* p. 94; Ayrinhac-Lydon, *Marriage Legislation,* n. 293; Payen, *De Matrimonio,* n. 2363.

Although canon 1122, § 2, employs the term "ipsa," the word is evidently placed there to denote the making of private interpellations by the convert in contradistinction to those made by the ordinary or with his authority. Were it the intention of the legislator to restrict this power to the convert personally, a more definitely qualifying term should have been used. Furthermore, there seems to be no solid reason to support the claim that a delegate may not effect that which the convert is empowered to do. This interpretation of the canon is strengthened by the fact that the Holy See has issued an instruction that whenever it is possible some responsible third person should be employed to secure the interpellations when they are privately made, lest the convert be prejudiced in his own case.[80]

However, if the convert does make the interpellations personally, whether with or without witnesses, either orally or by letter, or even secretly, there can be no doubt that they are valid and confer the right, at least in conscience, to contract another marriage, if they are properly proposed and answered. Whether or not they would be of value in the external forum is another question.[81] Although proof that the interpellations were validly made is regularly demanded before a convert is permitted to apply the Pauline privilege, the lawfulness of a second marriage already contracted by a convert may not be impugned solely on the grounds that evidence for the validity of the interpellations is lacking in the external forum.[82]

To prevent all challenging of the validity of the marriage and also all possible future interference from the unbeliever, the Church insists, at least for licit action, that the fact of the interpellations having been made be a matter of public record and capable of proof in the external forum. Hence, to be of value in the external forum, the Code states that the truth of the answers made by the unbeliever to the interpellations must be attested by at least two witnesses, or by some other legitimate form of proof.[83]

[80] Cf. *Monita ad Missionarios Provinciae Nankinensis,* n. 521, quoted in De Smet, *De Spons. et Matrim.,* n. 350, note 6; cf. also Payen, *De Matrimonio,* n. 2363; Vermeersch-Creusen, *Epitome,* II, n. 432; Cappello, *De Matrim.,* n. 779; Wernz-Vidal, *Ius Matrimoniale,* n. 632.

[81] Ayrinhac-Lydon, *Marriage Legislation,* n. 293; Payen, *De Matrimonio,* n. 2363.

[82] Cappello, *De Matrim.,* n. 779.

[83] Canon 1122, § 2; cf. also, *Glossa ordinaria*—"Debet adhibere testes, quod illa non vult ei cohabitare, ne impediatur postea contrahans."—ad v. "qui relinquitur," in c. 7, X, *de divortiis,* IV, 19.

The convert in making the private interpellations may not consider himself or his proxy as one of the witnesses. Two witnesses must be in attendance in addition to either of these. However, the interpellations are accepted in the external forum if the convert chooses not to appear before the unbeliever either personally or by proxy, but sends two trustworthy persons, who in the convert's name shall make the interpellations. These witnesses must give testimony from personal knowledge. Witnesses *de auditu alieno* do not suffice.[84]

The proxy or persons chosen to make the interpellations should secure the signature of the unbeliever to the document on which his answers appear, if this is possible.[85] If the unbeliever is reluctant to endorse the document, the substance of the interview must nevertheless be written and subscribed to by those who made the interpellations.

Under the category of "other legitimate forms of proof"[86] there may be listed letters written by the convert and the unbeliever. If there is no other avenue of approach to the unbeliever, then he may be interpellated by letter, provided that it is certain he really received the letter. Registered letters which demand a return card do not always prove this fact. Postal regulations under certain conditions allow others than the addressee to sign, and hence it may be doubtful whether the party to be interpellated actually received the letter. That no answer was forthcoming may be chargeable to other causes than the refusal of the infidel to answer. The answer may have been lost in transit or may not have been posted by the party to whom it was entrusted. However, if there has been received from the infidel a letter in which he substantially answers both questions in the negative, it is a recognized interpellation, but to be of value in the external forum the document must be authenticated by the affidavits of those who were in a position to know that it was really the unbeliever who wrote, that he acted freely and spontaneously,[87] and that no subterfuge or duress, least of all a bribe, was used to secure it.[88]

In so far as this is possible the ordinary or priest must exercise every caution before accepting evidence of this nature as proof that the interpellations were made, and they must be assured of the in-

[84] Payen, *De Matrimonio,* n. 2363.

[85] Payen, *op. cit.,* n. 2364.

[86] Canon 1122, § 2.

[87] Cappello, *De Matrim.,* n. 779; Putzer, *Commentarium in Facultates Apostolicas,* n. 129; Nau, *Manual on the Marriage Laws of the Code,* n. 142.

[88] Payen, *De Matrimonio,* n. 2364.

tegrity of those who furnish the affidavits. It is well known that there is at times a peculiar attitude of mind even with otherwise well disposed persons in questions of marriage—they think that no matter how a declaration of nullity or a dissolution was obtained the second marriage will be valid.[89] In extreme cases when other affidavits cannot be had to prove the unbeliever's letter to be genuine, the oath of the convert spouse, when it is supported by the proper presumption, will suffice.[90]

Other legitimate forms of proof acceptable in the external forum as evidence that the interpellations were made are the testimony of a pastor who by virtue of his office is a qualified witness[91] and, lacking any other means of proof, the testimony under oath of any Catholic to the fact that the interpellations were properly made.[92]

After the responses have been received privately they are to be sworn to by the convert or his proxy and the witnesses, and given to the ordinary or his delegate who will adjudicate the case in accordance with the evidence produced.

As in the juridic methods of making the interpellations, so also in the private method of proposing them, the convert may determine a certain period of time within which the unbeliever is to respond. However, in granting this time-allowance the convert should warn the unbelieving spouse that if he fails to make a response within the allotted time his silence will be construed as a negative answer.[93]

While the private interpellation is admitted as valid by the Church, and indeed also as licit if the juridic methods are impracticable in a given case, the greatest caution must be exercised in accepting evidence, especially when the convert reports a negative answer. In practice, if this procedure is followed, the services of some responsible third party, or of two trustworthy witnesses should be employed if that be at all possible.[94]

[89] Gregory, *The Pauline Privilege,* p. 95.

[90] Wanenmacher, *Canonical Evidence in Marriage Cases,* n. 115; Gregory, *The Pauline Privilege,* p. 95.

[91] Canon 1791, § 1; Gregory, *loc. cit.*

[92] Vermeersch-Creusen, *Epitome,* II, n. 432; Payen, *De Matrimonio* nn. 2363, 2364; Cappello, *De Matrim.,* n. 779.

[93] S.C.S. Off. (Cochinchin. Occident.), 12 iun. 1850—*Fontes,* n. 910; Triebs, *Praktisches Handbuch,* p. 715.

[94] Gregory, *The Pauline Privilege,* p. 96; De Smet, *De Spons. et Matrim.,* n. 350, note 6; Wanenmacher, *Canonical Evidence in Marriage Cases,* n. 115.

CHAPTER V

JURIDICAL EFFECT OF THE INTERPELLATIONS

Canon 1123. *Si interpellationes ex declaratione Sedis Apostolicae omissae fuerint, aut si infidelis eisdem negative responderit expresse vel tacite, pars baptizata ius habet novas nuptias cum persona catholica contrahendi, nisi ipsa post baptismum dederit parti non baptizatae iustam discedendi causam.*

Canon 1124. *Coniux fidelis, licet post susceptum baptismum denuo matrimonialiter cum parte infideli vixerit, ius tamen novas celebrandi nuptias cum persona catholica non amittit, ideoque potest hoc iure uti, si coniux infidelis, mutata voluntate, postea discedit sine iusta causa, vel iam non cohabitet pacifice sine contumelia Creatoris.*

In the preceding chapters there has been discussed the necessity of the interpellations and the manner in which they must be presented to the unbeliever; there now needs to be considered the juridic effect ensuing from the actual presentation of the interpellations. It is not to be thought that, since the Pauline privilege is a concession granted in favor of the faith, legitimately married converts may rashly be assured of applying it in their favor. Certain considerations must in justice be accorded to the unbelieving spouse of such a matrimonial alliance. As mentioned previously, the infidel party has legally acquired rights as the lawful husband (or wife) of the converted party and these rights cannot be denied him (or her). The unbelieving party forfeits them only by his desertion and by his confirmation of that fact as evidenced by his negative reply, expressed or tacit, to the interpellations,[1] unless a dispensation from the interpellations has been obtained from the Sovereign Pontiff in the event of some moral or physical impossibility relative to the making of the interpellations.[2]

The contingencies arising from the possible replies, or neglect of replies, to the interpellations have been anticipated through experience and provided for by the decrees of the Popes and the responses of the Sacred Congregations. Therefore, unless a dispensation intervenes, both

[1] Canon 1123; Vito, "Il Privilegio Paolino,"—*Perfice Munus,* XI (1936), 97; Triebs, *Praktisches Handbuch,* p. 715.

[2] Cf. *supra,* p. 32; also p. 105.

interpellations must be submitted to the unbelieving party [3] directly and without circumlocution, and both must be worded according to the accepted formula,[4] so that their full import may be understood.[5] Thus proposed, the interpellations will evoke responses from the infidel party which will allow of certain, definite courses of action for the convert.

Article I. Determination of the Effect Upon a Certified Answer

§ 1. *In an Affirmative Reply to Both Questions*

If the infidel party is interpellated according to the norms of canon 1121, and sincerely affirms his willingness not only to abide in peace with the converted party but also to embrace the faith, the convert is not conceded the right to marry anew, since the reasons which permit the use of the Pauline privilege fail to be present. If the converted party for a just cause, for example, in view of the sinful or scandalous life of the infidel spouse, had separated from the infidel, he or she may continue to live apart. But if the offending infidel is sincere in his answers to the interpellations, amends his life, and actually embraces the faith, he recovers the right to a common domestic life, for baptism removes all sin and the punishment due to it.[6]

If subsequently the unbelieving party fails to keep his pledges, then two courses of action are open to the convert, depending upon which promise the unbeliever is delinquent in observing. The convert may not apply the privilege if the unbeliever merely neglects for one reason or another to fulfill his promise of conversion and yet abides in peace. At most, in this contingency, the convert may effect a separation lasting to such a time as the unbeliever may be converted, when common marital relations should be re-established.[7]

[3] S.C. de Prop. Fide, (C.P. pro Sin. Tunk. Occid.), 5 mart. 1816, ad 2—*Coll.*, n. 704; E. Jombart, "Casus de Dissolutione Matrimonii Paganorum,"—*Periodica*, XIV (1925), p. 68, n. 74.

[4] Canon 1121, § 2.

[5] S.C.S. Off. (Mongoliae), 29 nov. 1882, ad 4—*Fontes*, n. 1075.

[6] Payen, *De Matrimonio*, nn. 2279, 2366; Vermeersch, *De Casu Apostoli*, n. 60.

[7] Canon 1131, § 2; cf. also Innocent III, "*Gaudemus in Domino,*" 22 apr. 1201—c. 8, X, *de divortiis*, IV, 19; Potthast, n. 1325.

But if the unbelieving party fails to observe peaceful cohabitation, his actions are construed to have effected a moral departure. Without again having to propose the interpellations the convert acquires the right to contract a new marriage with a Catholic.[8]

The note of sincerity must characterize the affirmation of the unbeliever to the interpellations. Occasionally an affirmative answer of the unbaptized party may lack this quality. It may be given to vex the convert or to prevent a second marriage. Hatred of religion or jealousy may also prompt such insincere responses.[9]

A mere suspicion that the unbeliever is feigning when he replies in the affirmative to the interpellations does not of itself justify the assumption of a negative construction. There must be serious, reasonable and substantial doubt about the unbeliever's veracity. If there is definite evidence of the infidel's malicious intent or ill-will prior to the making of the interpellations, then the ordinary may apply to the Holy See for a dispensation from them, or if he has the faculties to do so, he may dispense.[10] If the interpellations have already been made and substantial extrajudicial arguments can be adduced which demonstrate the unbeliever's ill-will, his affirmative responses may without further ado be construed as negative. Then the convert, without the making of further interpellations, may be declared free to contract a new marriage.[11] However, if certitude of the infidel's maliciousness is lacking, recourse should be had to the Holy See for a dispensation *ad cautelam* from the interpellations.

The Christian may also acquire the right to remarriage if the unbeliever, though sincere in answering the interpellations, later creates situations prejudicial to faith or morals.[12] In these circumstances the Christian may resort to the use of the Pauline privilege even if marital relations with the infidel party were re-established after the reception of baptism.[13]

[8] Canon 1124; S.C. de Prop. Fide, 26 iun. 1820—*Coll.*, n. 936; Feije, *De Imped. et Dispens. Matrim.*, n. 498; Petrovits, *The New Church Law*, n. 564; Payen, *De Matrimonio*, n. 2344, 1, 1°.

[9] S.C. de Prop. Fide, 30 mart. 1836—*Coll.*, n. 940; cf. also Feije who states: 'Invigilandum est ne subdole respondeat."—*De Imped. et Dispens. Matrim.*, n. 490, note 1.

[10] S.C.S. Off. (Mongoliae), 29 nov. 1882, ad 2—*Fontes*, n. 1075.

[11] Gasparri, *De Matrim.*, n. 1168; Payen, *De Matrimonio*, n. 2368, note 3.

[12] S.C.S. Off. (Mongoliae), 29 nov. 1882, ad 2, 3—*Fontes*, n. 1075; Vermeersch, *De Casu Apostoli*, n. 60; Cappello, *De Matrim.*, n. 780; Wernz-Vidal, *Ius Matrimoniale*, n. 632.

[13] Canon 1124; Petrovits, *The New Church Law*, n. 573; Payen, *De Matrimonio*, n. 2366; Ayrinhac-Lydon, *Marriage Legislation*, n. 295.

Furthermore, the Holy See permits the ordinary to decide whether or not there is possible the application of the privilege in those cases wherein the infidel spouse, after having answered the interpellations in the affirmative, unnecessarily delays in receiving baptism, thereby giving rise to the certified induction that he is not sincere or that the faith of the converted party is jeopardized.[14]

The right of the converted party to resort to the Pauline privilege is not lost even if the infidel consort is willing to comply with all the conditions required by law, but is so situated, even if through no fault of his own, that a restoration of conjugal relationship is a practical impossibility. Here a *de facto discessus* exists.[15] This condition is verified if the unconverted party is held in captivity or sequestration,[16] or even if a wife was sold by her own husband, provided the sale had taken place before his conversion. In a case of this kind proposed to the Holy Office, had the wife not been physically detained, the Christian convert would have received her back and would have endeavored to repair the injustice inflicted upon her by reason of the sale. Since it was not possible to redeem her, the Holy Office permitted the repentant convert to marry anew through the application of the Pauline privilege.[17]

It is to be recalled that the Holy See does not require a malicious departure on the part of the unbeliever, but merely the fact of a physical separation effected by the infidel party which is irremediable.[18]

[14] S.C.S. Off. (Tunkin. Orient.), 4 iul 1855—*Fontes*, n. 930; (Mongoliae), 29 nov. 1882, ad 3—*Fontes*, n. 1075; cf. also Gregory, *The Pauline Privilege*, p. 60, note 51; Ayrinhac-Lydon, *Marriage Legislation*, n. 295.

[15] "Quidam ad fidem nuper conversi interpellant coniugem infidelem, an velit converti vel saltem habitare pacifice. Respondet illa se quidem velle, sed detineri a secundo marito vel a creditore, qui illam abire non sinunt. Quaeritur, utrum in hoc casu coniux conversus possit ad alias transire nuptias." Resp: Affirmative, nempe conversum de quo agitur, si non est legitime ab Apostolica Sede dispensatus, teneri ex divino praecepto ad faciendam in praesenti casu una vice interpellationem alteri coniugi; posse autem pluries ex mera caritate. Expleta autem a converso hac divinitus iniuncta conditione, si pagana uxor ad ipsum non redierit intra iustum aliquod et rationabile temporis spatium, posse praefatum conversum licite et valide inire nuptias cum muliere tamen christiana, dummodo vir non sit causa impedimenti quo mulier detineatur."—S.S.C. Off. (Cochinchin. Occident.), 12 iun. 1850, ad 1—*Fontes*, n. 910; cf. also Cappello, *op. cit.*, n. 770; De Smet, *De Spons. et Matrim.*, n. 347; Feije, *De Imped. et Dispens. Matrim.*, n. 495

[16] S.C.S. Off. (Cochinchin. Occident.), 12 iun. 1850—*Fontes*, n. 910.

[17] S.C.S. Off. (Victoriae Nyanzae), 8 iul. 1891—*Fontes*, n. 1140.

[18] S.C.S. Off. (Cochinchin.), 1 aug. 1759—*Fontes*, n. 810; (Cochinchin. Occident.), 12 iun. 1850—*Fontes*, n. 910; cf. also Feije, *De Imped. et Dispens. Matrim.*, nn. 477, 495; Payen, *De Matrimonio*, n. 2286; Wernz, *Ius Decretalium*, IV, pars II, n. 702, note 62.

§ 2. *In an Affirmative or Negative Reply to Only One Question*

Since the Holy See can dispense from both interpellations it can likewise dispense from one or the other; the dispensation may be either plenary or partial.

If it is permitted to omit the first interpellation, namely, "will you be baptised," and to ask only, "will you abide in peace with the converted party," the convert's course of action relative to the application of the privilege will depend solely upon the certified affirmative or negative response the infidel party makes to this one question.

Likewise the second point of the interrogations may be dispensed, thus limiting the interpellation to the first question, namely, "will you be baptized."[19] If the unbelieving party responds in the affirmative to this single interrogation relative to conversion, the converted party may not enter a new marriage with a Catholic or, as frequently may be the case, a second marriage already attempted by the convert cannot be validated by the application of the Pauline privilege. In circumstances of this kind, however, the good will of the unbelieving spouse must be demonstrated. He must make the necessary overtures for actual conversion within a reasonable space of time after giving his affirmative response.

If the infidel maliciously delays or unnecessarily procrastinates in fulfilling his promise to embrace the faith then his actions, regardless of his words, may be construed as a refusal of baptism. In this contingency the converted party may be declared at liberty to enter new nuptials even if the unbeliever is willing to cohabit peaceably, for by the fact of not receiving baptism the infidel's actions are an indication of his will and may be interpreted as a negative reply to the only point of the interpellations the convert, by reason of dispensation, had to propose.

In the event that the unbelieving spouse gives a certified negative answer to the one question submitted to him, namely, that pertaining to his conversion, the departure is thereby immediately effected. Upon receiving such a response the Christian convert must without delay break all relations with the unbelieving party and may invoke the Pauline privilege if another marriage is contemplated.[20]

[19] Cappello, *De Matrim.*, n. 781; Petrovits, *The New Church Law*, n. 566; Wernz-Vidal, *Ius Matrimoniale*, n. 633; Nau, *Manual on the Marriage Laws of the Code*, n. 141; Feije, *De Imped. et Dispens. Matrim.*, n. 494.

[20] Const. St. Pius V, "*Romani Pontificis*," 2 aug. 1571—*C.I.C.*, Documentum VII; *Facultatum Apostolicarum Formula Tertia Maior*, n. 25; Payen, *De Matrimonio*, nn. 2366, 2367, 2410, 2447; Wernz-Vidal, *Ius Matrimoniale*, n. 633; Wernz, *Ius Decretalium*, IV, pars II, n. 704.

A. *In a Reply Affirmative for the First but Negative for the Second of the Two Questions*

If the unbeliever on being interpellated states his wish to be baptised, but because of circumstances for which the Christian is to blame refuses to continue or to resume domestic relations, then the convert, if the infidel's assertion be true, may not enter a second marriage. In this contingency the necessary condition of departure effected by the unbelieving party lacks fulfillment; it is rather the convert who is the cause of the separation.[21]

However, if the unbelieving spouse, although expressing a desire to be converted, unjustly refuses to live with the baptised consort, the marriage may be dissolved by the application of the Pauline privilege. It does not matter what are the motives on account of which the refusal is made, provided that the Christian party is not responsible for them.[22] Moreover, such a response may beget a presumption that the unbeliever lacks sincerity in responding in the affirmative to the first interpellation. If this can be proved, the infidel's response may be construed as a negative reply and remarriage may *a fortiori* be permitted to the convert.[23]

Should the unbelieving spouse, however, be sincere in his promise of conversion, but nevertheless unjustly refuses to live with the baptised consort or to live peaceably, then pastors and those in the care of souls, in view of the unbeliever's desire for conversion, should endeavor to compose the differences existing between the couple. But if in spite of all efforts to effect a reconciliation the infidel stubbornly refuses, and if the Christian since baptism is not responsible for the untoward situation, then the Pauline privilege may be invoked, "for a brother or sister is not under bondage in such cases, but God has called us to peace."[24] The marriage of the Christian, however, must precede the possible conversion of the unbelieving party.[25]

[21] Canon 1123.

[22] Petrovits, *The New Church Law*, n. 561; Cappello, *De Matrim.*, n. 770; De Smet, *De Spons. et Matrim.*, n. 347; Vermeersch, *De Casu Apostoli*, n. 60; Ayrinhac-Lydon, *Marriage Legislation*, n. 295.

[23] Gregory, *The Pauline Privilege*, p. 75; Ayrinhac-Lydon, *loc. cit.*

[24] I Cor., VII:15.

[25] S.C.S. Off. 26 apr. 1899—*Fontes*, n. 1222; *ASS*, XXXI (1898-99), 697-698; Payen, *De Matrimonio*, n. 2367; Ayrinhac-Lydon, *loc. cit.*

B. *In a Reply Negative for the First but Affirmative for the Second of the Two Questions*

In this hypothesis the unbelieving spouse on being interpellated refuses to consider entering the Church but pledges himself to continue cohabitation with the convert in a peaceful manner, to allow the neophyte the unrestricted practice of religion and to do nothing prejudicial to faith or morals.

The course of action open to the Christian spouse in this contingency has been the source of acute controversy in the history of the Pauline privilege, namely, whether such a response commands or permits the Christian to continue cohabitation, or allows him to separate without remarriage. Commentators are not agreed whether St. Paul's direction that the convert should continue the common life is a command or a counsel. St. Augustine [26] maintained that the Christian was free in his choice to separate if he formed no new alliance, but he held that the Apostle preferred to have the convert remain and work for the conversion of the pagan partner. The majority of Latin writers has followed the opinion of St. Augustine in counselling continued union, but in permitting separation without remarriage if the convert so desires.[27] Others held that the convert had to separate from the unbelieving spouse. They based their arguments on canon 63 of the IV Provincial Council of Toledo (633), which they understood thus: If the Jews who had convert Christian wives desired to remain with them, they had themselves to become Christians; if the Jews refused to embrace Christianity, a separation had to take place. As previously stated, this canon bears another interpretation [28] and the Council was purely local to Spain, but because Gratian included many of its canons in his collection, it was thought by some authors to be authentic law.[29] Gandulph of Bologna (late 12th century) taught that a Jewish convert was not only free to separate from his or her unbelieving spouse, but

[26] *De Coniugiis Adulterinis*, lib. 1, c. 13—*CSEL*, XLI, 362; *MPL*, XL, 459; c. 9, C. XXVIII, q. 1.

[27] St. Thomas Aquinas, in I Cor., VII, lib. 4, dist. 39, art. 3; Cabassutius, *Notitia Ecclesiastica Historiarum, Conciliorum, et Canonum invicem collatorum, veterumque iuxta, ac recentiorum Ecclesiae Rituum, ab ipsis Ecclesiae Christianae incunabilis, ad nostra usque tempora, secundum cuiusque saeculi seriem accurate Digesta* (Lugduni, 1680), p. 285, n. 17, Can. LXIII: Schmalzgrueber, *Ius Eccles. Universum*, lib. IV, tit. XIX, nn. 34, 35.

[28] Cf. p. 11.

[29] *Dictum* ad c. 2, C. XXVIII, q. 2; Schmalzgrueber, *Ius Eccles. Universum*, lib. IV, tit. XIX, n. 36.

could marry again "sive [infidelis] consentiat cohabitare, sive non . . ."[30] The same was taught by Robert of Flamborough (early 13th century).[31] These opinions, however, were precisely contrary to what had been affirmed in a decretal of Pope Clement III (1187-1191). After expressly enacting that convert Jews and Saracens were perfectly free to retain their unbelieving wives, if these were willing to remain with them, this Pope added that the converts might effect a separation if they wished, but that if the unbelieving partner was willing to abide peaceably, such a separation gave no right to form a new marriage.[32]

In the sixteenth and seventeenth centuries a group of Spanish theologians declared that the convert should always avail himself of the Pauline privilege if the unbeliever was unwilling to embrace the faith, especially if the unbelieving party was of Jewish extraction.[33]

The orthodox practice, however, was established by Pope Innocent III, (1198-1216) in his decretals in which he affirmed that the valid application of the privilege depended upon the departure effected by the infidel spouse. Regardless of the opinions expressed by individual theologians the principles enunciated by Innocent III have been the norm for any and every official action of the Church since that time.[34]

Thus Benedict XIV (1740-1758) quoted Innocent III as his authority for insisting on both interpellations and for permitting remarriage

[30] Schulte, *Die Glosse zum Dekret Gratians von ihren Anfängen bis auf die jüngsten Ausgaben (4. ed., Vienna, 1872)*, p. 52.

[31] *Summa de Matrimonio et Usuris ex Roberti Poenitentiali* (ed. Schulte, Gissae, 1868), p. XVII.

[32] Clement III, ep. "*Interrogatum*" (a. 1189),—Jaffé,*Regesta Romanorum Pontificum ab condita Ecclesia ad annum post Christum natum MCXCVIII* (ed. 2. correctam et auctam auspiciis Gulielmi Wattenbach curaverunt S. Loewenfeld, F. Kaltenbrunner, P. Ewald, 2 vols. in I, Lipsiae, 1885-1888), n. 16595, (hereafter cited as Jaffé). Mansi, XXII, 553; Hardouin, *Conciliorum Collectio Regia Maxima* (12 vols., Parisiis, 1715), XII, 562. Panormitanus stated:"Et ex hoc habes casum quotidianum in istis Iudaeis qui quandoque veniunt ad fidem, uxoribus remanentibus in Iudaeismo; possunt enim cum aliis mulieribus de novo contrahere si uxores eorum nolunt secum cohabitare vel non sine peccato."—c. 7, X, *De Divortiis*, IV, XIX.

[33] Cf. Sanchez, *De Matrim.*, lib. VII, disp. LXXIV, n. 9.

[34] "*Quanto te magis*," and "*Gaudemus in Domino*,"—c. 7, 8, X, *de divortiis*, IV, 19; Potthast, nn. 684, 1325.

to the convert only if a negative reply was given to both interrogations in the interpellations:

> ". . . volumus, ac decernimus, ut Haebraeus ad Fidem conversus, si uxorem Haebraeam habet, eam more solito interpellet, an etiam ipsa converti, et cohabitare velit sine contumelia Creatoris. Renuente autem muliere, liberum ei erit aliud matrimonium contrahere, iuxta verba Beati Apostoli Pauli in Epist. I ad Corinth., cap. 7, . . . Ut bene iam ante animadvertit clar. me. Praedecessor Noster Innocentius III in sua Decretali, quae incipit: *Quanto te divortiis*."[35]

Furthermore, unless a dispensation has been granted to omit the second question, no decision of the Sacred Congregations can be alleged in which it is allowed to invoke the Pauline privilege on the sole ground that the unbeliever refuses conversion; on the contrary, the decisions uphold the continued validity of the marriage contracted in infidelity.

> ". . . Si cohabitare absque Creatoris contumelia velint, et absque eo quod conversos ad mortale peccatum pertrahant, quamvis veram agnoscere Fidem noluerint, non posse conversos alias fideles accipere uxores."[36]

Thus when both interpellations are proposed to the unbelieving party and he declines conversion but is willing to live peaceably with the Christian consort, and there is no doubt as to his veracity, the Pauline privilege cannot be applied.

If the ordinary, regardless of the unbeliever's assertion that he will abide peaceably with the Christian convert, judges that the common life of this couple would constitute a grave spiritual danger for the convert fully warranting both answers of the infidel to be construed as negative, he may declare the convert at liberty to use the Pauline privilege.[37] And if the ordinary is aware of the convert's plight at the time that the interpellations are made, he may even dispense with the second interrogation if he has the faculties to do so and permit the converted party to divorce the infidel and to be married anew to

[35] Const. "*Apostolici ministrii,*" 16 sept. 1747, § 3—*Fontes,* n. 381.

[36] S.C.C., 23 ian. 1603, in Benedictus XIV, *De Synodo Dioecesani,* lib. XIII, c. 21, n. 1; S.C. de Prop. Fide (C.P. pro Sin. Tunkin. Occident.), 5 mart. 1816, ad 1, 2—*Fontes,* n. 4697.

[37] S.C.S. Off. litt. 7 aug. 1891, ad 4—*Fontes,* n. 1142; Feije, *De Imped. et Dispens. Matrim.,* n. 490; Payen, *De Matrimonio,* n. 2366; Gregory, *The Pauline Privilege,* p. 74.

a Catholic.[38] The ordinary is permitted to act thus in situations of this kind on the principle that, when there is serious doubt, the Pauline privilege enjoys the favor of the faith.[39]

If, in the judgment of the ordinary, the truthfulness of the answers of the unbeliever to the interpellations, namely, that he does not desire to embrace the faith but wishes to live in peace without offense to the Creator, cannot be questioned, then the convert may not consider another marriage through the use of the Pauline privilege, but at most may separate from the unbelieving spouse. Charity, however, should urge the Christian, if at all possible, to continue domestic relations with the infidel and to work, chiefly by the example of a good life, for his conversion.[40]

If the unbeliever fails at any time to keep his pledge of peaceful cohabitation by creating a state of either physical or moral departure—by leaving the convert without a just cause or by refusing to cohabit peaceably—the convert is immediately granted the right, without further interpellation,[41] to enter another marriage. The right of the convert to apply the privilege has not been forfeited by his renewing of conjugal relationship with the infidel party after the reception of baptism.[42]

§ 3. *In a Negative Reply to Both Questions*

If the unbeliever answers in the negative to both of the interpellations an effort must be made to ascertain the motives prompting him to reply thus. The need of this supplementary information cannot be

[38] S.C.S. Off. (Mongoliae), 29 nov. 1882, ad 2—*Fontes*, n. 1075; Ayrinhac-Lydon, *Marriage Legislation*, n. 295.

[39] Canon 1127. The Holy Office thus states the possible situation: "Licet infidelis, facta interpellatione, sine Creatoris contumelia se cohabitaturum polliceatur, pertinere ad Episcopum, ipsius onerata conscientia ut omni adhibita diligentia et perpensis singulorum casuum circumstantiis et moribus regionum, iudicet utrum parti ad fidem conversae permittenda sit cohabitatio iuxta ea quae traduntur a sa. me. Bened. XIV, *De Syn. Dioec.* lib. XIII, cap. 21, n. 1."—S.C.S. Off., litt. 7 aug. 1891—*Fontes*, n. 1142; cf. also Wanenmacher, *Canonical Evidence in Marriage Cases*, n. 417; De Smet, *De Spons. et Matrim.*, n. 355.

[40] St. Augustine, *De Coniugiis Adulterinis*, lib. I, c. 13—*CSEL*, XLI, 362; cf. also *MPL*, XL, 459; c. 9, C. XXVIII, q. 1; Feije, *De Imped. et Dispens. Matrim.*, n. 490.

[41] Payen, *De Matrimonio*, n. 2366; Feije, *op. cit.*, n. 492.

[42] Canon 1124.

over-emphasized, for if the unbeliever has a just cause warranting separation, the Christian may neither licitly nor validly apply the Pauline privilege.[43] The "just cause" alleged by the unbeliever, however, must be adjudicated in accordance with the norms of justice and reason.

The usual causes adduced are charges of moral lapses on the part of the convert, or of the presence of physical disease which renders cohabitation extremely difficult if not impossible. In regard to the former charge, the behavior of the unbeliever in departing would be justified if the convert, after the reception of baptism, were guilty of an uncondoned serious moral breach, for example, a sin of adultery. But the charge of adultery committed after baptism may not be alleged by the unbeliever as a motive for departure if he happens to be guilty of the same crime, or if he condones the offense in the convert. Nor may an offense of this nature be considered a just cause if it was committed by the convert before the reception of baptism, for the sacrament wipes out every stain and consequence of sin. Moreover, if the convert gave cause before baptism, for example, through an uncondoned act of adultery, it does not give the unbelieving spouse just cause for separation when the sin becomes known only after baptism. The cause must be given after baptism and at the same time be known and uncondoned by the infidel.[44]

In regard to the question of an infectious disease contracted by the convert it may be said that, if it renders common life impossible, the unbeliever is justified in departing at any time whether before or after baptism. In fact, departure may even be compulsory by reason of some quarantine malady, e.g., leprosy. If in this hypothesis the convert was morally responsible for contracting the disease the Pauline privilege may not be invoked, for the Christian, and not the infidel, is then the cause of the separation. If the disease was contracted innocently, the convert is nevertheless still the cause of the infidel's departure and for this reason cannot make use of the privilege to enter another marriage. But if in this contingency, notwithstanding the disease, the Christian wishes to marry another, who despite his knowledge of the sickness of the convert is ready to contract marriage with the latter, a petition may be sent to the Sovereign Pontiff for a dissolution in favor of the faith of the marriage contracted in infidelity.[45]

[43] Canon 1123.

[44] S.C.S. Off. 19 apr. 1899—*Fontes,* n. 1220; Gasparri, *De Matrim.,* n. 1152; Nau, *Manual on the Marriage Laws of the Code,* n. 142; Zitelli, *De Dispens. Matrim.,* p. 120.

[45] Gasparri, *De Matrim.,* n. 1152.

The mere allegation of the unbelieving spouse that the convert is responsible for his departure is not sufficient of itself to bar the convert from the lawful use of the Pauline privilege. His charges must be substantiated by at least a summary extrajudicial proof.[46]

If the unbeliever has no just cause whatsoever for his departure and replies in the negative to both interpellations, then the convert not only may but must separate—if a separation has not already taken place—from the contumacious spouse. The convert is immediately conceded the right to enter marriage with a Catholic if there be a desire to contract such a marriage.[47] By thus answering the interpellations the infidel has brought about the necessary condition of departure and has forfeited any legally acquired rights he has as the lawful husband or wife of the Christian. It matters not what motives prompt the unbeliever in his refusal to accept the terms of the interpellations, whether it be because of hatred of the faith, or because of reasons known only to himself, provided of course that the Christian party is not responsible after baptism for the infidel's attitude.[48]

Should there be children of the union contracted in infidelity, those who do not as yet enjoy the use of reason must, if possible, follow the converted party; and also those children in whom the use of reason is doubtful should accompany the convert in the separation for, in favor of the faith, the doubt may be presumed to point to the non-use of reason on their part. Those children who are evidently in the full possession of reason are to be urged and exhorted to go with the Christian consort, but they cannot be compelled.[49]

Article II. Determination of the Effect Upon a Doubtful Answer

At times the responses made by the non-Christian to the interpellations may, under certain conditions, be termed as equivalently negative and may be so evaluated. In this class is the doubtful or ambiguous answer, when the doubt or ambiguity of meaning is or will not be

[46] Nau, *Manual on the Marriage Laws of the Code*, n. 142.

[47] Benedictus XIV, const. "*Apostolici ministerii*," 16 sept. 1747—*Fontes*, n. 381; S.C.S. Off. (ad Vic. Ap. Yunnan), 23 iun. 1847, ad 1—*Fontes*, n. 903; (Siam), 17 iul. 1850—*Fontes*, n. 911; (Siam, 4 iul. 1855—*Fontes*, n. 931; (Coreae), 12 sept. 1855—*Fontes*, n. 934.

[48] Feije, *De Imped. et Dispens. Matrim.*, n. 492.

[49] Vermeersch, *De Casu Apostoli*, n. 63.

clarified by the unbeliever. While regularly such responses would scarcely be possible if the infidel is interpellated summarily and extrajudicially with the authority of the ordinary, it is conceivable that ambiguities could appear in the answers made to the private interpellations, due possibly to ignorance of the exact information desired or to malicious intent.

Answers which lack precision when they are made to the interrogations, or which may have a double meaning, may not be adjudicated immediately as the equivalent of a negative response unless it is certain from other sources of knowledge that a negative reply was intended. When certitude is lacking an effort must be made to solve the doubt or to make the equivocal expressions clear. In cases of this kind the unbeliever must again be summoned or approached for an explanation.

If this second attempt to interrogate the infidel party is successful inasmuch as he clarifies the issue, then the course of action open to the convert must be guided by the established norms for certified answers mentioned in the preceding article of this chapter. If a second attempt fails and yet it is known for certain that the unbeliever actually received the summons or that he was contacted by responsible witnesses but refused to be questioned further, he is to be notified that a period of grace, the duration of which is to be determined by the ordinary, is granted to him in which to clarify the meaning of his original vague statements and he is likewise to be warned that failure to act within the prescribed period of time will be tantamount to a negative response.[50]

If no answer is forthcoming from the unbelieving spouse at the expiration of the time allotted by the ordinary, then the Christian convert is free without further interpellations to apply the Pauline privilege. The lapse of the term assigned for answering the interpellations constitutes the tacit negative response recognized by the Code in the absence of any definite and positive reply from the interpellated party.[51] If the infidel, however, submits to a second interrogation and the doubt or ambiguity as to the meaning of his answers still remains, then the ordinary must suspend judgment and have recourse to the Holy See for a dispensation *ad cautelam* from the interpellations.[52]

[50] Payen, *De Matrimonio,* n. 2368.

[51] Canon 1123.

[52] S.C.S. Off. (Mongoliae), 29 nov. 1882, ad 2, 3—*Fontes,* n. 1075; Vermeersch, *De Casu Apostoli,* n. 60; Wernz-Vidal, *Ius Matrimoniale,* n. 632; Wernz, *Ius Decretalium,* IV, pars II, n. 703, note 81.

Article III. Determination of the Effect Upon a Formal Refusal to Give an Answer

In the making of the interpellations, whether it be by the summary extra-judicial procedure or by the private method, the unbeliever must be interrogated personally. No relative or friend may act as proxy to answer for him.[53] In the event that the unbeliever formally refuses to respond to the interpellations, the refusal indicates that at least he was personally approached and that he is aware of the conversion of his consort and likewise aware, in all probability, of what is desired of him.

If extrajudicial arguments substantiate the fact that the infidel's formal refusal to answer may be attributed to malice, the refusal may be construed as the equivalent of a negative reply, for example, if he manifests his feelings by a contemptuous silence when being questioned. Such an attitude is a presumptive confession of ill-will.[54] When such a contingency arises the infidel is to be notified that a definite period of time is allotted to him in which to make a civil reply to the interpellations, and he is to be admonished that failure to comply within the peremptory period will be regarded as a tacit negative reply to the questions,[55] which will permit his convert spouse to contract marriage anew with a Catholic.

A formal refusal to answer the interpellations, however, may not always be indicative of ill-will or malice on the part of the infidel. Especially may this be true if the separation occurred some time after the baptism of the convert. It is possible that the Christian may be the cause of this apparent vindictiveness. Hence the mere refusal to respond may not of itself be construed as a negative reply. Before this premise may be assumed an attempt must be made to ascertain the motives prompting the infidel's reluctance to answer, for if the convert is the cause of the separation the Pauline privilege is not applicable.[56]

Article IV. Determination of the Effect Upon the Simple Absence of an Answer

Canon 1123 states that if the unbaptized party has expressly or tacitly given a negative answer to the interpellations, the baptized

[53] Payen, *De Matrimonio*, n. 2366.

[54] Wanenmacher, *Canonical Evidence in Marriage Cases*, nn. 172, 177.

[55] Feije, *De Imped. et Dispens. Matrim.*, nn. 495, 496; Vermeersch, *De Casu Apostoli*, n. 60; Wernz-Vidal, *Ius Matrimoniale*, n. 632; Gregory, *The Pauline Privilege*, p. 75.

[56] Canon 1123.

consort has the right to contract a new marriage with a Catholic, unless after the reception of baptism he has given the unbaptized party a just cause for separation. In the category of the tacit negative reply is the absence of an answer to the interpellations.

Unless a dispensation from the interpellations has been obtained the infidel spouse must, as mentioned previously, either be personally interrogated, or if a negative response is to be deduced because of silence or refusal to answer the interpellations, then there must be some indication to the effect that the unbeliever is informed of what is expected of him.

While a formal refusal to respond is indicative of the fact that the unbeliever has been approached, the simple absence of an answer does not, without corroborating evidence, allow of this conclusion. Hence, before mere silence on the part of the infidel may be construed as the equivalent of a negative reply it must be established that an effort was made to secure the interpellations, at least by the private method, and that, though no answer was received, the infidel was not impeded from responding.[57] If these conditions are verified and no response is forthcoming, the infidel's silence may then be accepted as a negative response. His utter indifference or maliciousness is indicative of the fact that he wishes neither to embrace the faith nor to cohabit peaceably with the Christian consort.[58]

A tacit negative response may also be presumed if the infidel is known to have absconded for no other reason than to avoid being interpellated.[59]

In these contingencies it is customary, as it is when any answer to the interpellations is in doubt, to concede a prescribed period of time, the length of which is dependent upon the judgment of the ordinary, before the infidel's silence is interpreted as the equivalent of a negative reply. The admonition that his silence will be so construed must in some way be made known to him.[60] If it is not possible to warn the infidel party personally or even by letter, the admonition may be published in Catholic or secular newspapers or periodicals, through which channels it is presumed that he will be notified.[61] If the

[57] Feije, *De Imped. et Dispens. Matrim.*, n. 495.

[58] Payen, *De Matrimonio*, n. 2368.

[59] Wernz-Vidal, *Ius Matrimoniale*, n. 632.

[60] Nau, *Manual on the Marriage Laws of the Code*, n. 142.

[61] S.C. de Prop. Fide, *Formula Facultatum* III (Maior), *25; cf. also Vermeersch, *De Casu Apostoli*, n. 77.

peremptory period lapses and no word is heard from the infidel spouse in the interim, the convert may be declared free to marry anew by the application of the Pauline privilege.[62]

ARTICLE V. DETERMINATION OF THE EFFECT UPON THE LAPSE OF TIME AFTER A PREVIOUS ANSWER

§ 1. *The Question of Time Elapsed*

The question of the effect of the lapse of time upon the value of the interpellations after a previous answer has been given may be studied from the viewpoint of the infidel and also from the viewpoint of the convert.

The law concedes to the infidel spouse the right to ask for a reasonable length of time for deliberation before giving a certified answer to the interpellations.[63] Though usually this request will be granted, it need not necessarily and always be conceded. The matter is left by the law to the prudent judgment of the ordinary who alone is authorized to refuse or to grant such a wish.[64] However, charity and justice demand that this right be not ordinarily denied to the unbeliever. Likewise, a prescribed period of time may also be allotted to the unbeliever to clarify a previous answer to the interrogations if the response is doubtful or ambiguous; to make answer if the infidel has formally refused to reply; or to answer if an effort to make the interpellations has met with nothing but silence.[65]

The ordinary is to specify the length of time within which the infidel must give an answer. As individual cases and circumstances differ, the Code does not suggest the specific time to be allotted, but requires the ordinary to use his own judgment. Authors indicate that normally a period of one month is suitable and serves as a sufficient extension of time. The authors are likewise of the opinion that the prescribed period of time should be considered as *tempus utile*,[66] for in the acquisition or the loss of rights available time becomes an important

[62] Payen, *De Matrimonio*, n. 2368; Feije, *loc. cit.*

[63] Canon 1122, § 1.

[64] Gasparri, *De Matrim.*, n. 1143; Cappello, *De Matrim.*, n. 779.

[65] Payen, *De Matrimonio*, n. 2368.

[66] Canon 35; Gregory, *The Pauline Privilege*, p. 93; Cappello, *De Matrim.*, n. 780.

factor. *Tempus utile* is the time granted either by law or by man for the exercise and prosecution of one's rights, in the sense that times does not lapse if one is ignorant of his rights or unable to act within the allotted time. The ignorance here referred to is that which may be present in a man diligent and alert to protect his rights, not that which is the fruit of culpable negligence. When one does not know that he is in possession of a certain right, time does not run against him; thus in matters that are prejudicial to his rights the time begins to run from the day on which he first obtained knowledge of the response required. The same rule is applicable if one is physically or juridically impeded from acting at a specific time.[67]

It is to be recalled that the infidel spouse possesses legally acquired rights as the lawful husband or wife of the converted party and that the question of keeping or forfeiting these rights is involved in the making of the interpellations.[68] For the fulfillment of an obligation the concession of *tempus utile* in general should not be presumed. There must be evidence in a given situation that it was intended expressly by the law, by some agreement, or at least that it was tacitly and implicitly acknowledged. Hence, since authors consider the matter of response to the interpellations serious enough to warrant the sanctioned use of *tempus utile,* ordinaries should make that concession when granting a prescribed period of time in which the infidel party is to make a certified answer to the interpellations. Otherwise a duration of time which suffers no interruption *(tempus continuum)* must be presumed, and the lack of the period of grace conceded by *tempus utile* may deprive a well-meaning unbeliever of an equitable opportunity to consult the exercise and maintenance of his rights derived from his marital status.

In the act of granting to the infidel spouse a time-allowance in which he may answer the interpellations the ordinary should admonish him, either personally, by letter, or by publication in a newspaper, that failure to reply within the given period of time will be interpreted as the equivalent of a negative answer to the interpellations.[69]

§ 2. *The Factor of Continuity in the Previous Answer*

Once the interpellations have been properly made, the subsequent lapse of time has no effect upon the answer received. They need never

[67] Cicognani, *Canon Law,* p. 691.

[68] Vito, "Il Privilegio Paolino,"—*Perfice Munus,* XI (1936), 97.

[69] Canon 1122, § 1; "Mora sua cuilibet nociva est."—Reg. 25, R.J., in VI°.

be repeated, no matter how long a time may elapse before the converted party decides to take another consort if a negative answer was given, provided that the conversion of the other party does not precede such a step.[70] Nor has the lapse of time any effect on the juridical continuity inherent in the answered interpellations if the convert after baptism has lived maritally with the unbaptized party, for without repeating the interpellations the convert may apply the Pauline privilege at any time if the infidel spouse, after having replied to the interpellations in the affirmative, becomes of a different mind, and departs without a just cause, or refuses to live peaceably with the convert, without insult to the Creator.[71]

The only factor that would render the negatively answered interpellations ineffective relative to the application of the Pauline privilege by the convert would be the conversion of the infidel partner during the lapse of time which precedes the contraction of the contemplated second marriage on the part of the original convert. Otherwise their continuity perdures.[72]

After the convert has remarried by reason of applying the Pauline privilege charity will urge him to bring that fact to the attention of the former consort who has remained in infidelity, by stating that nothing now bars the infidel party from legitimately entering new nuptials or from validating a marriage already attempted. A copy of the official record of the convert's marriage may also be sent to the former infidel spouse. This act of kindness may have untold favorable consequences and may influence the unbeliever to investigate the doctrine of the Church and finally to embrace the faith.[73]

Article VI. The Convert in Resorting to the Pauline Privilege May Contract Marriage Only With a Catholic

With the fulfillment of the certified conditions requisite for the use

[70] S.C.S. Off. (Cochinchin.), 1 aug. 1759, ad 5—*Fontes*, n. 810; (Tunkin. Orient.), 4 iul, 1855—*Fontes*, n. 930; (Natal), 11 iul. 1866— *Fontes*, n. 996; Nau, *Manual on the Marriage Laws of the Code*, n. 142; Petrovits, *The New Church Law*, n. 564; Payen, *De Matrimonio*, n. 2342; Feije, *De Imped. et Dispens. Matrim.*, n. 498, note 3; Wernz-Vidal, *Ius Matrimoniale*, n. 632; Gasparri, *De Matrim.*, n. 1143; Vermeersch, *De Casu Apostoli*, n. 57.

[71] Payen, *De Matrimonio*, n. 2344, 1, 1°; Feije, *De Imped. et Dispens. Matrim.*, n. 497; Nau, *Manual on the Marriage Laws of the Code*, n. 142; Ayrinhac-Lydon, *Marriage Legislation*, n. 296.

[72] Payen, *De Matrimonio*, n. 2342; Petrovits, *The New Church Law*, n. 564; Gregory, *The Pauline Privilege*, p. 72.

[73] Payen, *De Matrimonio*, n. 2368, note 5.

of the Pauline privlege, canon 1123 states that "*. . . pars baptizata ius habet novas nuptias cum persona catholica contrahendi . . .;*" and canon 1124 reasserts the same thought, "*. . . ius tamen novas celebrandi nuptias cum persona catholica non amittit. . . .*" Hence it is clearly the mind of the Church that the convert, in resorting to the use of the privilege should form an alliance with a Catholic person only. This is a logical deduction from the doctrine of the privilege. The Pauline concession was granted solely in favor of the faith [74] and to remove obstacles prejudicial to the convert's faith and morals. For the neophyte to contract a second union with a non-Catholic, baptized or unbaptized, would to a great extent defeat the purpose of the privilege, and the very element of the danger of perversion that it seeks to remove would still exist. The usual effect would flow from a marriage of this type attempted without the proper dispensation, namely, if attempted with an infidel it would be invalid, and if attempted with a baptized non-Catholic, it would be illicit.[75]

However, the Sovereign Pontiff for grave reasons may dispense from the impediments of disparity of worship and mixed religion in favor of converts wishing to invoke the Pauline privilege.

> "Iuxta exposita mulierem esse baptizandam, et praevia interpellatione primi viri, prout de iure, si renuat, data dispensatione disparitatis cultus, matrimonio copuletur secundo viro pagano, servatis servandis, praesertim circa educationem filiorum." [76]

The gravity of the reasons for which this particular dispensation was allowed is gathered from the petition prompting this favorable response. The woman catechumen had become separated from her heathen husband prior to her knowledge of Christianity and both she and her lawful husband had formed new unions with other pagans. Because of the subsequent alliances contracted by both partners, the husband would neither take back the prospective convert nor would the local customs of the place permit her to return to him. Furthermore, there were already children born to the woman by reason of the second union. Because of these serious reasons and because of the pledge of the woman to educate her children in the faith, the Holy Father was moved to allow her to receive baptism, to grant the dispensation of disparity of cult and to permit her, by reason of the

[74] Cappello, *De Matrim.*, n. 785.

[75] De Smet, *De Spons. et Matrim.*, n. 353 ter.

[76] S.C.S. Off. (Coreae), 12 sept. 1855, ad 1—*Fontes*, n. 934.

privilege accruing to her newly embraced faith, to contract marriage with her pagan consort.

In another instance where the reasons were not as urgent or grave, the petition for a similar dispensation was denied, as the problem was solvable in other ways. In this case the woman desiring conversion was willing, if necessary, to separate from her second pagan partner. The solution of the Holy Office is as follows:

> "Mulier certior facta de nullitate secundi matrimonii, separata a secundo viro et sufficienter instructa, baptizetur; . . . mulier nubere possit alteri viro catholico." [77]

What has been stated regarding the grave reasons demanded by the Holy See for the granting of a dispensation from the impediment of disparity of cult likewise applies to a dispensation from the impediment of mixed religion.[78] It is with great reluctance that either is granted and the favor is conceded only in cases of sheer necessity.

The faculty granted in the common indult sent quinquennially by the Sacred Congregation of the Holy Office to ordinaries to dispense from these impediments does not suffice in connection with the Pauline privilege.[79] If the convert wishes to marry a heretic, schismatic or infidel, the ordinary is obliged to petition the Holy See for a special dispensation.[80] The same is likewise true of ordinaries in mission territories who enjoy the faculties issued by the Sacred Congregation for the Propagation of the Faith.[81] They may not dispense from these impediments by reason of their ordinary faculties.

When ordinaries foresee the need of such dispensations, the Holy See will, on their request, grant them the necessary faculties to dispense from these impediments for a determined number of years.[82]

[77] S.C.S. Off. (Vic. Ap. Yunnan.), 23 iun. 1847, ad 1—*Fontes,* n. 903.

[78] Payen, *De Matrimonio,* n. 2224.

[79] Payen, *op. cit.,* n. 2223.

[80] Vermeersch-Creusen, *Epitome,* II, 432, 2; Wernz-Vidal, *Ius Matrimoniale,* n. 631; Gregory, *The Pauline Privilege,* p. 99; Ayrinhac-Lydon, *Marriage Legislation,* n. 296; Vromant, *Facultates Apostolicae quas S.C. de Prop. Fide delegare solet Ordinariis Missionum,* n. 342.

[81] "In casibus de quibus agitur R.P.D. Vicarius Apostolicus, adeoque missionarii ab eo deputati non possunt dispensare super disparitate cultus vi facultatis III Formulae."—S.C. de Prop. Fide, decr., 29 aug. 1866—*Coll.,* n. 1297; cf. also S.C.S. Off. (Siam), 22 nov. 1871, Quaesit. 2—*Fontes,* n. 1019.

[82] S.C.S. Off. (Siam), 17 iul. 1850—*Fontes,* n. 911; cf. also Payen, *loc. cit.*

However, those to whom this extraordinary faculty is granted are admonished in the indult that the favor must be exercised with the utmost care and that the dispensations are to be granted only for the most urgent of reasons.[83]

In cases of extreme necessity and where there is danger of death ordinaries, pastors and approved confessors, by virtue of the law itself, may dispense from these impediments in connection with the Pauline privilege. In view of the circumstances they may do this, lacking the special faculties usually demanded.[84]

If a dispensation from the interpellations has been granted by the Holy See, it in no way automatically carries with it a dispensation from the impediments of disparity of worship or of mixed religion. On the contrary a dispensation from the interpellations is granted expressly for the purpose of permitting the convert to contract marriage anew with a Catholic. Cappello [85] even doubts if a convert, availing himself of the Pauline privilege by reason of a dispensation from the interpellations, could validly contract marriage with a baptized non-Catholic, unless a direct papal dispensation from this impediment was secured.

If a dispensation from the impediment of disparity of cult has been invalidly conceded to a convert, for example, an ordinary dispenses by reason of his general faculties, the marriage is invalid since it is contracted with a diriment impediment of the divine ecclesiastical law. In this hypothesis the only procedure is to effect a separation of the couple, or to secure the proper papal dispensation, if the reasons warranting such a favor are sufficient, and to marry them according to the proper form. The Church will not grant a radical sanation in cases which involve an impediment of the natural or of the divine law.[86]

A response of the Holy Office [87] stated that the vicar apostolic to whom the reply was addressed was not, in connection with the Pauline privilege, to dispense from the impediment of disparity of cult by reason of Formula III of his general faculties, but that the couple in whose favor he had issued such a dispensation were not to be disturbed but

[83] S.C.S. Off., *loc. cit.*

[84] Canons 1043, 1044, 1045; Cf. also Vermeersch-Creusen, *Epitome*, II, 433, 2; Payen, *De Matrimonio*, n. 2224.

[85] *De Matrim*, n. 785, 5.

[86] Canon 1139, § 2; cf. also Payen, *De Matrimonio*, n. 2225.

[87] S.C.S. Off. (Siam), 22 nov. 1871, Quaesit. 2—*Fontes*, n. 1019.

rather left in good faith. The vicar apostolic was advised that in the future he should have recourse to the Holy See in each individual case.

If a dispensation from the impediment of mixed religion happens to be invalidly conceded to a convert who has made the interpellations, the subsequent marriage, though gravely illicit, is nevertheless valid, if the regular form of marriage has been observed.[88]

CHAPTER VI

DISPENSATION FROM THE INTERPELLATIONS

The formal interpellations, asking whether the unbelieving party will accept the faith or, alternatively, cohabit peacefully, are generally a matter of strict obligation.[1] But whatever be the origin or compelling force of the obligation to propose them to the unbeliever, the Church, for a weighty and just cause, can and does dispense from the interpellations so that the converted party, without any admonition to the infidel, can validly and licitly celebrate a new marriage. In some cases this is done by means of a dispensation in law,[2] and in other cases by means of special faculties whereby the dispensation may be granted.[3]

When speaking of the relaxation of the necessity of the interpellations the Code uses the term "declare" rather than "dispense." The text reads: "*nisi Sedes Apostolicae aliud declaraverit;*"[4] and, "*Si interpellationes ex declaratione Sedis Apostolicae omissae fuerint.*"[5] Evidently the Code deliberately refrains from using terminology which indicates the granting of a dispensation from the interpellations, for the reason that what may often be called a dispensation rather con-

[88] Payen, *De Matrimonio*, n. 2225.

[1] Canon 1121, § 2.

[2] Canon 1125; Wernz-Vidal, *Ius Matrimoniale*, n. 633; Wernz, *Ius Decretalium*, IV, pars II, n. 704.

[3] Facultates S.C. de Prop. Fide, *Formula III (Maior)*, nn. 25, 26, 27; *(Minor)*, nn. 24, 25, 26, 27; cf. also Vermeersch-Creusen, *Epitome*, II, n. 435; Vermeersch, "Commentaria de Formulis Facultatum, etc.,"—*Periodica*, XI (1923), p. (139).

[4] Canon 1121, § 2.

[5] Canon 1123.

stitutes a comprehensive declaration that the Pauline privilege is applicable in a certain case in which there happens to be no need to make the interpellations. Thus, when the interpellations are useless inasmuch as it is known that the infidel spouse has departed, the Church may declare them not to be necessary, as in the case wherein the bad will of the infidel is certain, and the interpellations by the very nature of things appear superfluous. But the Holy See by ecclesiastical law [6] reserves to itself the right to declare when the interpellations may be omitted, lest the objective departure of the infidel be not certain. In this case, then, the Church intends the declaration to imply not only an exemption from the making of the interpellations but also a dissolution of the marriage contracted in infidelity should it later develop that the infidel was converted at the time the second marriage occurred.[7]

Previous to the Code the common expression was that of *dispensing* from the interpellations. Gregory XIII in his constitution "*Populis*" uses the expression "*concedimus facultatem dispensandi.*" This was also the terminology employed in the faculties granted by the Sacred Congregations prior to the Code, and the identical expression is used by the Congregations today.[8] In accord with the common way of speaking, the use of the word "dispensation" will be retained here.

Article I. The Church's Power to Grant a Dispensation

The opinions advanced as to the basis of the papal power to dispense from the interpellations and the arguments regarding the exercise of this power have been treated at length in the chapter on the necessity of the interpellations.[9]

The reader will recall that two explanations are offered as to the origin of the Pauline privilege and that the opinion regarding the need of the interpellations is conditioned upon one's opinion relative to the source from which the Pauline privilege itself derives.

Some authors assert that the Pauline privilege is of immediate divine origin, instituted by Christ and promulgated by St. Paul. By

[6] Canon 1121, § 2.

[7] Burton, *A Commentary on Canon 1125*, p. 92; Gregory, *The Pauline Privilege*, p. 76; Payen, *De Matrimonio*, n. 2403.

[8] S.C.S. Off. (Denver.), 15 nov. 1934—Protoc. Num., 2619/34.

[9] Cf. *supra*, p. 49ff.

reason of this premise, these authors conclude that this privilege points to the sole and only power granted to the Church whereby the bond of marriage contracted and consummated in infidelity may be severed.[10]

Those who advance this opinion have laboriously endeavored to explain the constitutions of Popes Paul III, St. Pius V, and Gregory XIII consistently with their view.[11] Benedict XIV [12] gave it as his opinion that it was the purport of the constitutions simply to grant a dispensation from the canonical process of the interpellations. He admitted that the formal inquiry whether the unbelieving spouse was willing either to accept the faith or alternatively to cohabit peaceably could for a weighty and just cause be dispensed in the face of a physical or moral difficulty in the making of an interrogation which could be acknowledged as needless. It is true, as Benedict XIV asserted, that a dispensation from the interpellations was possible, but the constitutions do not admit of this restricted explanation. The permission accorded by St. Pius V to the polygamous convert to retain the wife who should accept baptism with him implies much more than a mere exemption from the making of the interpellations.

Benedict XIV did admit that the clause in the constitution of Gregory XIII, which declared that, even if it appeared that the other partner was in fact a baptized Christian at the time of the second marriage, this latter union was nevertheless to be held as valid, presented special difficulties. According to him it was to be interpreted as signifying that the ecclesiastical court had to decline the admission of any evidence which impugned the marriage on these grounds, and the statement that the infidel party would have been willing to abide peacefully, or was already a baptized Christian, had to be rejected without inquiry, and the second marriage had to be upheld.[13]

If this opinion were correct, then one would correspondingly be asked to believe that the Pope directed the ecclesiastical courts to uphold a union even when there was plain evidence that it was no marriage at all. To do this would have been a flagrant violation of the

[10] Benedictus XIV, *De Synodo Dioecesana,* lib. VI, cap. 4, n. 3; Schmalzgrueber, *Ius Eccles. Universum,* lib. IV, tit. 19, n. 58; Feije, *De Imped. et Dispens. Matrim.*, nn. 601-602.

[11] "*Altitudo,*" 1 iun. 1537; "*Romani Pontificis,*" 2 aug. 1571; "*Populis,*" 25 ian. 1585—*C.I.C.,* Documenta VI, VII, VIII.

[12] *De Synodo Diocesana,* lib. XIII, cap. 21, n. 5.

[13] Benedictus XIV, *De Synodo Dioecesana, loc. cit.*

natural and positive divine law. It has ever been a recognized principle of ecclesiastical jurisprudence that a marriage never becomes a *res iudicata.*[14] A case which deals with the juridical question of the validity or nullity of a marriage may always be reopened, if fresh evidence is forthcoming. The Church would never allow an invalid union to claim the sanction of prescription.[15]

Other authors who held with Benedict XIV that the use of the Pauline privilege constituted the sole exception to the indissolubility of a marriage contracted and consummated in infidelity attempted a different solution. They asserted that the two Popes were in fact interpreting the Pauline privilege and applying it to special circumstances. There is, however, an insuperable objection to this viewpoint. Such an interpretation would involve a positive amplification of the privilege by extending it beyond the limits prescribed by the Apostle. It is hardly necessary to point out that if God has, as these authorities stated, made this the sole exception to a law which under all other circumstances is of the strictest obligation, then its limits must be accepted precisely as they have been marked out. Not even a Pope could extend the exception to make it apply to a case not comprehended within these limits.[16]

On the other hand, it is contended by many authors[17] that the dispensations granted by the Sovereign Pontiffs in their constitutions cannot be brought under the Pauline privilege, for these authors state that these constitutions taken in their natural and obvious sense are not applications of the privilege, but dispensations granted by papal authority for the purpose of dissolving the marriages contracted between unbaptized persons; that the concessions granted are rather an exercise of a special vicarious power possessed by the Roman Pontiffs; and that the Pauline privilege is a specific entity within the generic and more comprehensive privilege of the faith.[18]

[14] Canon 1903; cf. also Coronata, *Institutiones Iuris Canonici,* III, n. 1424; Vermeersch-Creusen, *Epitome,* III, nn. 245, 295; Joyce, *Christian Marriage,* p. 495.

[15] E.g., Feije, *De Imped. et Dispens. Matrim.,* nn. 494, 496.

[16] Wernz, *Ius. Decretalium,* IV, pars II, n. 702, note 62; Burton, *A Commentary on Canon 1125,* p. 82; Payen, *De Matrimonio,* n. 2443.

[17] Gasparri, *De Matrim.,* n. 1161; Vermeersch-Creusen, *Epitome,* II, n. 434; Noldin-Schmitt, *Summa Theologiae Moralis,* III, n. 525; Wernz, *Ius Decretalium,* IV, pars II, n. 705, note 93; Cappello, *De Matrim.,* n. 791; Payen, *De Matrimonio,* n. 2446; Joyce, *Christian Marriage,* p. 496.

[18] Ayrinhac-Lydon, *Marriage Legislation,* n. 299; Burton, *A Commentary on Canon 1125,* p. 85; Kieda, "Direct Dissolution of a Legitimate Marriage by Papal Authority,"—*The Jurist,* II (1942), 134-144.

Those who subscribe to this opinion hold that the Pauline privilege is of mediate divine origin; that the favor was both instituted and promulgated by St. Paul in virtue of his participation in the apostolic authority. Hence there is no need to postulate any special and immediate divine intervention in the granting of the privilege. This argument likewise urges the convenience of basing in the same apostolic authority the power used by the Popes in dissolving legitimate marriages.[19]

This opinion seems to be more capable of being harmonized with the actions of the Popes in declaring certain legitimate marriages to be dissolved in favor of the faith, for the Roman Pontiffs have used this power and still are using it. Of necessity one must deduce the existence of the power from the use of it. The right depends upon the fact. If the fact be certain, then the right also must be certain. The fact cannot be denied, for certain dispensations granted by the Holy See are not mere declarations or comprehensive interpretations of the Pauline privilege, but dissolutions of marriages contracted in infidelity.[20]

The fact, too, that the constitutions of Popes Paul III and St. Pius V demand no interpellations implies an exercise of power different from a mere application of the possibilities inherent in the use of the Pauline privilege, especially in cases wherein the will of the unbaptized party is not known. St. Pius V does not even invoke the privilege; he simply acts *"apostolicae potestatis plentitudine."*[21]

The existence of papal power to dissolve legitimate marriages is further shown in the provision of canon 1127. Through the application of this canon, in favor of the faith, a marriage contracted in infidelity may be considered null if its validity remains doubtful after due inquiry. The doubt, however, can not change the objective order, that is, it can not make a factually valid marriage to be null. Yet as long as the insoluble doubt continues the Church practically deals with the doubtfully valid marriage as if it were an invalid union, and thus of necessity implicitly grants a dispensation from the existing bond if in actual reality the doubtfully valid marriage exists as a valid legitimate union.[22]

[19] Woods, *The Constitutions of Canon 1125*, p. 18; Cappello, *De Matrim.*, n. 767.

[20] Kieda, *ibid.*, p. 136; Cappello, *De Matrim.*, n. 790.

[21] Ayrinhac-Lydon, *loc. cit.*

[22] Cf. canon 1119.

In view of the actions of the Popes, therefore, one should maintain that the Pauline privilege is merely a special case of the exercise of a general power conceded by Christ to the Church, that the compulsory need of the interpellations is founded only on ecclesiastical law,[23] and that as the author of this requirement the Church may dispense from one or both of the interpellations as she sees fit.[24]

The problem now, therefore, is to see wherein the power was granted. It is freely admitted that the indissolubility of marriage is a precept of the natural and positive divine law. It is divine law that all marriages are intrinsically indissoluble, for whether the parties be unbaptized or Christian the partners in a valid marriage cannot of their own will sever the bond of their union. But not all marriages are extrinsically indissoluble. The precepts of the natural law are of two kinds. There are laws from which even God Himself cannot dispense. He cannot give a man license to blaspheme, to bear malice, or to give rein to his lower passions. Here the natural law arises from the very nature of things. But there are also precepts which are not involved in the nature of things, but are consequent on some free action of man. Thus natural law bids a man to fulfill a vow once it has been made, but a dispensation from a vow is possible.[25] The obligation to observe the indissolubility of the marriage contract is also in this category of precepts.

Man cannot always foresee in which circumstances it would be for his greater good that the obligations he has freely assumed should cease to bind. Hence it is expedient that it be within the jurisdiction of a superior at times to grant dispensations. It is to be noted, however, that a dispensation in any matter which takes its obligations from the natural law is not properly a dispensation, that is, it is not a relaxation of the law itself. The precise effect of the dispensation from the bond of marriage is to loose a married person from the obligation that followed upon the free exchange of marriage consent. The act, once placed, cannot be recalled, but God can release man from the obligation He has attached to the act. In effecting this release God employs the Church as acting with vicarious power in His name.[26] Cicognani [27] states the matter thus: In

[23] Scherer, *Handbuch des Kirchenrechts*, II, p. 563; Lehmkuhl, *Theologia Moralis*, II, nn. 929-932; Cappello, *De Matrim.*, n. 777.

[24] De Smet, *De Spons. et Matrim.*, n. 353; Wernz-Vital, *Ius Matrimoniale*, n. 632, note 70.

[25] Joyce, *Christian Marriage*, p. 442.

[26] Triebs, *Praktisches Handbuch*, pp. 213-214; Burton, *A Commentary on Canon 1125*, pp. 87-88.

[27] *Canon Law*, p. 589.

such cases the Roman Pontiff has power to dispense and he exercises this power with respect to the action of the human will rather than to the law, by freeing a person, for a just cause, from the obligation of a promise freely made, and he does this in virtue of a power divinely delegated to him.

When there is no question of the absolute law of nature the Sovereign Pontiffs therefore can, if there be an adequate cause, dispense a man from any obligation by which he may be bound. In so doing the Popes are exercising the power of loosing, the use of which Christ has assured us will be ratified in heaven. Since in the matter of legitimate marriages the binding force of the law of nature and of the law of God is not absolute, but such as to admit of relaxation, the Pope has authority as the Vicar of Christ to grant the dispensation in question.[28]

Article II. The Causes That Warrant the Use of This Power

In cases of the Pauline privilege the right to use the privilege is self-executory,[29] but some summary extrajudicial formalities of procedure are prescribed for the purpose of a just control and for the verification of the freedom to marry anew. This procedure must likewise be observed when there is a question of dispensing from the interpellations. A dispensation from the interpellations cannot be granted unless there is present a just and reasonable cause. The fact must be ascertained by a summary extrajudicial investigation,[30] and the testimony to this fact should be executed in writing in order to prevent any future controversy involving the convert personally or others, for example, defamatory charges or legal suits brought by the infidel spouse against the ordinary or pastor alleging alienation of affection.[31]

What causes, then, are requisite in order to justify the Sovereign

[28] "The marriages contracted between unbelievers, though they are true marriages, are yet not reckoned as being so confirmed *(rata)* that, in case of necessity, they cannot be dissolved."—Const. Gregory XIII, "*Populis,*" 25 ian. 1585—*C.I.C.*, Documentum VIII; cf. also Joyce, *Christian Marriage*, p. 491.

[29] Wanenmacher, *Canonical Evidence in Marriage Cases*, n. 5.

[30] S.C.S. Off. (ad Vic Ap. Iaponiae Merid.), 4 febr. 1891, ad finem—*Fontes*, n. 1130; Petrovits, *The New Church Law*, n. 566; Gregory, *The Pauline Privilege*, p. 78; Cappello, *De Matrim.*, n. 781; Wernz-Vidal, *Ius Matrimoniale*, n. 633; Wernz, *Ius Decretalium*, IV, pars II, n. 704.

[31] Putzer, *Commentarium in Facultates Apostolicas*, n. 130.

Pontiff in granting a dispensation? In general terms the Holy See has adduced as just causes the impossibility or the uselessness of making the interpellations and the grave danger that may arise to a convert personally, to his children, or to a Christian community by reason of an attempt to interpellate the unbelieving spouse.[32] The anticipated harm, together with the damage resulting, must be foreseen and the possibility of such conclusions must be founded on solid reasons, not on mere presumptions.[33] In particular such causes are divided into two classes, ordinary and extraordinary.[34]

The ordinary causes justifying the Roman Pontiff to grant a dispensation from the interpellations may be listed as follows: (1) if a polygamous (polyandrous) convert cannot recall which of his (her) heathen consorts was the first and legitimate wife (husband);[35] (2) if the infidel party's place of residence is not known;[36] (3) if the distance to the infidel's domicile is so excessive as to cause great difficulty for the convert in presenting the interpellations, which difficulty may consist in the necessary length of the journey, its cost, its inconvenience and the consequent damage suffered;[37] (4) if the infidel party's home is located at some far distant place to which safe access cannot be gained because of a state of war or because the region is infested with guerillas;[38] (5) if the first legitimate wife is unknown and it would be very difficult to find her;[39] (6) if the infidel party, after

[32] Gasparri, *De Matrim.*, n. 1149; Payen, *De Matrimonio*, n. 2414; Gregory, *loc. cit.*

[33] Gregory, *The Pauline Privilege*, p. 80; Wanenmacher, *Canonical Evidence in Marriage Cases*, n. 98.

[34] Facultates S.C. de Prop. Fide, *Formula III (Maior)*, n. 26; *(Minor)*, n. 25; S.C.S. Off. (Cheni-si et Chan-si), 23 nov. 1769, ad 4—*Fontes*, n. 825; Payen, *De Matrimonio*, nn. 2408, 2409, 2413, 2414; Gregory, *op. cit.*, p. 79.

[35] Paulus III, const. "*Altitudo*," 1 iun. 1537—*C.I.C.*, Documentum VI; Cappello, *De Matrim.*, n. 781; Wernz-Vidal, *Ius Matrimoniale*, n. 633, note 80; Petrovits, *The New Church Law*, n. 567.

[36] Gregorius XIII, const. "*Populis*," 25 ian. 1585—*C.I.C.*, Documentum VIII; Petrovits, *loc. cit;* Cappello, *loc. cit;* Wernz-Vidal, *loc. cit;* Vermeersch, *De Casu Apostoli*, n. 78; Gregory, *The Pauline Privilege*, p. 79.

[37] Cappello, *loc. cit;* Vermeersch, *loc. cit;* Wernz-Vidal, *loc. cit;* Gregory, *loc. cit;* Veermeersch-Creusen, *Epitome*, II, n. 435; Putzer, *Commentarium in Facultates Apostolicas*, n. 130; Payen, *De Matrimonio*, n. 2426.

[38] Cappello, *loc. cit;* Wernz-Vidal, *loc. cit;* Vermeersch-Creusen, *loc. cit;* Putzer, *loc. cit;* Gregory, *loc. cit.*

[39] St. Pius V, const. "*Romani Pontificis*," 2 aug. 1571—*C.I.C.*, Documentum VII; S.C.S. Off. (Siam), 22 nov. 1871—*Fontes*, n. 1019; Gregory, *loc. cit;* Wernz-Vidal, *Ius Matrimoniale*, n. 633, note 80.

being admonished, fails to intimate his intentions within the specified time;[40] (7) if there is a well founded belief that the promises of the infidel party are fictitious;[41] (8) if it is judged with certainty that the interpellations are absolutely useless;[42] (9) if grave necessity urges that a dispensation be granted.[43] The necessity granted in this contingency must approximate that necessity in which ordinaries are permitted to dispense from the matrimonial impediments, namely, if there is present the danger of death, or if an impediment is discovered only after everything has been prepared for the wedding and the ceremony cannot be delayed or postponed without probable danger of grave evil while a dispensation is secured from the Sovereign Pontiff;[44] (10) if there is serious doubt as to whether the polygamous neophyte has actually given proper matrimonial consent to any of his heathen consorts.[45] In these cases there may not even be need explicitly to seek a papal dispensation from the interpellations. When the curia considers the question of validity in these contingencies, the favor of the law rests rather upon the conversion of the infidel with the privilege of a new marriage than upon the supposed former marriage. If there is any solid probability of nullity the presumption for the validity of the marriage gives way in these cases.[46]

De Smet rightly calls attention to the fact that when the matrimonial consent is the subject of doubt in these contingencies, the

[40] S.C.S. Off. (Mongoliae), 29 nov. 1882—*Fontes,* n. 1075; Petrovits, *loc. cit;* Gregory, *loc. cit;* Vermeersch, *De Casu Apostoli,* nn. 78, 79.

[41] S.C.S. Off. (Mongoliae), 29 nov. 1882, ad 2—*Fontes,* n. 1075; Petrovits, *loc. cit.*

[42] Vermeersch, *op. cit.,* n. 78; Gregory, *loc cit.*

[43] S.C.S. Off., 11 aug. 1859: "Quoties coniugem infidelem nec Christi fidem amplecti, nec sine contumelia Creatoris cum converso velle cohabitare certo constet, Episcopi tamquam Apostolicae Sedis delegati, et Vicarii Apostolici, dispensare poterunt super interpellatione, dummodo urgeat necessitas, nec tempus suppetat recurrendi ad S. Sedem."—*Fontes,* n. 954; cf. also S.C.S. Off., instr. (ad Superior. Mission. Peguan.), 11 iun. 1760—*Fontes,* n. 811.

[44] Canons 81, 1043, 1045; cf. also Vermeersch, *loc. cit;* Putzer, *loc. cit;* Gregory, *loc. cit.*

[45] S.C.S. Off., 8 iun. 1836—*Fontes,* n. 874; Cappello, *loc. cit;* Wernz-Vidal, *loc. cit;* Petrovits, *loc. cit;* Putzer, *loc. cit.*

[46] The Holy Office has explicitly stated that there is a presumption of nullity in such cases: "Si . . . examinato casu particulari supersit dubium, stet pro nullitate matrimonii, in favorem fidei."—S.C.S. Off., 18 maii, 1892, ad 1—*Fontes,* n. 1156; cf. also S.C.S. Off., 26 apr. 1899—*Fontes,* n. 1222.

presumption may stand for the nullity of the marriage contracted in infidelity, but that it need not be so applied, for the parties are to be permitted to continue their wedded life, unless scandal would arise from their cohabitation or danger would ensue to the faith of the baptized party.[47] The presumption militates against the validity of the infidel marriage only when it serves the interests which favor the true faith.[48]

To explain the theological basis of the presumption in such cases Wernz-Vidal[49] have recourse to the dispensing power of the Sovereign Pontiff whereby he, in cases that are not *de facto* invalid, and that do not come under the Pauline privilege, may dissolve the marriages of infidels if they were not consummated after the conversion of the parties, otherwise there would be attributed to the verdict of a human judge the force and effect of altering the objective truth of a thing in a case wherein a subjective doubt regarding the validity of a particular marriage would coincide with its objective validity.

What might be listed here as a weighty cause justifying the Roman Pontiff to dispense from the interpellations, though not generally listed by the authors, is insanity. In a case submitted from China [50] the Sacred Congregation for the Propagation of the Faith declared the insanity of the pagan spouse to be a sufficient cause for a dispensation from the interpellations.

Article III. The Juridical Value of the Granted Dispensation

The ordinary juridical effect or force of a dispensation from the interpellations is to confer on the converted party the right to resort to the Pauline privlege and to enter a second marriage with a Catholic: "*Si interpellationes ex declaratione Sedis Apostolicae omissae fuerint, . . . pars baptizata ius habet novas nuptias cum persona catholica contrahendi.*" [51]

At times, however, a dispensation from the interpellations is the

[47] *De Spons. et Matrim.*, n. 319, (5).

[48] S.C.S., instr. (ad Ep. S. Alberti), 9 dec. 1874—*Fontes*, n. 1036.

[49] *Ius Matrimoniale*, n. 44.

[50] S.C. de Prop. Fide (C.P. pro Sin. Sutchuen.), 5 mart. 1787, ad 1—*Fontes*, n. 4615; Payen, *De Matrimonio*, n. 2413.

[51] Canon 1123; cf. also De Smet, *De Spons. et Matrim.*, n. 353; Gregory, *op. cit*, p. 88; Ayrinhac-Lydon, *Marriage Legislation*, n. 294.

equivalent of a dissolution of the marriage contracted in infidelity, for over and above the effect of dispensing from the interpellations there is attached to a dispensation the extraordinary juridical value which upholds the validity of a second marriage of a convert even if subsequent investigation should disclose the fact that the absent party wanted to live peaceably, or desired to be converted, or actually was converted at the time of the other's marriage.[52] That this singular effect flows from a dispensation is proved by the constitution of Pope Gregory XIII [53] and the constitution and writings of Benedict XIV.[54] It is to be noted that these declarations of the Roman Pontiffs relative to this unique juridic effect of a dispensation from the interpellations cannot be treated as though they were mere isolated incidents, unsupported by subsequent action of the Holy See. On the contrary, the decisions have served as precedents; the example set by these Pontiffs has been followed by responses of the Sacred Congregation to the same effect.

A close examination of the concluding sentence of Gregory XIII's constitution reveals that it implies not only a dispensation from the interpellations, but by way of precaution, an act which dissolves the bond of the legitimate marriage, which certainly exceeds the terms of the Pauline privilege.

> "Quae quidem matrimonia, etiamsi postea innotuerit coniuges priores infideles suam voluntatem iuste impeditos declarare non potuisse, et ad fidem etiam tempore transacti secundi matrimonii conversos fuisse, nihilominus rescindi numquam debere, sed valida et firma, prolemque inde suscipiendam legitimam fore decernimus." [55]

The same thought was clearly expressed in the Epistle *"In suprema"* of Benedict XIV to the Papal Nuncio at Venice:

> "Praeterea matrimonia inter neophytos huiusmodi, et alios fideles, et Catholicos alias rite contracta, etiamsi postmodum

[52] Wernz-Vidal, *Ius Matrimaniale,* n. 634; Petrovits, *The New Church Law,* n. 570; Wanenmacher, *Canonical Evidence in Marriage Cases,* n. 98; Cappello, *De Matrim.,* nn. 781-782; De Smet, *loc. cit;* Nau, *Manual on the Marriage Laws of the Code,* n. 145; Gregory, *loc. cit;* Putzer, *Commentarium in Facultates Apostolicas,* n. 130.

[53] *"Populis,"* 25 ian. 1585—*C.I.C.,* Documentum VIII.

[54] Const. *"Apostolici ministerii,"* 16 sept. 1747—*Fontes,* n. 381; *De Synodo Dioecesana,* lib. XIII, cap. 21, n. 5.

[55] Gregorius XIII, const. *"Populis,"* 25 ian. 1585—*C.I.C.,* Documentum VIII.

innotuerit priores coniuges infideles, . . . suam voluntatem significare minime potuisse, vel ad fidem etiam tempore secundi matrimonii conversos fuisse, ullo unquam tempore rescindi minime debere, sed illa semper firma, valida, et inviolabilia existere et fore, dicta auctoritate decernas et declares, plenam et amplam facultatem et potestatem, eadem auctoritate, tenore praesentium, tribuimus et impertimur; salva tamen semper in praemissis autctoritate Congregationis eorumdem Cardinalium." [56]

Furthermore, in his capacity as a private author, Benedict XIV stated:

"Primum enim matrimonium eo ipso momento, et quidem irrevocabiliter, solutum remanet, quo coniux conversus ad alias nuptias cum fideli transivit; sive quia in hanc libertatem vindicatus fuerit iure divino, propterea quod infidelis coniux iudicialiter interpellatus, evangelicae veritati, aut innocuae cohabitationi se denegaverit; sive quia peculiares rerum circumstantiae viam aperuerint indulto apostolico, quo sublata fuit interpellandi necessitas: quod quidem indultum, quum nulli conditioni sit alligatum, secundi matrimonii validitatem et firmitatem perpetuo asserit, et reditum intercludit ad prima connubia, etiamsi quis probare contenderet, primo coniugi interpellato non fuisse liberum respondere, vel eum iam tunc christiani religioni amplectendae paratum fuisse, immo ante illam diem, qua secundum matrimonium a coniuge converso celebratum fuit, ipsum quoque Christo nomen dedisse, et baptismum suscepisse." [57]

In a case from Japan the Sacred Congregation of the Holy Office in its decision followed the precedent set by these Pontiffs:

"Matrimonium vero eius cum quo dispensatum fuerit, etiamsi postea innotuerit coniugem infidelem suam voluntatem iuste impeditam declarare non potuisse, et ad fidem etiam tempore initi matrimonii conversum fuisse, nihilominus numquam rescindi, sed validum esse debebit." [58]

[56] 16 ian. 1747—*Fontes,* n. 353; cf. also Wernz-Vidal, *Ius Matrimoniale,* n. 634; Gregory, *The Pauline Privilege,* p. 88; Joyce, *Christian Marriage,* p. 490.

[57] *De Synodo Dioecesana,* lib. XIII, cap. 21, n. 5.

[58] S.C.S. Off. (ad Vic. Ap. Iaponiae Merid.), 4 febr. 1891—*Fontes,* n. 1130; cf. also Wernz-Vidal, *op. cit.,* n. 634; Cappello, *loc. cit;* Petrovits, *loc. cit;* Vermeersch-Creusen, *Epitome,* II, n. 436; Vermeersch, *De Casu Apostoli,* n. 84.

The making of the interpellations does not produce such an extraordinary and far-reaching juridic effect as that which is achieved by a dispensation.[59] The interpellations are rendered ineffective relative to the application of the Pauline privilege by the convert if later on it is disclosed that the unbelieving spouse was likewise converted prior to the convert's second marriage. In this event the original marriage stands and the second nuptials must be terminated.

It is in the process of settling this point of difference between the juridical effect of the interpellations and that of a dispensation that authors disagree. Some argue that a dispensation is nothing more than an extensive declaration that the Pauline privilege may be rightfully used in virtue of the supreme power of the Sovereign Pontiff which authorizes its use, while others insist that he grants a true dispensation by which the marriage contracted in infidelity is dissolved. This problem has been discussed in Article I of this chapter, to which the reader is herewith referred.[60] Whichever side of the controversy is supported, the final solution is the same and admits the absolute severance of the first marriage and the validity of the second.[61]

Article IV. The Continuity of Effect in the Granted Dispensation

Prior to the Code, if a dispensation from the interpellations was granted but the convert failed to avail himself of the favor by entering a second marriage within one year, it was necessary to secure a new dispensation.[62] The same requirement exists today for the licitness of a second marriage, although the validity of the dispensation would not seem to be impaired, since the Code is silent on the necessity of such a renewal.[63] This assumption is based on the principle enunciated

[59] S.C.S. Off. (Cochinchin.), 1 aug. 1759, ad 5—*Fontes,* n. 810; (Tunkin. Orient.), 4 iul. 1855—*Fontes,* n. 930; Nau, *op. cit.,* n. 142; Petrovits, *op cit.,* n. 564; Payen, *op. cit.,* n. 2342; *Feije, De Imped. et Dispens. Matrim.,* n. 498, note 3; Wernz-Vidal, *Ius Matrimoniale,* n. 632.

[60] Cf. *supra,* p. 106.

[61] Wernz-Vidal, *op. cit,* n. 635; Cappello, *De Matrim.,* nn. 789-792; Petrovits, *The New Church Law,* n. 570; Gregory, *The Pauline Privilege,* p. 89.

[62] S.C. de Prop. Fide (C.P. pro Sin. Sutchuen.), 26 iun. 1820—*Fontes,* n. 4717.

[63] Wernz-Vidal, *Ius Matrimoniale,* n. 632; Cappello, *De Matrim.,* n. 781; De Smet, *De Spons. et Matrim.,* n. 353; Vermeersch, *De Casu Apostoli,* nn. 75, 76; Gregory, *The Pauline Privilege,* p. 80.

in canon 6, 6°, which in substance is that all disciplinary laws of the old law, which are neither explicitly nor implicitly contained in the Code, have lost all force of law with the exception of the laws contained in the approved liturgical books and laws derived from the natural and the positive divine law. The Sacred Congregation of the Council rendered an interpretation of canon, 6, 6°,[64] which declared that this repeal applied only to general laws, not to particular ones. That a renewal of a dispensation from the interpellations after the lapse of a year was always necessary, was accepted prior to the Code as general law. Hence, since this necessity is neither explicitly nor implicitly demanded by the Code, it would seem that the disciplinary law given in the response of the Sacred Congregation for the Propagation of the Faith is abolished.

Likewise, since the interpellations once made need not be repeated, even if the convert refrains from entering a new union for a considerable time, it appears by analogy that a dispensation once granted will remain in force, providing that the unbelieving spouse continues in infidelity.[65]

However, inasmuch as a dispensation from the interpellations has the extraordinary juridic effect of simultaneously acknowledging as valid the second marriage of the convert should subsequent investigation reveal the fact that the infidel spouse also had embraced the faith at the time when this second marriage was celebrated, it is not the desire of the Church that the granted dispensation have this effect indefinitely. Therefore, although the dispensation would be valid in its effective force unless a time-limit were expressly indicated in the terms of the rescript, it would be gravely illicit to use the favor after the expiration of a year from the date of its granting. The silence of the Code does not seem to void this regulation.[66]

Though the second marriage of the convert is acknowledged as valid when it is later revealed that the pagan consort was also baptized prior to the wedding, a convert can neither validly nor licitly make use of a dispensation from the interpellations to enter marriage anew if he is aware of the conversion of the formerly unbelieving spouse. If the conversion of the other party in the interim is known to the first convert, a dispensation, like the interpellations, ceases to be of value for the application of the Pauline privelege.[67] What is the reason for this difference in the effect of the dispensation, namely,

[64] *AAS,* XII (1920), 43; cf. also Bouscaren, *Canon Law Digest,* I, 51.

[65] Cappello, *loc. cit;* Petrovits, *The New Church Law,* n. 566.

[66] Wanenmacher, *Canonical Evidence in Marriage Cases,* n. 99.

[67] Petrovits, *The New Church Law,* n. 566.

that *post factum* the second marriage of the convert is recognized as valid, while *ante factum* it is not? The reason may be stated thus. From the late twelfth century the principle has been accepted in the use of the Pauline privilege that the bond of the existing marriage contracted in infidelity is dissolved only when the converted party has contracted the new marriage. The same would be true in regard to a marriage dissolved by the exercise of the papal power to dispense the bond which is granted in the dispensation from the interpellations. Gasparri,[68] relative to this question, states that the relationship between the two cases (use of the Pauline privilege, and exercise of papal power to dispense the bond) is of an analogous character. Hence, as in the use of the privilege God desired the bond of the first marriage to continue up to the moment when the second valid marriage begins, so in the case of a papal dispensation of this type the same must be said to be His will until the contrary is established. Now a dispensation from the interpellations is primarily intended to dispense only from the interpellations. The added juridic effect of declaring valid the second marriage of the convert when it is later revealed that the formerly infidel spouse was also a Christian at the time, is granted solely by the will of the Sovereign Pontiff to cover this specific contingency. The dispensation is not intended primarily as a dissolution of the legitimate bond of marriage. Hence, if certified knowledge is had of the other party's conversion prior to the second marriage of the convert, the dispensation ceases to be of value in the application of the privilege.

If a dispensation was granted to a convert to enter marriage with a specified person, that dispensation could not be used validly to permit the convert's union with any other party, for dispensations are to be interpreted strictly. However, if the dispensation was granted merely with the permission to remarry, the convert could enter another union with any Catholic person whom he desired to take as his partner in his new marriage.[69]

Article V. The Authority Competent for Granting of the Dispensation

§ 1. *By Means of the Common Law*

Canon 1125. *Ea quae matrimonium respiciunt in constitutionibus Pauli III Altitudo, 1 iun. 1537; S. Pii V Romani*

[68] *De Matrim.*, n. 1167.

[69] Vermeersch, "Quaesita de Usu Privilegii Fidei,"—*Periodica*, XVII (1928), 241*-243*.

Pontificis, 2 aug. 1571; Gregorii XIII Populis, 25 ian. 1585, quaeque pro peculiaribus locis scripta sunt, ad alias quoque regiones in eisdem adiunctis extenduntur.

In the common law the sole source of a dispensation from the interpellations is exemplified in canon 1125. With the incorporation in the Code of the contents of these papal constitutions therein mentioned, the concessions formerly granted in favor of particular places are now extended "*ad alias quoque regiones in eisdem adiunctis.*" Formerly there was doubt as to whether the privileges granted by these papal constitutions could be applied in other places or only in those countries to which they were addressed.

Though the Code has settled this question and has extended the concessions of the constitutions beyond the territorial limits originally defined, a doubt now arises as to the import of the phrase "*in eisdem adiunctis.*" Does this phrase mean that the application of the provisions of the constitutions to other countries is dependent upon the presence of the same circumstances which gave rise to the necessity for the legislation in the particular places? Or does it mean that the provisions are applicable in any country today to cases in which the circumstances are identical with those for which the legislation was originally given?

If the application is limited to countries rather than to cases wherein the circumstances are the same, this would circumscribe the usefulness of the concessions, since few places in the world today have social or political circumstances that could be called identical with those existing in the sixteenth century. While polygamy is still practised in many pagan countries, and while the vice of successive polygamy is certainly not unknown in so-called Christian countries that are predominantly Protestant, still the circumstances in relatively few countries could be called the same as those which existed in the particular regions to which the legislation was first directed.[70] This opinion limits the application of the concessions to definite countries and regions rather than to individual cases.[71]

Augustine[72] states that the circumstances must affect countries, not persons or particular cases. He does not believe that the United States, or even our Indian reservations, can claim to be in the category intended

[70] Gregory, *The Pauline Privilege,* p. 87, note 83.

[71] Cf., Burton, *A Commentary on Canon 1125,* pp. 25-29.

[72] *A Commentary on Canon Law,* V, 364.

by canon 1125. On the other hand, Gregory[73] holds with Augustine that the constitutions do apply to regions in which the circumstances are the same, but he states that our Indian reservations and vast Negro colonies of the South may be regarded as constituting such regions. He bases his opinion upon the fact that polygamy is still very common among many American Indian tribes and that pastors working for the conversion of the Negroes testify that it is not unusual to find converts who cannot recall how many consorts they have had or when or under what circumstances they entered these various unions. Hence Gregory concludes that ordinaries who meet with these conditions as common to a given region should not hesitate in applying the provisions of canon 1125.

The second opinion—that the concessions of the constitutions are applicable in any country to individual cases in which the circumstances are the same as those for which the legislation was originally enacted—is more commonly held today.[74] Vermeersch[75] argued for it, especially with reasons drawn from the condition of the regions originally contemplated in the constitutions, from the significance of the text of canon 1125, and from the mind of the legislator.

It is scarcely possible that the Code intended to exclude from the use of the grants of the constitutions the territories for which they were first given, yet today even those places are not in the same circumstances in which the missionaries found them in the sixteenth century. And if, in post-Code times, because of the changed circumstances in those countries the constitutions could not be used, it may be asked whether there is any place in the world where they could be used? Even prior to the Code the concessions had been extended to localities other than those to which they were addressed. When the occasion arose and when necessity demanded that they be applied in places in which these extraordinary conditions were present, the Holy See readily granted permission for their use by means of special indults, demanding, however, that a summary extrajudicial investigation be made.[76] Thus, for example, Pope Paul V granted the faculty to the Bishop of Naples for a particular case;[77] and Benedict XIV al-

[73] *Op. cit.*, p. 87.

[74] Burton, *op. cit.*, p. 114; Woods, *The Constitutions of Canon 1125*, p. 73; Cappello, *De Matrim.*, n. 787.

[75] "De Canone 1125 eiusque vi extensiva," *Periodica*, XX (1931), 1*-5*.

[76] Benedictus XIV, *De Synodo Dioecesana*, lib. XIII, cap. 21, nn. 3, 6; Mansella, *De Imped. Matrim.*, p. 108.

[77] S.C.C., *Neapolitana*, 21 iun. 1611—Benedictus XIV, *De Synodo Dioecesana*, lib. XIII, cap. 21, n. 6.

lowed for use in regard to Jewish and Turkish converts the same permission to the Nuncio of Venice as that which had been granted in the constitution "*Populis*."[78]

Furthermore, the universal extension of the concessions seems evident from the opposition between, "*quae pro peculiaribus locis scripta sunt*," and "*ad alias quoque regiones*." The canon makes the provisions applicable to "*alias quoque regiones*" which are not among the "*peculiaria loca*," but if the same circumstances had to be present in the *regiones* as were present in the original *peculiaria loca* then they too would be "*peculiaria loca*." Since the canon does not localize the use of the concessions, there is little reason to doubt that the phrase "*in eisdem adiunctis*" was meant by the legislator to refer not to countries or regions, but to cases wherever they may occur. From a study of the canon and the changes made in the terminology during the formation of the Code, Woods[79] concludes that it was the intention of the legislator to extend the provisions of the constitutions to make their application available for *cases* in all parts of the world if the same circumstances obtain.

The constitutions of Popes Paul III and St. Pius V apply only to polygamist converts. The constitution "*Altitudo*" of Paul III[80] allows of no choice among the polygamist's marital partners if he can recall which of them was his first wife.[81] In this case he is to retain her and dismiss the others, always excepting the possible use of the Pauline privilege. The special favor this constitution grants, however, is that if the polygamist cannot recall the woman with whom he first contracted marriage, he may choose any one with whom he had marital relations prior to his conversion in order to contract marriage with her. In this contingency no interpellations are required. The essential condition for the use of the favor is that the convert be not able to remember the identity of his first wife.[82] If another woman other than the first wife is elected, a renewal of consent is demanded.[83]

[78] Ep. "*In suprema*," 16 ian. 1745—*Fontes*, n. 353.

[79] *The Constitutions of Canon 1125*, pp. 73-82.

[80] 1 iun. 1537—*C.I.C.*, Documentum VI.

[81] Vermeersch, "Commentaria de Formulis Facultatum, etc."—*Periodica*, XI (1923), (138).

[82] Burton, *A Commentary on Canon 1125*, p. 143.

[83] Augustine, *A Commentary on Canon Law*, V, 363.

The force of the constitution "*Romani Pontificis*" of Pope St. Pius V[84] is to be found in its application to the case of a polygamist convert whose first wife is certainly known and could be interpellated if the Pauline privilege were to be used. If in such a case it would be a very severe demand to separate the convert from one of the marital consorts with whom he has lived and who is willing to be baptized with him, there is no necessity to make any interpellation of the first wife; the convert may retain as his lawful wife the woman with whom he is living if she embraces the faith. Inasmuch as the constitution does not require any renewal of consent, it is evident that the factor of conversion is the decisive element which makes possible the dissolution of the earlier marriage, for it is in favor of the faith that the second marriage is acknowledged as a valid union.

Neither of these constitutions required that the heathen party be subjected to any form of interpellation, since the Popes were exercising their apostolic power of dispensing from the legitimate bond of marriage. Apparently the application of the Pauline privilege in no way occupied their minds.[85]

The barbarous treatment inflicted upon the victims of the slave trade toward the end of the sixteenth century[86] was the occasion for the constitution "*Populis*" of Pope Gregory XIII.[87] This constitution, unlike those of Paul III and St. Pius V, made no distinction between polygamist and monogamist. The concession therein granted could be used for the benefit of either type.[88] Furthermore, while the former constitutions mentioned nothing about the interpellations, this constitution of Gregory granted to local ordinaries, pastors and approved Jesuit confessors who labored in Angola, Ethiopa, Brazil, and other Indian regions the faculty of dispensing from the making of the interpellations. By the promulgation of the present Code this provision was made part of the Church's universal law. When cases similar to those for which Gregory's legislation was ordinarily given arise, the Holy See authorizes all local ordinaries, pastors, and those

[84] 2 aug. 1571—*C.I.C.*, Documentum VII..

[85] Benedictus XIV, *De Synodo Dioecesana,* lib. XIII, cap. 21, n. 4; Fahrner, *Geschichte des Unauflöslichkeitsprinzips*, p. 275; Gregory, *op. cit.*, p. 39.

[86] Cf. Burton, *op. cit.*, pp. 63-64.

[87] 25 ian. 1585—*C.I.C.*, Documentum VIII.

[88] Mansella, *De Imped. Matrim.*, p. 111; Feije, *De Imped. et Dispens. Matrim.*, n. 474; Gregory, *op. cit.*, p. 39.

members of the Society of Jesus who are approved to hear confessions,[89] to dispense from the interpellations when it is evident that the infidel spouse cannot be reached, or that he has not given his reply within the peremptory period of time allowed for the making of a reply. The only restriction to this concession is the necessity of proving at least by a summary extrajudicial investigation that this impossibility or failure to respond truly exists. The text of the constitution does not allow of the omission of the interpellations under any other circumstances, as, for example, when their uselessness is foreseen. The granting of a dispensation from the making of the interpellations is restricted within the following conditions as expressed in the words of the constitution: *"Dummodo constet, etiam summarie et extraiudicialiter, coniugem absentem moneri legitime non posse, aut monitum intra tempus in eadem monitione praefixum suam voluntatem non significasse.*[90]

The causes generally listed as pointing to the impossibility which is presupposed by the constitution obtain if the couple is forceably separated and a messenger cannot be sent to a hostile country where the absent infidel spouse is known to be, or if it is not known where the infidel party is. If the interpellations can be made but only after a long journey, the difficulty cannot be called more than a moral impossibility. When asked whether the words *"moneri legitime non posse"* could be understood to include the moral as well as the physical impossibility of making the interpellations, the Holy Office passed over the direct question without an answer.[91] Later, in a reply to an inquiry concerning what distance or circumstances in connection with a journey were to be considered as sufficient to consider the making of the interpellations to be impossible, the Sacred Congregation responded that such a distance suffices which, when all things are considered, causes great difficulty.[92] A great difficulty is not synonymous with a physical impossibility, but it may constitute a moral impossibility. The more common opinion of authors is that a grave

[89] Cf. Burton, *A Commentary on Canon 1125,* p. 174, for a discussion on the question of the communication of privileges among the religious orders. Cf., also Jone, "Wie müssen die Interpellationen bei Anwendung des Paulinischen Privilegs gemacht werden,"—*LQS,* LXXX (1927), 336-342, who holds that quasi-pastors and apparently all confessors are now included in the grant originally given to approved Jesuit confessors; Vermeersch-Creusen, *Epitome,* doubting, II, n. 435.

[90] Gregorius *XIII, "Populis,"* 25 ian. 1585—*C.I.C.,* Documentum VIII.

[91] S.C.S. Off. (Ind. Orient.), 13 ian. 1757—*Fontes,* n. 807.

[92] S.C.S., Off. (Mongoliae), 29 nov. 1882, ad 1—*Fontes,* n. 1075.

moral impossibility of this type suffices to omit the interpellations in accordance with the meaning of the canon.[93]

The serious nature of the matter, however, demands caution against a too easy persuasion that it is impossible to make the interpellations. Circumstances are as various as cases and places, and the gravity of the difficulty or danger which may be accounted as a moral impossibility must be left to the prudent judgment of the ordinary or priest who uses the faculty after the summary extrajudicial inquiry has been made.

The constitution of Gregory XIII likewise provided for a dispensation from the interpellations when the unbeliever, whether absent or present, failed to signify his intention within the specified time granted him for the making of a reply. The appropriate period of time which should be allowed to the infidel party to make a reply will vary with circumstances. A period of a month *(tempus utile)* is usually suggested,[94] with perhaps some extensions or limitations in accord with the dictates of charity as well as those of justice. The unbeliever is to be informed that his failure to answer within the allotted time will be construed as a negative answer and that his convert spouse will be declared free to enter new nuptials with a Catholic.

In practice the provisions of the constitution *"Populis,"* now extended by canon 1125 to the same kinds of cases in any part of the world, contemplate the procedure for the use of the Pauline privilege when there are difficulties in the matter of making the interpellations. (1) The marriage of the converted party, in whose interest the favor of the constitution is being used, must have been contracted in infidelity. (2) From a summary extrajudicial examination it must appear that it is at least morally impossible to interpellate the unbelieving spouse or, if he was interpellated, that he has not answered within the specified time. The results of the inquiry are to be committed to writing. Though a written statement to this effect is not required for the valid use of the granted dispensation, it is a document which the ordinary should demand for the chancery files; it should be demanded of both pastors and privileged confessors, even though they be exempt religious, together with a testimonial that

[93] Payen, *De Matrimonio*, n. 2409; Cappello, *De Matrim.*, n. 787; Burton. *A Commentary on Canon 1125*, p. 169.

[94] Cf. *supra*, p. 99; Vermeersch, *De Casu Apostoli*, n. 59; Gregory, *The Pauline Privilege*, pp. 92-93; Burton, *A Commentary on Canon 1125*, p. 171.

the dispensation has been granted, when the dispensation is given in the external forum or in the internal non-sacramental forum.[95]

The power of dispensing given by the constitution of Gregory XIII is connected with the office of local ordinaries[96] and of pastors[97] in any part of the world. The power is therefore ordinary,[98] may be delegated,[99] and may be used in both the external and internal forums.[100] Furthermore, local ordinaries and pastors may use the power to dispense from the interpellations for their own subjects wherever the subjects may be, and to dispense anyone actually living within their territory.[101] The same is true of those priests to whom the local ordinaries and pastors have delegated the power without restriction. Those who enjoy the use of this power by delegation may subdelegate it, but only in individual cases.[102]

The effect of the dispensation is, like that of a direct dispensation issued by the Sovereign Pontiff, not alone to permit the legitimate omission of the interpellations but to certify as valid the second marriage of the convert should subsequent investigation reveal the fact that the absent party of the first marriage was also a baptized convert prior to the new marriage, or that he was legitimately prevented from answering the interpellations within the allotted time.[103]

§ 2. *By Means of Ordinary Power*

The Catholic Church possesses, by divine institution, the power of jurisdiction or government. By the will of Christ the Church is

[95] Cappello, *De Matrim.*, n. 787; Burton, *A Commentary on Canon 1125*, pp. 171, 176; Vermeersch, *De Casu Apostoli*, n. 79; Payen, *op. cit.*, n. 2409.

[96] Cf. canon 198, §§ 1, 2.

[97] Cf. canon 451, §§ 1, 2.

[98] Cf. canon 197; cf. also Vermeersch-Creusen, *Epitome*, II, n. 435; Burton, *op. cit.*, p. 173.

[99] Cf. canon 199, § 1.

[100] Cf. canon 202, § 3.

[101] Vermeersch-Creusen, *loc. cit.*

[102] Cf. canon 199, § 3.

[103] Wernz-Vidal, *Ius Matrimoniale*, n. 634; Cappello, *De Matrim.*, nn. 781-782; Petrovits, *The New Church Law*, n. 570; De Smet, *De Spons. et Matrim.*, n. 353.

a juridically perfect and supreme society and therefore in its own right exercises the functions necessary for its government.[104]

Canon 197 states that ordinary power of jurisdiction is that which by the law itself is attached to an office. Those who possess the public power of jurisdiction conferred by an office are termed, in juridical parlance, ordinaries. Canon 198 states that by the term "local ordinaries" are to be understood in law: the Roman Pontiff, and within their respective territories the residential bishop, abbot and prelate *nullius* (and their vicars general), the administrator, the vicar and the prefect apostolic. Likewise those persons who, in case of a vacancy of the above mentioned offices, succeed to the office during the vacancy by the provisions of the law or through approved constitutions are termed local ordinaries.

A. *The Roman Pontiff*

The first and, therefore, the supreme ordinary is the Sovereign Pontiff. The universal extent of the Roman Pontiff's jurisdiction is gathered from the text of canon 218 which states that, as the successor to the primacy of St. Peter, he enjoys not only the primacy of honor, but also supreme and full power of jurisdiction over the universal Church in matters of faith and morals as well as in such matters as pertain to the discipline and government of the Church throughout the whole world. This power is episcopal, ordinary and immediate, and extends over each and every church, and over each and every pastor as well as over all the faithful, and is independent of all human authority.

Hence the Pope's ordinary power of jurisdiction is without limits, and its scope is merely defined, not determined, by ecclesiastical legislation. This primacy is of divine sanction and is bestowed on the Sovereign Pontiff by Christ Himself. He does not receive it from his electors and consequently no human power can set any bounds to it or take it away from him.[105]

By reason of his office and by ordinary power, therefore, the Roman Pontiff is authorized to dispense anywhere in the world, for a just

[104] Canon 196; cf. also, Ottaviani, *Institutiones Iuris Publici Ecclesiastici* (2. ed., 2 vols., Romae: Typis Polyglottis Vaticanis, 1935-36), I, n. 88 sq.

[105] Vermeersch-Creusen, *Epitome,* I, 333; Augustine, *A Commentary on Canon Law,* II, 210; Ayrinhac, *Constitution of the Church in the New Code of Canon Law* (London-New York: Longmans, Green and Co., 1930), n. 9, (hereafter cited as *Constitution of the Church*); Coronata, *Institutiones Iuris Canonici,* I, 309.

cause, from the necessity of making the interpellations; given the condition of departure effected by the unbelieving spouse, the Pope may permit a legitimately married convert, for a grave reason, to marry anew any Catholic without the least warning whatsoever to the infidel partner.

B. *The Sacred Congregation of the Holy Office*

From ancient times the Roman Pontiffs have employed the help of various colleges of clerics in the government of the Church. With the Church's rapid growth in Europe and in the far flung mission territories the business of the Holy See, increasing in proportion, demanded the establishment of standing committees of Cardinals and other dignitaries to assist the Popes. Thus arose, as occasion demanded, the various Congregations, each attending to a specific portion of the affairs directly falling within the realm of papal administration. Through these agencies the Pope habitually exercises administrative and executive power.[106] In each of the Congregations, Tribunals and Offices, that discipline is maintained and those rules for the transaction of business are followed which have been prescribed by the Roman Pontiff.[107] Much of the routine business is conducted directly by the Congregations with their clients, but canon 244 states that nothing of importance or of an extraordinary character shall be decided by the Congregations apart from their previous consultation with the Sovereign Pontiff.

The Holy Office, as we know the Sacred Congregation today, is the outgrowth of inquisitorial tribunals, authorized and instituted by Gregory IX (1232). In the sixteenth century the organization was revamped and the work was completed and approved by the constitution *"Immensa"* of Sixtus V, January 22, 1587.[108] Sixtus V gave the Congregation, then called the Office of the Inquisition, a plan of operation which has been retained practically to this day. With the passage of time the custom arose of referring to this Congregation as the Holy Office.[109]

[106] Ayrinhac, *The Constitution of the Church*, n. 37.

[107] Cf. canon 243.

[108] *Thesaurus Resolutionum Sacrae Congregationis Concilii*, IV, 392-401.

[109] Santi, *Praelectiones Iuris Canonici*, I, 288; Bargilliat, *Praelectiones Iuris Canonici* (25. ed., 2 vols., Parisiis: Berche et Tralin, 1909), n. 450; Coronata, *Institutiones Iuris Canonici*, I, 339; Ayrinhac, *Constitution of the Church*, n. 38; Woywod, *A Practical Commentary on the Code of Canon Law*, n. 187.

In the year 1908 Pius X, in preparation for the publication of the Code, effected another reorganization of the Roman Curia, and detailed the rules and regulations whereby its various branches were to be governed. In his constitution[110] Pius X used only the term Holy Office in referring to this particular Congregation, as the Code now does. The Popes reserve to themselves the office of prefect of this congregation.[111]

Under the present legislation among the categories of affairs assigned to the Holy Office for adjudication are certain types of marriage cases, including those which involve the Pauline privilege. Canon 247 states that this Congregation has exclusive jurisdiction in whatever pertains, directly or indirectly, in law or in fact, to the privilege.[112] In the category of what pertains to the Pauline privilege may be listed dispensations from the interpellations. Thus the Congregation of the Holy Office is competent to grant, for just and weighty causes, dispensations from the interpellations.

C. The Ordinary in the Case of an Extreme Emergency

The Holy Office has declared that bishops and vicars apostolic may dispense from the interpellations when grave necessity urges and there is no time to refer the matter to the Holy See, and when it is certain from summary extrajudicial evidence that the unbelieving spouse will neither be converted nor consent to live in peace with the convert.[113]

There now arises the question whether this approval to act in urgent cases still holds. The answer is in the affirmative. Canon 81 states the general principle that the ordinary may dispense in urgent cases.[114] That this principle is applicable to a dispensation from the interpellations derives from canon 20, directing that, when the present law does not provide for a particular situation, one is to be guided by definite

[110] Const. "*Sapienti consilio,*" 29 iun. 1908—*Fontes,* n. 682.

[111] Coronata, *loc. cit.;* Ayrinhac, *loc. cit.*

[112] Cf. Ayrinhac, *op. cit.,* n. 39; Coronata, *loc. cit.*

[113] S.C.S. Off., 11 aug. 1859—*Fontes,* n. 954.

[114] Canon 81: "Ordinaries other than the Roman Pontiff cannot dispense from the general laws of the Church, even in a particular case, unless this power has been conceded to them explicitly, or unless recourse to the Holy See is difficult, while there is danger of grave harm in delay, and the case is one in which the Holy See usually dispenses."—Woywod, *A Practical Commentary on the Code of Canon Law,* n. 58; cf. also canons 15 and 209.

norms among which are the laws given for parallel cases, and by the style and practice of the Roman Curia. Canons 1043 and 1045, §§ 1 and 2, give a parallel law in a very similar matter, for they provide that the ordinary may dispense from the impediments in urgent cases, just as the Holy Office in the pre-Code response provided for a dispensation from the interpellations. Moreover, the above-mentioned decree of the Holy Office certainly states what was, at least, the manner and practice of the Curia in such cases. Some doubt arises as to whether this pre-Code decree is expressive of the present practice of the Curia; as long, however, as no contrary practice is established, one is safe in basing a course of action on this principle.[115]

§ 3. *By Means of Delegated Power*

While ordinary jurisdiction is that which by the law itself is attached to an office, delegated jurisdiction, according to canon 197, §1, is that which has been commissioned to a person.[116] Delegated jurisdiction is not attached to the office itself but accrues to a person by reason of a special commission which may be bestowed by the law or which may be derived directly from the competent authority. Hence a delegated jurisdiction is not exercised in one's own name, but in the name of and by the commission of another. The Pope, who by reason of his office has ordinary power of jurisdiction, may delegate it to another, either wholly or partially.[117] Jurisdiction delegated by the Roman Pontiff can be subdelegated unless the party chosen was delegated for personal reasons and qualifications, or unless the act of subdelegation was expressly forbidden.[118]

A. *The Papal Nuncio, Internuncio, and Apostolic Delegate*

The index of general faculties granted after the Code by the Holy See to Nuncios, Internuncios and Apostolic Delegates gives no hint of a delegated power to dispense from the interpellations.[119]

[115] Wanenmacher, *Canonical Evidence in Marriage Cases,* n. 97.

[116] Cf. S.C.S. Off., litt. encycl. 20 febr. 1888—*Fontes,* n. 1109.

[117] Augustine, *A Commentary on Canon Law,* II, 175.

[118] Cf. canon 199, §§ 1, 2.

[119] Cf. Vermeersch-Creusen, *Epitome,* I, 872, for the index of Faculties granted to Nuncios, Internuncios and Apostolic Delegates. Cf. also Burton, *A Commentary on Canon 1125,* pp. 106-107.

However, the Apostolic Delegate to the United States of America, at least, is empowered by special faculties given him by the Sacred Congregation of the Holy Office to dispense from the interpellations in individual cases and under specified conditions which must be verified before the dispensation may be issued. The faculty possessed by the United States Delegation, as well as the conditions under which it is possible for the Delegation to act, is expressed in a letter of the Delegate addressed to the ordinaries of the United States.[120] The letter reads as follows:

> "Since the Ordinaries of this country are obliged from time to time to seek dispensations from the interpellations which are required for the lawful use of the Pauline privilege, the Supreme Sacred Congregation of the Holy Office has thought it opportune to grant the faculty to dispense from the interpellations to the Apostolic Delegation.
>
> "When, therefore, in an individual case, *there is danger in delay and no time for recourse to the Holy See,* Your Excellency may direct requests for this dispensation to the Apostolic Delegation. The petition, moreover, must state that the following conditions, by which the faculty is circumscribed, are verified in the case: 'Dummodo adhibitis prius omnibus diligentiis (etiam per publicas ephemerides, ubi fieri possit) certo constiterit, ex processu saltem summario et extraiudiciali coniugem infidelem omnino reperiri nequivisse, aut interpellationem fieri non posse sine evidenti periculo gravis damni aut coniugi iam ad fidem converso aut christianis inferendi."

It will be noted that, if time permits and there is no danger in delay, the dispensation must be secured through the normal channels, namely, by having recourse directly to the Holy See. If recourse to the Sovereign Pontiff is neither feasible nor possible in a given case, then the appeal for the dispensation may be directed to the Apostolic Delegate, provided, of course, that the other conditions mentioned in the letter of the delegated faculty are fulfilled.

B. *The Local Ordinaries*

By a decree of the Consistorial Congregation[121] the faculties previously granted to ordinaries other than those subject to the Congregation

[120] Apos. Delegation U.S.A., litt. 17 iul., 1935, No. 116/35.

[121] 25 apr. 1918—*AAS,* X (1918), 190-192.

for the Propagation of the Faith were supressed May 19, 1918, when the Code became operative law. It was thought that the Code, which was officially in effect as of that date, would render the former faculties superfluous, and since some of the faculties contained in the old formulas were at variance with the codified law, it was surmised that confusion would result if they continued in force. Furthermore, it was felt that canon 1125 was broad enough in scope to cover any former faculties pertinent to the privilege of the faith or the *Casus Apostoli.*

Not long after the Code went into effect, however, it became evident that in addition to the powers therein conceded them, bishops still had need of at least some of the quinquennial faculties which they formerly enjoyed. Hence, provision was made for the faculties by the various Congregations according to their competence. But in order to obviate the necessity of applying to each Congregation separately, Pius XI in 1923 [122] decreed that bishops not subject to the Congregation for the Propagation of the Faith or to the Congregation for the Oriental Church were to procure these faculties through the Sacred Consistorial Congregation.[123] The new formula of faculties issued by the Consistorial Congregation contained nothing in regard to dispensations from the interpellations.

The ordinaries of the United States were frequently empowered to dispense from the interpellations under the pre-Code faculties,[124] but unless they are the recipients of special indults they must, since the promulgation of the Code, depend on the common law or appeal to the Holy See for the necessary dispensation for individual cases.

The Holy See will grant ordinaries the power to dispense from the interpellations for a definite number of cases and, in fact, advises them to apply for this faculty if the need is foreseen.[125] For reference, the post-Code faculty as issued by the Holy Office reads as follows:

> Dispensandi pro decem casibus coniugem fidelem supra interpellatione coniugis in infidelitate relicti, si quidem

[122] Motu Propr. "Post datum." 20 apr. 1923—*AAS*, XV (1923), 193-194.

[123] The Index of Faculties granted after the Code by the Holy See to Nuncios, Internuncios, and Apostolic Delegates is given in Vermeersch-Creusen, *Epitome,* I, 872; cf. also, Burton, *A Commentary on Canon 1125,* pp. 106-107.

[124] Facultates Apostolicae, *Formula* I, *C. D. E.*—Cf. Putzer, *Commentarium in Facultates Apostolicas,* n. 97; Facultates speciales—*AKKR,* XCVII (1917), 433.

[125] S.C.S. Off. (Portland), 18 iun. 1884—*Fontes,* n. 1088.

adhibitis prius omnibus diligentiis (etiam per publicas ephemerides, ubi fieri possit) certo constiterit, saltem summarie et extraiudicialiter coniugem infidelem omnino reperiri nequivisse. Hanc facultatem Episcopus nemini subdelegare potest, sed ipse per se exercere debet.

In singulis autem casibus expressa fiat mentio Apostolicae delegationis (C. 1057).

Ordinarius, his casibus expletis, S. Officio referat de circumstantiis in quibus, singulis vicibus, his facultatibus usus fuerit.[126]

The delegated power wherewith ordinaries dispense the normally required interpellations may be used only when there is a sufficient cause at hand. Otherwise the dispensation is exposed to the danger of being invalidly granted. The causes warranting the Sovereign Pontiff to grant an individual dispensation from the interpellations establish the norms for the application of the power of dispensing as granted by the indult.[127] It is to be noted that the indult cited reserves the exercise of the faculty to the bishop personally and does not allow any subdelegation in the matter.

C. *The Bearers of Special Faculties*

In addition to the individual indults which permit the granting of dispensations from the making of the interpellations, there are also special faculties which are issued by the Sacred Congregation for the Propagation of the Faith in favor of those ordinaries who are subject to this Congregation inasmuch as they labor in missionary countries, where frequently there arise extraordinary cases which do not allow of sufficient time for recourse to the Holy See.

The pre-Code faculties granted to these ordinaries were in effect until January 1, 1920, when all formulas of faculties, "ordinary" and "extraordinary," were superseded by new formulas prepared in view of the provisions of the Code.[128] Where the faculties in use before the Code were divided into "ordinary" and "extraordinary," the present

[126] S.C.S. Off. (Denver), 15 nov. 1934—Protoc. Num. 2619/34.

[127] Cf. *Supra*, p. 111.

[128] Vermeersch, "Commentaria de Formulis Facultatum, etc.,"—*Periodica*, XI (1923), n. 29, p. (70). This author refers the reader to the letter of the S.C. de Prop. Fide, 1 iul. 1919, protoc. 1522/19.

system classifies three formulas, of which the second and third are subdivided into "*Maior*" and "*Minor.*" This classification of major and minor is founded on the distinction of persons, for the former are addressed to vicars and prefects who enjoy the episcopal character, while the latter are intended for the use of lesser dignitaries inasmuch as they have not received episcopal consecration.[129]

Among these special faculties, those which concern the power of granting dispensations from the making of the interpellations are to be found in the Third Formula, both major and minor, listed as numbers 25, 26, 27 and 24, 25, 26, respectively.[130] The major faculties, of which the minor are duplicates, are listed as follows:

> *25. "Dispensandi super interpellatione coniugum in infidelitate relictorum pro omnibus casibus ordinariis, dummodo scilicet adhibitis antea omnibus diligentiis, etiam per publicas ephemerides ad reperiendum locum ubi coniux infidelis habitat, iisque in irritum cessis, constet saltem summarie et extraiudicialiter coniugem absentem moneri legitime non posse, aut monitum infra tempus in monitione praefixum suam voluntatem non significasse."
>
> *26. "Itemque dispensandi super interpellatione coniugis in infidelitate relicti, siquidem certo constiterit, saltem summarie et extraiudicialiter, interpellationem fieri non posse sine evidenti gravis damni aut coniugi iam ad fidem converso, aut christianis inferendi periculo."
>
> *27. "Permittendi ut, accendente gravi causa, interpellatio coniugis infidelis ante baptismum partis quae ad fidem convertitur fieri possit; nec non, gravi pariter de causa, ab eadem interpellatione, ante baptismum partis quae convertitur, dispensandi, dummodo hoc in casu ex processu saltem summario et extraiudiciali constet interpellationem fieri non posse, vel fore inutilem."[131]

The local ordinaries, subject to the Congregation for the Propagation

[129] Iglesias, *Brevis Commentarius in Facultates quas S.C. de Prop. Fide dare solet Missionariis* (Taurini-Romae, 1924), p. 16; Gregory, *The Pauline Privilege,* p. 82.

[130] Vermeersch-Creusen, *Epitome,* I, n. 873; Burton, *A Commentary on Canon 1125,* p. 108; cf. also Jone, "Die Interpellationen bei Anwendung des Paulinischen Privilegs,"—*LQS,* XXX (1927), 338-340.

[131] Blat, *De Sacramentis,* III, pars I, n. 532 and page 726; Vermeersch-Creusen, *Epitome,* I, p. 633; Wernz-Vidal, *Ius Matrimoniale,* n. 633, note 79.

of the Faith, to whom these faculties are addressed, are listed in canon 198, § 1. Such ordinaries are residential bishops, abbots and prelates *nullius*, together with vicars general, administrators, vicars and prefects apostolic. The faculties may be subdelegated either absolutely or conditionally, and they may be made available for use either habitually or for a single given case.[132] However, those to whom the faculty to dispense from the making of the interpellations has been subdelegated by the ordinary, may not further subdelegate this power for the faculties do not permit it.[133]

Unless they contain a direct statement to the contrary, or were given to a definite individual because of his personal qualifications, the faculties which are granted by the Holy See to the Bishop and to others mentioned in canon 198, § 1, do not become inoperative with the lapse from office of the ordinary to whom they were given, but pass on to the succeeding ordinary.[134]

In order that the validity of a marriage contracted by the Christian convert with a dispensation from the making of the interpellations may not be later contested, the granting of the dispensation should be noted in the parish book of marriages and in the curial register, together with the reason for the dispensation, for example, that it has been extrajudicially ascertained that the infidel spouse could not be found; that he had been taken captive, etc. Should future controversy develop, the fact that the interpellations were made or that a dispensation was granted can then be proved from the notation in the original documents, or from the record in the parish registers or in the books of the curia.[135]

[132] Facultates S.C. de Prop. Fide, Normae interpretations, n. XI; cf. also Vermeersch, "Dissertatio,"—*Periodica*, XI (1923), pp. (75), (141).

[133] Canon 199, § 5; cf. also Vermeersch, "Dissertatio,"—*Periodica*, XI (1923), p. (75).

[134] Keene, *Religious Ordinaries and Canon 198*, The Catholic University of America Canon Law Studies, n. 135 (Washington, D. C.: The Catholic University of America Press, 1942), p. 23.

[135] Wanenmacher, *Canonical Evidence in Marriage Cases*, nn. 355, 372.

CONCLUSIONS

From this study of the doctrine of the interpellations in relation to the Pauline privilege it is evident that, though the Church is willing, with the charity of Christ, to grant every possible concession in favor of the faith, she is likewise, with the justice of Christ, deeply concerned in upholding the sanctity and the indissolubility of the marriage bond, whether it is the bond between Christians or between infidels. This conclusion is suggested by reason of the rigorous view adopted by the Church in her insistence on the necessity of the interpellations and the grave reasons she demands before allowing a dispensation from them. Nowhere in all the literature on law is there a greater attempt to safeguard justice than in the laws of the Church and its interpretative instructions regarding them. The Church seeks only objective truth, and with regard to the interpellations her one desire is to marshal out by means of them those facts which have a direct bearing on the unbeliever's departure, since this is the *sine qua non* condition for the use of the Pauline privilege.

Since the Pauline privilege had become a doctrine less of theory and more of practice by reason of the missionary expansion of the sixteenth century and the increase in the number of non-Catholics subsequent to the Protestant Reformation, the Roman Pontiffs continually stressed the importance of contacting the unbelieving spouse and of proposing the interpellations. Insistence on this necessity has now been canonized.

The investigation and research made by the writer on the topic convinces him that the mind of the Church and the opinion of canonists is that, in cases of the Pauline privilege, the interpellations must invariably be made or, if that procedure is either not possible or not feasible in a given case, the proper dispensation from them must regularly be secured for the valid use of the Pauline privilege. Canon 1121 states: "*Antequam coniux conversus . . . valide contrahat matrimonium debet . . . partem non baptizatam interpellare;*" and canon 1123 reads: "*Si interpellationes ex declaratione Sanctae Sedis omissae fuerint aut si infidelis negative responderit expresse vel tacite, pars baptizata ius habet novas nuptias . . . contrahendi.*" From the text of these two canons it is evident that the right to remarry is granted by ecclesiastical law only when the interpellations have been made or when a dispensation has been obtained. It appears, therefore, that canon law not only considers the unbeliever's departure as a necessary condition for the valid use of the Pauline privilege but also the manner of proof.

If ordinaries foresee the need of papal dispensations from the interpellations, the necessity should be anticipated by securing from the Sacred Congregation of the Holy Office faculties to dispense in a determined number of cases.

In regard to dispensations from the interpellations granted by the constitution of Gregory XIII, "*Populis,*" it appears to the writer that ordinaries of the United States are either unaware of their power or are loath to use the extraordinary faculty to dispense given to them in the common law by reason of canon 1125. While there is a lack of uniformity of opinion among authors as to what constitutes the "*eadem adiuncta*" under which the grant is made available, the more common opinion is that the Code makes available the concessions of the papal constitutions for all cases similar to those for which the favors were first conceded and does not limit their application to definite regions. Canon 1127 inclines one not to be timid in one's appraisal of which circumstances may rightly be considered as forming a similar case.

APPENDIX

The following formularies[1] are suggested with the hope that they may prove to be of some assistance to those who must deal with matrimonial problems which involve the use of the Pauline privilege.

FORMULARY I

The convert's petition addressed to the ordinary and asking that the unbelieving spouse be interpellated. This document must be signed by the convert personally and by the convert's pastor.

Your Excellency:

N.N., born (*date*) in (*city, diocese, state*), now a baptized Catholic having domicile in (*parish, diocese*) with due reverence wishes to say: that before his/her baptism he/she had contracted marriage according to the local customs of non-Catholics with N.N., also not baptized and who at the present time resides at (*address, city, state*); he/she now desires the aforesaid N.N., still not baptized, to be interpellated according to the laws of the Church for the purpose that he/she may again cohabit with the same N.N., or be permitted to enter new nuptials through the use of the Pauline privilege. The petitioner humbly asks Your Excellency through the undersigned pastor, that the canonical interpellations be made according to the prescripts of canon 1121.

(*Place and date*) (*Signed*) N. N.
Pastor

(*Seal of Parish*) (*Signed*) N. N.
Petitioner

FORMULARY II

The letter of the ordinary delegating a pastor or a priest to interpellate the unbelieving spouse of a convert. Unless the ordinary makes the interpellations personally, the delegate chosen by him should be notified in writing.

[1] Muniz, *Procedimientos Eclesiásticos* (2. ed., 3 vols., Barcelona, 1928), II, n. 508.

Reverend dear Father:

You are hereby delegated to interpellate, according to the norms of canon 1121, N.N., unbaptized, now residing at (*address, city, state*), whose spouse N.N., being converted to the Catholic faith, now desires to enter Christian nuptials through the use of the Pauline privilege.
(*Place and date*)

(*Signed*) N. N.
Chancellor
(*Curial Seal*)

(*Signed*) N. N.
Bishop of N. N.

FORMULARY III

The letter of citation sent by the delegate of the ordinary to the unbelieving spouse, containing the substance of the interpellations and requesting the party's appearance at a stated time and place to give his answers to the interrogations. Two copies are to be made of all citations: the original to be communicated to the person summoned, the copy to be kept in the chancery files.[2]

By the commission of the Most Reverend N. N., Bishop of N. N., and at the request of N. N., a convert to the Catholic Church, I, the undersigned, hereby request N. N., the consort of the above mentioned N. N., to express and declare on (*date*), at (*time*), at (*address and city*), whether: (1) he/she wishes to embrace the Holy Catholic faith and with a sincere heart receive baptism, as his/her consort has done; and if he/she is not willing to do this, whether: (2) he/she is willing and disposed to cohabit peacefully with N. N., without blaspheming Almighty God, namely, that such cohabitation will not be a source of mortal sin for N. N. (*name of convert*). And I herewith inform the aforesaid N. N. (*name of infidel*) that if he/she refuse to be baptized and declares that he/she will not cohabit peacefully, the aforesaid N. N. (*name of convert*) will be free to proceed to another matrimonial alliance with a Catholic person.
(*Place and date*)

(*Signed*) N. N.
Delegate of the Bishop

(*Curial Seal*)

[2] Canon 1716.

FORMULARY IV

The formula for reporting the actual presentation of the interpellations to the unbelieving spouse.

I, N. N., Pastor/Assistant Pastor of N. N. Church, (*address, city, state*), having been authorized by His Excellency, the Most Reverend Ordinary of the Diocese of N. N., in accordance with canon 1122, to serve the required canonical interpellations to N. N., (*name of infidel*) of (*address, city, state*), consort of N. N., (*name of convert*) a convert from infidelity, who now petitions permission to remarry in the Catholic faith by virtue of the Pauline privilege, do hereby certify that on the (*day, month, year*), I personally interviewed N. N. (*name of infidel*), the respondent in this case, and presented to him/her the interpellations. The said interpellations are based on the words of St. Paul in the First Epistle to the Corinthians, VII, 12:16.

"If any brother has an unbelieving wife and she consents to live with him, let him not put her away. And if any woman has an unbelieving husband and he consents to live with her, let her not put away her husband.

"For the unbelieving husband is sanctified by the believing wife, and the unbelieving wife is sanctified by the believing husband; otherwise your children would be unclean, but, as it is, they are holy.

"But if the unbeliever departs, let him depart. For a brother or sister is not under bondage in such cases, but God has called us to peace."

I explained the doctrine of the Pauline privilege to the respondent and asked him/her the following questions:

1. Are you willing to embrace the Holy Catholic faith and with a sincere heart to receive the sacrament of baptism, as your consort has done? (*Space for the reply of the unbelieving spouse.*)

2. If you do not wish to be baptized, will you agree to live peacefully with your converted spouse, without blaspheming the Creator, that is, will you permit him/her to practice freely the Catholic religion, allow the children who have been born or who may yet be born of the union to be baptized and reared in the Catholic faith, and live in such a manner that

the faith of the convert will not in any way be endangered or weakened? (*Space for the answer of the unbeliever.*)

When the unbelieving spouse N. N. answered both interpellations in the negative, I then informed him/her that the converted party N. N. will be permitted in accordance with the doctrine of St. Paul to contract another marriage with a Catholic.

(*Place and date*) (Rev.) N. N.
Delegate

(*Seal of Parish*)

(N.B. Every endeavor must be made to secure a truthful and positive YES or NO in the responses.)

BIBLIOGRAPHY

Sources

Acta Apostolicae Sedis, Commentarium Officiale, Romae, 1909—

Acta et Decreta Concilii Plenarii Baltimorensis Tertii, A.D. MDCCCLXXXIV, 2. ed., Baltimorae: Typis Ioanni Murphy et Sociorum, 1894.

Acta et Decreta Sacrorum Conciliorum Recentiorum, Collectio Lacensis, 7 vols., Friburgi Brisgoviae, 1870-1890.

Acta Sanctae Sedis, 41 vols., Romae, 1865-1908.

Annuario Pontificio per L'anno 1936, Cìttá del Vaticano: Tipografia Poliglotta Vaticana, 1936.

Appendix ad Bullarium Pontificium Sacrae Congregationis de Propaganda Fide, 2 vols., Romae: Typis Collegii Urbani, (no date given on title page.)

Canones et Decreta Concilii Tridentini, ed. novissima, Romae: Typographia Polyglotta S.C. de Prop. Fide, 1882.

Codex Iuris Canonici Pii X Pontificis Maximi iussu digestus, Benedicti Papae XV auctoritate promulgatus, Romae: Typis Polyglottis Vaticanis, 1934.

Codicis Iuris Canonici Fontes, cura Emi. Petri Card. Gasparri editi, 9 vols., Romae: Typis Polyglottis Vaticanis, 1925-1939. (Vols., VII-IX *ed. cura et studio Emi Iustiniani Card. Serédi.*

Collectanea Constitutionum, Decretorum, Indultorum ac Instructionum S. Sedis ad usum Societatis Missionum ad exteros, 2 ed., Hongkong, 1905.

Collectanea S. Congregationis de Propaganda Fide, 2 vols., Romae: Typographia Polyglotta S.C. de Prop. Fide, 1907.

Corpus Iuris Civilis, 3 vols., Berolini: apud Weidmannos, 1928-1929: Vol. I, ed. stereotypa quinta decima, *Institutiones*—Paul Krueger; *Digesta,*—Theodorus Mommsen, retractavit Paul Krueger.

Corpus Scriptorum Ecclesiasticorum Latinorum, 68 vols., Vindobonae-Tempsky, 1866-1936.

Decretales D. Gregorii Papae IX, una cum Glossis Restitutae, Romae, 1582.

Decretum Gratiani emendatum et notationibus illustratum, una cum Glossis, Gregorii XIII Pont. Max. iussu editum, 2 vols., Romae, 1582.

Denzinger, Henr. et Bannwart, Clem., *Enchiridion Symbolorum Definitionum et Declarationum de Rebus Fidei et Morum,* 18. et 20. ed., Friburgi Brisgoviae: Herder, 1932.

Hardouin, Jean, *Conciliorum Collectio Regia Maxima,* 12 vols., Parisiis, 1715.

Jaffé, Philippus, *Regesta Romanorum Pontificum ab condita Ecclesia ad annum post Christum natum MCXCVIII,* ed. 2, correctam et auctam auspiciis Gulielmi Wattenbach curaverunt S. Loewenfeld, F. Kaltenbrunner, P. Ewald, 2 vols. in I, Lipsiae, 1885-1888.

Mansi, Ioannes, *Sacrorum Conciliorum Nova et Amplissima Collectio,* 53 vols. in 59, Paris-Arnhem-Leipzig, 1901-1927.

Pallottini, S., *Collectio Omnium Conclusionum et Resolutionum Quae in Causis Propositis apud Sacram Congregationem Cardinalium S. Concilii Tridentini interpretum Prodierunt ab eius institutione anno MDLXIV ad MDCCCLX, distinctis titulis alphabetico ordine per materias digestas, cura et studio Salvatoris Pallottini,* 18 vols., Romae, 1868-1895.

Regesta Pontificum Romanorum, ed. Augustus Potthast, 2 vols., Berolini, 1874-1875.

Thesaurus Resolutionum Sacrae Congregationis Concilii, 167 vols., Romae, 1718-1908.

Authors

Acosta, Joseph, *De Natura Novi Orbis et de Promulgatione Evangelii apud Barbaros sive De Procuranda Indorum Saluti Libri Sex,* Salmanticae, 1589.

Aquinas, St. Thomas, *Divi Thomae Aquinatis Opera,* 2 ed., 28 vols., Venetiis, 1775-1788.

Ayrinhac, H. A., *Constitution of the Church in the New Code of Canon Law,* London-New York: Longmans, Green and Company, 1930.

Ayrinhac, H. A.-Lydon, P. J., *Marriage Legislation in the New Code of Canon Law,* revised ed., New York: Benziger Brothers, 1935.

[Bachofen], Charles Augustine, *A Commentary on the New Code of Canon Law,* 8 vols., St. Louis: Herder, 1925-1938; vol. V, 5. revised ed., 1935.

Ballerini, A.-Palmieri, D., *Opus Theologicum Morale,* 3 ed., 7 vols., Prati, 1898-1901.

Bargilliat, M., *Praelectiones Juris Canonici,* 25. ed., 2 vols., Parisiis: Berche et Tralin, 1909.

Benedictus XIV, *De Synodo Dioecesana,* 2 vols., Romae: Typographia S.S. de Prop. Fide, 1806.

Blat, Albertus, *Commentarium Textus Codicis Iuris Canonici,* 5 vols, in 7, Romae: Collegio Angelico, 1921-1938. Vol. I, 1921; Vol. II, pars I, ed. altera, 1921; Vol. II, partes II et III, 3 ed., 1938; Vol. III, pars I, 2. ed., 1924; Vol. III, partes II et III, 2. ed., 1934; Vol. IV, 1927; Vol. V, 1924.

Bouscaren, T. Lincoln, *The Canon Law Digest,* 2 vols. and Supplement-1941, Milwaukee: Bruce, 1934-1941.

Burton, Francis J., *A Commentary on Canon 1125,* The Catholic University of America Canon Law Studies, n. 121, Washington, D. C.: The Catholic University of America Press, 1940.

Cabassutius, Ioannes, *Notitia Ecclesiastica Historiarum, Conciliorum, et Canonum invicem collatorum veterumque iuxta, ac recentiorum Ecclesiae Rituum, ab ipsis Ecclesiae Christianae incunabilis, ad nostra usque tempora, secundum cuiusque saeculi seriem accurate Digesta,* Lugduni, 1680.

Cappello, Felix M., *Tranctatus Canonico-Moralis de Sacramentis,* 3 vols. in 6, Taurini: Marietti, 1932-1939. Vol. I, 3. ed., 1938; Vol. II, pars I, 3. ed., 1938; Vol. II, pars II, 1932; Vol. II, pars III, 1935; Vol. III, pars I, 4. ed., 1939; Vol. III, pars II, 4. ed., 1939.

Catholic Encyclopedia, 15 vols., New York, 1907-1912.

Cecil, Russell L., *A Text Book of Medicine by American Authors,* 3. ed., Philadelphia and London: W. B. Saunders Company, 1934.

Cicognani, A. G., *Canon Law,* 2. revised ed., Philadelphia, Dolphin Press, 1935.

Cornelius a Lapide, *Commentaria in Scripturam Sacram,* ed. A. Crampon, Vol. XVIII, *In Epistolas Divi Pauli,* Parisiis, 1866.

Coronata, Matthaeus Conte a, *Institutiones Iuris Canonici,* 5 vols., Taurini: Marietti, 1933-1939. Vols. I et II, 2. ed., 1939; Vol. III, 1933; Vol. IV, 1935; Vol. V, 1936.

Costello, John Michael, *Domicile and Quasi-Domicile,* The Catholic University of America Canon Law Studies, n. 60, Washington, D. C.: The Catholic University of America, 1930.

De Becker, Julius, *De Sponsalibus et Matrimonio Praelectiones Canonicae,* 2. ed., Lovanii, 1903.

De Smet, Aloysius, *Tractatus Theologico-Canonicus de Sponsalibus et Matrimonio,* 4. ed., Brugis: Car. Beyaert, 1927.

Esmein, A.-Génestal, R.-Dauvillier, J., *Le Mariage en Droit Canonique,* 2 vols., Paris: Sirey, 1929-1935.

Fahrner, Ignaz, *Geschichte des Unauflöslichkeitsprinzips und der vollkommenen*

Scheidung der Ehe im kanonischen Recht, Freiburg im Breisgau, 1903

Feije, Henricus, *De Impedimentis et Dispensationibus Matrimonialibus*, 3. ed., Lovanii, 1885.

Freisen, Joseph, *Geschichte des Canonischen Eherechts bis zum Verfall der Glossenliteratur*, Paderborn: Schöningh, 1893.

Gasparri, Petrus Card., *Tracatus Canonicus de Matrimonio*, ed. nova ad mentem Codicis I.C., 2 vols., Typis Polyglottis Vaticanis, 1932.

Gregory, Donald J., *The Pauline Privilege*, The Catholic University of America Canon Law Studies, n. 68, Washington, D. C.: The Catholic University of America, 1931.

Hostiensis, Cardinalis (Henricus de Segusio), *Commentaria in V Libros Decretalium*, 5 vols. in 3, Venetiis, 1581.

Iglesias, *Brevis Commentarius in Facultates quas S.C.de Prop. Fide dare solet Missionariis*, Taurini-Romae, 1924.

Joyce, George H., *Christian Marriage, A Doctrinal and Historical Study*, London and New York: Sheed and Ward, 1933.

Keene. Michael J., *Religious Ordinaries and Canon 198*, The Catholic University of America Canon Law Studies, n. 135, Washington, D. C.: The Catholic University of America Press, 1942.

Leage, R. W.-Ziegler, C.H., *Roman Private Law*, 2. ed., London: Macmillan and Co., Ltd., 1937.

Lehmkuhl, Augustinus, *Theologia Moralis*, 5 ed., 2 vols., Friburgi Brisgoviae, 1888.

MacRory, Joseph, *The Epistles of St. Paul to the Corinthians*, St. Louis: Herder, 1915.

Mansella, Joseph, *De Impedimentis Matrimonium Dirimentibus ac de Processu Iudiciali in Causis Matrimonialibus*, Romae: Typographia S.C., de Prop. Fide, 1861.

Migne, Jacques Paul, *Patrologiae Cursus Completus, Series Latina*, 221 vols., Parisiis, 1844-1864.

——————,*Patrologiae Cursus Completus, Series Graeca*, 161 vols., Parisiis, 1856-1864.

Muniz, T., *Procedimientos Eclesiásticos*, 2. ed., 3 vols., Barcelona, 1928.

Nau, Louis J., *Manual on the Marriage Laws of the Code of Canon Law*, 2. ed., New York: Pustet, 1934.

Noldin, H., et Schmitt, A., *Summa Theologica Moralis iuxta Codicem Iuris Canonici*, 31. ed., 3 vols., Oeniponte: Pustet, 1932.

Ojetti, Benedictus, *Synopsis Rerum Moralium et Iuris Pontificii*, Romae, 1899.

Ottaviani, Alaphridus, *Institutiones Iuris Publici Ecclesiastici*, ed. altera emendata et aucta, 2 vols., Typis Polyglottis Vaticanis, 1935-1936.

Panormitanus (Nicolaus de Tudeschis), *Commentaria in Quinque Libros Decretalium*, 5 vols. in 7, Venetiis, 1588.

Payen, G., *De Matrimonio in Missionibus ac Potissimum in Sinis Tractatus Practicus et Casus*, 2 ed., 3 vols., Zi-ka-wei, China: Typographia T'ou-Sé-Wé, 1935-1936.

Pesch, Christianus, *Praelectiones Dogmaticae*, 3. ed., Vol. VII, *De Sacramentis*, Pars II, Friburgi Brisgoviae, 1909.

Petrovits, Joseph, *The New Church Law on Matrimony*, 2. ed., Philadelphia: McVey, 1926.

Pontius, Basilius, *De Sacramento Matrimonii Tractatus cum Appendice de Matrimonio Catholici cum Haeretico*, 2. ed., Bruxellis, 1627.

Putzer, Joseph, *Commentarium in Facultates Apostolicas*, Ilchester College, Maryland: Typis Cong. Sanctissimi Redemptoris, 1893.

Robertus Flamesburiensis, *Summa de Matrimonio et usuris ex Roberti Poenitentiali*, edited by J. F. Schulte, Gissae, 1868.

Sabetti, A.-Barrett, T., *Compendium Theologiae Moralis,* 33. ed., New York-Cincinnati: Pustet, 1931.

Salmanticenses, *Cursus Theologiae Moralis,* 6 vols., Venetiis, 1728; Vol. I., Tract. IX, *De Matrimonio.*

Sanchez, Thomas, *De Sancto Matrimonii Sacramento Disputationum Libri Tres,* 3 vols., Venetiis, Apud Ioannem Guerilium, 1614.

Santi, Franciscus, *Praelectiones Iuris Canonici,* 4 vols., Ratisbonae-Neo Eboraci-Cincinnati: Pustet, 1886.

Scherer, Rudolph Ritter von, *Handbuch des Kirchenrechts,* 2 vols., Graz, 1886-1898.

Schulte, J. F. von, *Die Glosse zum Dekret Gratians von ihren Anfängen bis auf die jüngsten Ausgaben,* 4 ed., Vienna, 1872.

Schmalzgrueber, Franciscus, *Ius Ecclesiasticum Universum,* 5 vols. in 12. Romae: Typographia Rev. Cam. Apostolicae, 1843-1845.

Souter, Alexander, *A Study of Ambrosiaster,* Cambridge, 1905.

Stokes, John H., *Dermatology and Syphilology for Nurses,* 2. ed., Philadelphia and London: W. B. Saunders Company, 1937.

Triebes, Franz, *Praktisches Handbuch des geltenden kanonischen Eherechts in Vergleichung mit dem deutschen staatlichen Eherecht,* Breslau: Ostdeutsche Verlagsantalt, 1933.

Vazquez, Gabriel, *Commentariorum ac Disputationum in Primam Secundae Sancti Thomae Tomus Primus,* Lugduni, 1620.

Vermeersch, Arthurus, *De Casu Apostoli seu De Fidei Privilegio,* Brugis, 1911.

Vermeersch, A.-Creusen, J., *Epitome Iuris Canonici.* 5 ed., 3 vols., Mechliniae-Romae: Dessain, 1934-1937.

Vlaming, Th. M., *Praelectiones Iuris Matrimonii,* 3. ed., 2 vols., Bussum in Hollandia, 1919-1921.

Vromant, G., *Facultates Apostolicae quas S.C. de Prop. Fide delegare solet Ordinariis Missionum, Commentaria in Formulam Tertiam,* Louvain, 1926.

Wanenmacher, Francis, *Canonical Evidence in Marriage Cases,* Philadelphia: Dolphin Press, 1935.

Wernz, Franciscus X., *Ius Decretalium,* 2. ed., 6 vols. in 10 toms., Romae et Prati, 1905-1913.

Wernz, F.X.-Vidal, Petrus, *Ius Canonicum ad Codicis Normam Exactum,* 7 toms. in 8 vols., Romae: Apud Aedes Universitatis Gregorianae, 1923-1938; *Ius Matrimoniale,* Vol. V, 2. ed., 1928.

Woods, Edward F., *The Constitutions of Canon 1125 and Their Application in the United States,* Milwaukee: Bruce, 1935.

Woywod, Stanislaus, *A Practical Commentary on the Code of Canon Law,* 2 vols., New York: Joseph F. Wagner, 1925.

Zitelli, *De Dispensationibus Matrimonialibus iuxta Recentissimas Sac. Urbis Congreg. Resolutiones Commentarii,* Romae: Typis Soc. Edit. Rom., 1887.

ARTICLES

Arendt, G., "Quomodo in favorem fidei solvatur a S. Pontifice matrimonium in infidelitate contractum, nota theologico-canonica circa canonem 1127," *ETL,* I (1924), 174-184.

Jemolo, "Il Privilegio Paolino dal principio del secolo XI agli albori del XV,"—*Studi Sassaresi,* II (1923), 243-335.

Jombart, E., "Casus de Dissolutione Matrimonii Paganorum,"—*Periodica,* XIV (1925), 68-74.

Jone, H., "Wie müssen die Interpellationen bei Anwendung des Paulinischen Privilegs gemacht werden,"—*LQS,* LXXX (1927), 336-348.

Kieda, Francis J., "Direct Dissolution of a Legitimate Marriage by Papal Authority,"—*The Jurist,* II (1942), 134-144.
Kuttner, Stephen, "The Father of the Science of Canon Law,"—*The Jurist,* I (1941), 2-19.
Lämmer, "Die Interpellatio coniugis infidelis und die päpstliche Dispens von derselben,"—*AKKR,* XI (1864), 246-250.
Ott, "Card. C. Tarquini über das Paulinische Privileg,"—*AKKR,* L (1883), 224-237.
Vermeersch, A., "Commentaria de Formulis Facultatum Quas S. Congr. de Propaganda Fide Concedere Solet,"—*Periodica,* XI (1923), (33)-(144).
——————, "Quaesita de Usu Privilegii Fidei,"—*Periodica,* XVII (1928), 241*-243*.
——————, "De Canone 1125 eiusque vi extensiva,"—*Periodica,* XX (1931), 1*-5*.
Vito, P., "Il Privilegio Paolino,"—*Perfice Munus,* XI (1936), 97-102.

Periodicals

Analecta Ecclesiastica, Romae, 1893-1911.
Archiv für katholisches Kirchenrecht, Innsbruck, 1857-1861; Mainz, 1862—
Ecclesiastical Review, The (originally *The American Ecclesiastical Review*), Philadelphia, 1889—
Ephemerides Theologicae Lovanienses, Lovanii-Brugis, 1924—
Perfice Munus, Torino, 1926—
Periodica de Re Canonica et Morali utilia praesertim Regiliosis et Missionariis, Brugis, 1905—
The Jurist, Catholic University of America, Washington, D. C., 1941—
Theologisch-praktische Quartalschrift, Linz, 1832—

List of Abbreviations

AAS—*Acta Apostolicae Sedis.*
AER—*The Ecclesiastical Review.*
ASS—*Acta Sanctae Sedis.*
AKKR—*Archiv für katholisches Kirchenrecht.*
C.I.C.—*Codex Iuris Canonici.*
Coll.—*Collectanea S. Congregationis de Propaganda Fide,* ed., 1907.
Coll. Hong.—*Collectanea Constitutionum, Indultorum ac Instructionum ad usum Societatis Missionum ad exteros,* 2 ed.
CSEL—*Corpus Scriptorum Ecclesiasticorum Latinorum.*
ETL—*Ephemerides Theologicae Lovanienses.*
Fontes—*Codicis Iuris Canonici Fontes.*
Mansi—*Sacrorum Conciliorum Nova et Amplissima Collectio.*
MPG—Migne, *Patrologia Series Graeca.*
MPL—Migne, *Patrologia Series Latina.*
Periodica—*Periodica de Re Canonica et Morali.*
S.R.R.—*Sacra Romana Rota.*

INDEX

BIOGRAPHICAL NOTE

Edward Martin Woeber was born April 4, 1903, at Denver, Colorado. He received his primary and secondary education in St. Joseph School and Regis High School, Denver. His college studies were pursued at Regis College and St. Thomas Seminary, Denver, and from the latter institution he received the degree of Master of Arts on the completion of his course in philosophy. He followed his theology course at St. Thomas Seminary and was ordained to the priesthood at Denver and for the Archdiocese of Denver, June 9, 1929, by His Excellency, the Most Reverend Patrick A. McGovern, Bishop of Cheyenne. In September of the year 1939 he matriculated in the School of Canon Law at the Catholic University of America. From this pontifical institution he received the degree of the Baccalaureate in Canon Law in June, 1940, and the degree of the Licentiate in Canon Law in June, 1941.

CANON LAW STUDIES

1. Freriks, Rev. Celestine A., C.PP.S., J.C.D., Religious Congregations in Their External Relations, 121 pp., 1916.
2. Galliher, Rev. Daniel M., O.P., J.C.D., Canonical Elections, 117 pp., 1917.
3. Borkowski, Rev. Aurelius L., O.F.M., J.C.D., De Confraternitatibus Ecclesiasticis, 136 pp., 1918.
4. Castillo, Rev. Cayo, J.C.D., Disertacion Historico-Canonica sobre la Potestad del Cabildo en Sede Vacante o Impedida del Vicario Capitular, 99 pp., 1919 (1918).
5. Kubelbeck, Rev. William J., S.T.B., J.C.D., The Sacred Penitentiaria and its Relations to Faculties of Ordinaries and Priests, 129 pp., 1918.
6. Petrovits, Rev. Joseph, J.C., S.T.D., J.C.D., The New Church Law On Matrimony, X-461 pp., 1919.
7. Hickey, Rev. John J., S.T.B., J.C.D., Irregularities and Simple Impediments in the New Code of Canon Law, 100 pp., 1920.
8. Klekotka, Rev. Peter J., S.T.B., J.C.D., Diocesan Consultors, 179 pp., 1920.
9. Wanenmacher, Rev. Francis, J.C.D., The Evidence in Ecclesiastical Procedure Affecting the Marriage Bond, 1920 (Printed 1935).
10. Golden, Rev. Henry Francis, J.C.D., Parochial Benefices in the New Code, IV-119 pp., 1921 (Printed 1925).
11. Koudelka, Rev. Charles J., J.C.D., Pastors, Their Rights and Duties According to the New Code of Canon Law, 211 pp., 1921.
12. Melo, Rev. Antonius, O.F.M., J.C.D., De Exemptione Regularium, X-180 pp., 1921.
13. Schaaf, Rev. Valentine Theodore, O.F.M., S.T.B., J.C.D., The Cloister, X-180 pp., 1921.
14. Burke, Rev. Thomas Joseph, S.T.D., J.C.D., Competence in Ecclesiastical Tribunals, IV-117 pp., 1922.
15. Leech, Rev. George Leo, J.C.D., A Comparative Study of the Constitution, "Apostolicae Sedis" and the "Codex Juris Canonici," 179 pp., 1922.
16. Motry, Rev. Hubert Louis, S.T.D., J.C.D., Diocesan Faculties According ing to the Code of Canon Law, II-167 pp., 1922.
17. Murphy, Rev. George Lawrence, J.C.D., Delinquencies and Penalties in the Administration and Reception of the Sacraments IL-121 pp., 1923.
18. O'Reilly, Rev. John Anthony, S.T.D., J.C.D., Ecclesiastical Sepulture in the New Code of Canon Law, II-129 pp., 1923.
19. Michalicka, Rev. Wenceslas Cyril, O.S.B., J.C.D., Judicial Procedure in Dismissal of Clerical Exempt Religious, 107 pp., 1923.
20. Dargin, Rev. Edward Vincent, S.T.B., J.C.D., Reserved Cases According to the Code of Canon Law, IV-103, pp. 1924.
21. Godfrey, Rev. John A., S.T.B., J.C.D., The Right of Patronage According to the Code of Canon Law, 153 pp., 1924.
22. Hagedorn, Rev. Francis Edward, J.C.D., General Legislation on Indulgences, II-154 pp., 1924.
23. King, Rev. James Ignatius, J.C.D., The Administration of the Sacraments to Dying Non-Catholics, V-141 pp., 1924.
24. Winslow, Rev. Francis Joseph, O.F.M., J.C.D., Vicars and Prefects Apostolic, IV-149 pp., 1924.
25. Correa, Rev. Jose Servelion, S.T.L., J.C.D., La Potestad Legislativa de la Iglesia Catolica, IV-127 pp., 1925.

26. Dugan, Rev. Henry Francis, A.M., J.C.D., The Judiciary Department of the Diocesan Curia, 87 pp., 1925.
27. Keller, Rev. Charles Frederick, S.T.B., J.C.D., Mass Stipends, 167 pp., 1925.
28. Paschang, Rev. John Linus, J.C.D., The Sacramentals According to the Code of Canon Law, 129 pp., 1925.
29. Piontek, Rev. Cyrillus, O.F.M., S.T.B., J.C.D., De Indulto Exclaustrationis necnon Saecularizationis, XIII-289 pp., 1925.
30. Kearney, Rev. Richard Joseph, S.T.B., J.C.D., Sponsors at Baptism According to the Code of Canon Law, IV-127 pp., 1925.
31. Bartlett, Rev. Chester Joseph, A.M., LL.B., J.C.D., The Tenure of Parochial Property in the United States of America, V-108 pp., 1926.
32. Kilker, Rev. Adrian Jerome, J.C.D., Extreme Unction, V-425 pp., 1926.
33. McCormick, Rev. Robert Emmett, J.C.D., Confessors of Religious, VIII-266 pp., 1926.
34. Miller, Rev. Newton Thomas, J.C.D., Founded Masses According to the Code of Canon Law, VII-93 pp., 1926.
35. Roelker, Rev. Edward G., S.T.D., J.C.D., Principles of Privilege According to the Code of Canon Law, XI-166 pp., 1926.
36. Bakalarczyk, Rev. Richardus, M.I.C., J.U.D., De Novitiatu, VIII-208 pp., 1927.
37. Pizzuti, Rev. Lawrence, O.F.M., J.U.L., De Parochis Religiosis, 1927 (Not printed).
38. Bliley, Rev. Nicholas Martin, O.S.B., J.C.D., Altars According to the Code of Canon Law, XIX-132 pp., 1927.
39. Brown, Mr. Brendan Francis, A.B., LL.M., J.U.D., The Canonical Juristic Personality with Special Reference to Its Status in the United States of America, V-212 pp., 1927.
40. Cavanaugh, Rev. William Thomas, C.P., J.U.D., The Reservation of the Blessed Sacrament, VIII-101 pp., 1927.
41. Doheny, Rev. William J., C.S.C., A.B., J.U.D., Church Property: Modes of Acquisition, X-118 pp., 1927.
42. Feldhaus, Rev. Aloysius H., C.PP.S., J.C.D., Oratories, IX-141 pp., 1927.
43. Kelly, Rev. James Patrick, A.B., J.C.D., The Jurisdiction of the Simple Confessor, X-208 pp., 1927.
44. Neuberger, Rev. Nicholas J., J.C.D., Canon 6 or the Relation of the Codex Juris Canonici to the Preceding Legislation, V-95 pp., 1927.
45. O'Keefe, Rev. Gerald Michael, J.C.D., Matrimonial Dispensations, Powers of Bishops, Priests and Confessors, VIII-232 pp., 1927.
46. Quigley, Rev. Joseph, A.B., A.M., J.C.D., Condemned Societies, 139 pp., 1927.
47. Zaplotnik, Rev. Johannes Leo, J.C.D., De Vicariis Foraneis, X-142 pp., 1927.
48 Duskie, Rev. John Aloysius, A.B., J.C.D., The Canonical Status of the Orientals in the United States, VII, 196 pp., 1928.
49. Hyland, Rev. Francis Edward, J.C.D., Excommunication, Its Nature, Historical Development and Effects, VIII-181 pp., 1928.
50. Reinmann, Rev. Gerald Joseph, O.M.C., J.C.D., The Third Order Secular of Saint Francis, 201 pp., 1928.
51. Schenk, Rev. Francis J., J.C.D., The Matrimonial Impediments of Mixed Religion and Disparity of Cult, XVI-318 pp., 1929.
52. Coady, Rev. John Joseph, S.T.D., J.U.D., A.M., The Appointment of Pastors, VIII-150 pp., 1929.
53. Kay, Thomas Henry, J.C.D., Competence in Matrimonial Procedure, VIII-164 pp., 1929.

54. Turner, Rev. Sidney Joseph, C.P., J.U.D., The Vow of Poverty, XLIX-217 pp., 1929.
55. Kearney, Rev. Raymond A., A.B., S.T.D., J.C.D., The Principles of Delegation, VII-149 pp., 1929.
56. Conran, Rev. Edward James, A.B., J.C.D., The Interdict, V-163 pp., 1930.
57. O'Neil, Rev. William H., J.C.D., Papal Rescripts of Favor, VII-218 pp., 1930.
58. Bastnagel, Rev. Clement Vincent, J.U.D., The Appointment of Parochial Adjutants and Assistants, XV-257 pp., 1930.
59. Ferry, Rev. William A., A.B., J.C.D., Stole Fees, V-135 pp., 1930.
60. Costello, Rev. John Michael, A.B., J.C.D., Domicile and Quasi-Domicile, VII-201 pp., 1930.
61. Kremer, Rev. Michael Nicholas, A.B., S.T.B., J.C.D., Church Support in the United States, VI-1930.
62. Angulo, Rev. Luis, C.M., J.C.D., Legislacion de la Iglesia sobre la intencion en la aplication de la Santa Misa, VII-104 pp., 1931.
63. Frey, Rev. Wolfgang Norbert, O.S.B., A.B., J.C.D., The Act of Religious Profession, VIII-174 pp., 1931.
64. Roberts, Rev. James Brendan, A.B., J.C.D., The Banns of Marriage, XIV-140 pp., 1931.
65. Ryder, Rev. Raymond Aloysius, A.B., J.C.D., Simony, IX-151 pp., 1931.
66. Campagna, Rev. Angelo, Ph.D., J.U.D., Il Vicario Generale del Vescovo, VII-205 pp., 1931.
67. Cox, Rev. Joseph Godfrey, A.B., J.C.D., The Administration of Seminaries, VI-124 pp., 1931.
68. Gregory, Rev. Donald J., J.U.D., The Pauline Privilege, XV-165 pp., 1931.
69. Donohue, Rev. John F., J.C.D., The Impediment of Crime, VII-110 pp., 1931.
70. Dooley, Rev. Eugene A., O.M.I., J.C.D., Church Law on Sacred Relics, IX-143 pp., 1931.
71. Orth, Rev. Raymond Clement, O.M.C., J.C.D., The Approbation of Religious Institutes, 171 pp., 1931.
72. Pernicone, Rev. Joseph M., A.B., J.C.D., The Ecclesiastical Prohibition of Books, XII-267 pp., 1932.
73. Clinton, Rev. Connell, A.B., J.C.D., The Paschal Precept, IX-108 pp., 1932.
74. Donnelly, Rev. Francis B., A.M., S.T.L., J.C.D., The Diocesan Synod, VIII-125 pp., 1932.
75. Torrente, Rev. Camilo, C.M.F., J.C.D., Las Processiones Sagradas, V-145 pp. 1932.
76. Murphy, Rev. Edwin J., C.PP.S., J.C.D., Suspension Ex Informata Conscientia, XI-122 pp., 1932.
77. Mackenzie, Rev. Eric F., A.M., S.T.L., J.C.D., The Delict of Heresy in its Commission, Penalization, Absolution, VII-124 pp., 1932.
78. Lyons, Rev. Avitus E., S.T.B., The Collegiate Tribunal of First Instance, XI-147 pp., 1932.
79. Connolly, Rev. Thomas A., J.C.D., Appeals, XI-195 pp., 1932.
80. Sangmeister, Rev. Joseph V., A.B., J.C.D, Force and Fear as Precluding Matrimonial Consent, V-211 pp., 1932.
81. Jaeger, Rev. Leo A., A.B., J.C.D., The Administration of Vacant and Quasi-Vacant Episcopal Sees in the United States, IX-229 pp., 1932.
82. Rimlinger, Rev. Herbert T., J.C.D., Error Invalidating Matrimonial Consent, VII-79 pp., 1932.

83. Barrett, Rev. John D. M., SS., J.C.D., A Comparative Study of the Third Plenary Council of Baltimore and the Code, IX-221 pp., 1932.
84. Carberry, Rev. John J., Ph.D., S.T.D., J.C.D., The Juridical Form of Marriage, X-177 pp., 1934.
85. Dolan, Rev. John L., A.B., J.C.D., The Defensor Vinculi, XII-157 pp., 1934.
86. Hannan, Rev. Jerome D., A.M., S.T.D., LL.B., J.C.D., The Canon Law of Wills, IX-517 pp., 1934.
87. Lemieux, Rev. Delisle A., A.M., J.C.D., The Sentence in Ecclesiastical Procedure, IX-131 pp., 1934.
88. O'Rourke, Rev. James J., A.B., J.C.D., Parish Registers, VII-109 pp., 1934.
89. Timlin, Rev. Bartholomew, O.F.M., A.M., J.C.D., Conditional Matrimonial Consent, X-381 pp., 1934.
90. Wahl, Rev. Francis X., A.B., J.C.D., The Matrimonial Impediments of Consanguinity and Affinity, VI-125 pp., 1934.
91. White, Rev. Robert J., A.B., LL.B., S.T.D., J.C.D., Canonical Ante-Nuptial Promises and the Civil Law, VI-152 pp., 1934.
92. Herrera, Rev. Antonio Parra, O.C.D., J.C.D., Legislacion Ecclesiastica sobre el Ayuno y la Abstinencia, XI-191 pp., 1935.
93. Kennedy, Rev. Edwin J., J.C.D., The Special Matrimonial Process in Cases of Evident Nullity, X-165 pp., 1935.
94. Manning, Rev. John J., A.B., J.C.D., Presumption of Law in Matrimonial Procedure, XI-111 pp., 1935.
95. Moeder, Rev. John M., J.C.D., The Proper Bishop for Ordination and Dismissorial Letters, VII-135 pp., 1935.
96. O'Mara, Rev. William A., A.B., J.C.D., Canonical Causes for Matrimonial Dispensations, IX-155 pp., 1935.
97. Reilly, Rev. Peter, J.C.D., Residence of Pastors, IX-81 pp., 1935.
98. Smith, Rev. Mariner T., O.P., S.T.L., J.C.D., The Penal Law for Religious, VII-169 pp., 1935.
99. Whalen, Rev. Donald W., A.M., J.C.D., The Value of Testimonial Evidence in Matrimonial Procedure, XIII-297 pp., 1935.
100. Cleary, Rev. Joseph F., J.C.D., Canonical Limitations on the Alienation of Church Property, VIII-141 pp., 1936.
101. Glynn, Rev. John C., J.C.D., The Promoter of Justice, XX-337 pp., 1936.
102. Brennan, Rev. James H., S.S., A.M., S.T.B., J.C.D., The Simple Convalidation of Marriage, VI-135 pp., 1937.
103. Brunini, Rev. Joseph Bernard, J.C.D., The Clerical Obligations of Canons 139 and 142, X-121 pp., 1937.
104. Connor, Rev. Maurice, A.B., J.C.D., The Administrative Removal of Pastors, VIII-159 pp., 1937.
105. Guilfoyle, Rev. Merlin Joseph, J.C.D., Custom, XI-144 pp., 1937.
106. Hughes, Rev. James Austin, A.B., A.M., J.C.D., Witnesses in Criminal Trials of Clerics, IX-140 pp., 1937.
107. Jansen, Rev. Raymond J., A.B., S.T.L., J.C.D., Canonical Provisions for Catechetical Instruction, VII-153 pp., 1937.
108. Kealy, Rev. John James, A.B., J.C.D., The Introductory Libellus in Church Court Procedure, XI-121 pp., 1937.
109. McManus, Rev. James Edward, C.SS.R., J.C.D., The Administration of Temporal Goods in Religious Institutes, XVI-196 pp., 1937.
110. Moriarity, Rev. Eugene James, J.C.D., Oaths in Ecclesiastical Courts, X-115 pp., 1937.

111. Rainer, Rev. Eligius George, C.SS.R., J.C.D., Suspension of Clerics, XVII-249 pp., 1937.
112. Reilly, Rev. Thomas F., C.SS.R., J.C.D., Visitation of Religious, VI-195 pp., 1938.
113. Moriarty, Rev. Francis E., C.SS.R., J.C.D., The Extraordinary Absolution from Censures, XV-334 pp., 1938.
114. Connolly, Rev. Nicholas P., J.C.D., The Canonical Erection of Parishes, X-132 pp., 1938.
115. Donovan, Rev. James Joseph, J.C.D., The Pastor's Obligation in Prenuptial Investigation, XII-322 pp., 1938.
116. Harrigan, Rev. Robert J., M.A., S.T.B., J.C.D., The Radical Sanation of Invalid Marriages, VIII-208 pp., 1938.
117 Boffa, Rev. Conrad Humbert, J.C.D., Canonical Provisions for Catholic Schools, X-211 pp., 1939.
118. Parsons, Rev. Anscar John, O.F.M. Cap., J.C.D., Canonical Elections, XII-236 pp., 1939.
119. Reilly, Rev. Edward Michael, A.B., J.C.D., The General Norms of Dispensation, X-156 pp., 1939.
120. Ryan, Rev. Gerald Aloysius, A.B., J.C.D., Principles of Episcopal Jurisdiction, XII-172 pp., 1939.
121. Burton, Rev. Francis James, C.S.C., A.B., J.C.D., A Commentary on Canon 1125, X-222 pp., 1940.
122. Miaskiewicz, Rev. Francis Sigismund, J.C.D., Supplied Jurisdiction According to Canon 209, XII-340 pp., 1940.
123. Rice, Rev. Patrick William, A.B., J.C.D., Proof of Death in Prenuptial Investigation, VIII-156 pp., 1940.
124. Anglin, Rev. Thomas Francis, M.S., J.C.D., The Eucharistic Fast, VIII-183 pp., 1941.
125. Coleman, Rev. John Jerome, J.C.D., The Minister of Confirmation, VI-153 pp., 1941.
126. Downs, Rev. John Emmanual, A.B., J.C.D., The Concept of Clerical Immunity, XI-163 pp., 1941.
127. Esswein, Rev. Anthony Albert, J.C.D., Extrajudicial Penal Powers of Ecclesiastical Superiors, X-144 pp., 1941.
128. Farrell, Rev. Benjamin Francis, M.A., S.T.L., J.C.D., The Rights and Duties of the Local Ordinary Regarding Congregations of Women Religious of Pontifical Approval, V-195 pp., 1941.
129. Feeney, Rev. Thomas John, A.B., S.T.L., J.C.D., Restitutio in Integrum, VI-169 pp., 1941.
130. Findlay, Rev. Stephen William, O.S.B., A.B., J.C.D., Canonical Norms Governing the Deposition and Degradation of Clerics, XVII-279 pp., 1941.
131. Goodwine, Rev. John, A.B., S.T.L., J.C.D., The Right of the Church to Acquire Property, VIII-119 pp., 1941.
132. Heston, Rev. Edwin Louis, C.S.C., Ph.D., S.T.D., J.C.D., The Alienation of Church Property in the United States, XII-222 pp., 1941.
133. Hogan, Rev. James John, A.B., S.T.L., J.C.D., Judicial Advocates and Procurators, VIII-200 pp., 1941.
134. Kealy, Rev. Thomas M., A.B., Litt.B., J.C.D., Dowry of Women Religious, IX-152 pp., 1941.
135. Keene, Rev. Michael James, O.S.B., J.C.D., Religious Ordinaries and Canon 198, V-164 pp., 1942.
136. Kerin, Rev. Charles A., S.S., M.A., S.T.B., J.C.D., The Privation of Christian Burial, XVI-279 pp., 1941.

137. Louis, Rev. William Francis, M.A., J.C.D., Diocesan Archives, X-101 pp. 1941.
138. McDevitt, Rev. Gilbert Joseph, A.B., J.C.D., Legitimacy and Legitimation, X-247 pp., 1941.
139. McDonough, Rev. Thomas Joseph, A.B., J.C.D., Apostolic Administrators, X-217 pp., 1941.
140. Meier, Rev. Carl Anthony, A.B., J.C.D., Penal Administrative Procedure Against Negligent Pastors, XI-240 pp., 1941.
141. Schmidt, Rev. John Rogg, A.B., J.C.D., The Principles of Authentic Interpretation in Canon 17 of the Code of Canon Law, XII-331 pp., 1941.
142. Slafkosky, Rev. Andrew Leonard, A.B., J.C.D., The Canonical Episcopal Visitation of the Diocese, X-197 pp., 1941.
143. Swoboda, Rev. Innocent Robert, O.F.M., J.C.D., Ignorance in Relation to the Imputability of Delicts, IX-271 pp., 1941.
144. Dubé, Rev. Arthur Joseph, A.B., J.C.D., The General Principles for the Reckoning of Time in Canon Law, VIII-299 pp., 1941.
145. McBride, Rev. James T., A.B., J.C.D., Incardination and Excardination of Seculars, XX-585 pp., 1941.
146. Król, Rev. John J., J.C.L., The Defendant in Contentious Trials, IX-207 pp., 1942.
147. Comyns, Rev. Joseph J., C.SS.R., J.C.L., The Papal and Episcopal Administration of Church Property.
148. Barry, Rev. Garrett Francis, O.M.I., J.C.L., Violation of the Cloister.
149. Bolduc, Rev. Gatien, C.S.V., A.B., S.T.L., J.C.L., Les études dans les religions cléricales.
150. Boyle, Rev. David John, M.A., J.C.L., The Juridic Effects of Moral Certitude on Pre-Nuptial Guarantees.
151. Canavan, Rev. Walter Joseph, M.A., Litt.D., J.C.L., Profession of Faith.
152. Desrochers, Rev. Bruno, A.B., Ph.L., S.T.B., J.C.L., Le Premier Concile Plénier de Québec et le Code de Droit Canonique.
153. Dillon, Rev. Robert Edward, A.B., J.C.L., Common Law Marriage.
154. Dodwell, Rev. Edward John, Ph.D., S.T.B., J.C.L., The Time and Place for the Celebration of Marriage.
155. Donnellan, Rev. Thomas Andrew, A.B., J.C.L., The Obligation of the Missa pro Populo.
156. Eltz, Rev. Louis Anthony, A.B., J.C.L., Cooperators in Crime.
157. Gass, Rev. Sylvester Francis, M.A., J.C.L., Ecclesiastical Pensions.
158. Guiniven, Rev. John Joseph, C.SS.R., J.C.L., The Precept of Hearing Mass on Sundays and Holy Days of Obligation.
159. Gulczynski, Rev. John Theophilus, J.C.L., The Desecration and Violation of Churches.
160. Hammill, Rev. John Leo, M.A., J.C.L., The Obligations of the Traveler according to Canon 14.
161. Haydt, Rev. John Joseph, A.B., J.C.L., Reserved Benefices.
162. Huser, Rev. Roger John, O.F.M., A.B., J.C.L., The Crime of Abortion in Canon Law.
163. Kearney, Rev. Francis Patrick, A.B., S.T.L., J.C.L., The Principles of Canon 1127.
164. Linahen, Rev. Leo James, S.T.L., J.C.L., De Absolutione Complicis In Peccato Turpi.
165. McCloskey, Rev. Joseph Aloysius, A.B., J.C.L., The Subject of Ecclesiastical Law according to Canon 12.

166. O'Neill, Rev. Francis Joseph, C.SS.R., J.C.L., The Dismissal of Religious in Temporary Vows.
167. Prince, Rev. John Edward, A.B., S.T.B., J.C.L., The Diocesan Chancellor.
168. Riesner, Rev. Albert Joseph, C.SS.R., J.C.L., Apostates and Fugitives from Religious Institutes.
169. Stenger, Rev. Joseph Bernard, J.C.L., The Mortgaging of Church Property.
170. Waldron, Rev. Joseph Francis, A.B., J.C.L., The Minister of Baptism.
171. Willett, Rev. Robert Albert, J.C.L., The Probative Value of Documents in Ecclesiastical Trials.
172. Woeber, Rev. Edward Martin, M.A., J.C.L., The Interpellations.

www.ingramcontent.com/pod-product-compliance
Lightning Source LLC
LaVergne TN
LVHW050227080826
844660LV00012B/490

* 9 7 8 0 8 1 3 2 2 3 6 1 2 *